AMERICAN
POLITICAL
THEOLOGY

AMERICAN POLITICAL THEOLOGY

HISTORICAL PERSPECTIVE AND THEORETICAL ANALYSIS

edited by

Charles W. Dunn

PRAEGER SPECIAL STUDIES • PRAEGER SCIENTIFIC

New York • Philadelphia • Eastbourne, UK
Toronto • Hong Kong • Tokyo • Sydney

Library of Congress Cataloging in Publication Data

Dunn, Charles W.
    American political theology.

    Bibliography: p.
    Includes index.
    1. Religion and politics--United States--History.
2. Theology, Doctrinal--United States--History.
I. Title.
BL2525.D86 1984   322'.1'0973   84-13308
ISBN 0-03-071843-0
ISBN 0-03-071844-9 (pbk.)

Published and Distributed by the
Praeger Publishers Division
(ISBN Prefix 0-275)
of Greenwood Press, Inc.,
Westport, Connecticut

Published in 1984 by Praeger Publishers
CBS Educational and Professional Publishing,
a Division of CBS Inc.
521 Fifth Avenue, New York, NY 10175 USA

56789 052 987654532

Printed in the United States of America
on acid-free paper

PREFACE

Few subjects arouse emotions like religion and politics. And when combined, few subjects raise more obstacles to balanced and scholarly analysis. Many strong and competing biases among both religious and political groups together with a scholar's own ideological and theological convictions make it difficult to examine the issues raised with 20/20 vision.

Several years ago I began to think about the relationships between religion and politics, especially with respect to how forms of theology may affect presidential policy making in view of the theological positions taken by Presidents Carter and Reagan. First this led to a new lecture in my American Presidency class, then to a paper at an American Political Science Association convention, later to two more papers at professional meetings and to two articles in *Presidential Studies Quarterly* and *Humanities in Society*, and finally to this book.

Only after several years of study did it occur to me that a book on the subject might be in order. While there are many excellent works on politics and religion, they generally do not treat the questions of how, why, and when they intersect. That is this book's purpose.

The study of these heatedly disputed issues often causes one to wonder if it is worth the effort or should it ever have been started. My consolation rests in the words of Theodore Roosevelt, who said: "It's not the critic that counts, but the credit belongs to the man who is in the arena, whose face is marred by dust and sweat and blood, who if he succeeds, knows the triumph of high achievement and who if he fails at least fails while daring greatly."

It would be presumptuous for anyone to think he could write on the subjects of politics and theology and have his conclusions universally accepted; thus, the purpose of this book is to explore the links between the two and to suggest new ways of thinking about them. In the process, conclusions reached here may be tested, and accepted or rejected elsewhere.

I am attempting here to reduce the bias and emotion often associated with these issues by providing diagrams, paradigms, and figures that constitute a more neutral point of reference or more value-free framework for consideration of the relationships between politics and theology in America.

I am much indebted to several persons for their patience, research and typing assistance, and critiques, including my wife Carol, Tommy Strickland, Susan Hollinger and Greg Usry.

Charles W. Dunn
January 26, 1984
Clemson University

CONTENTS

AMERICAN
POLITICAL
THEOLOGY

1 INTRODUCTION TO THE THEORY OF AMERICAN POLITICAL THEOLOGY

> . . . *any coherent and viable society rests on a common set of moral understandings about good and bad, right and wrong, in the realm of individual and social action. It is almost as widely held that these common moral understandings must also in turn rest upon a common set of religious understandings that provide a picture of the universe in terms of which the moral understandings make sense. Such moral and religious understandings produce both a basic cultural legitimation for a society which is viewed as at least approximately in accord with them, and a standard of judgment for the criticism of a society that is seen as deviating too far from them.*[1]
>
> ROBERT N. BELLAH

While much has been written about politics and religion, the subject of the impact of theology on American politics has hardly been touched. The importance of this scholarly oversight has been noted by a variety of scholars in a diversity of disciplines.

Political scientist Seymour Martin Lipset concludes that "there is an understandable reluctance to deal with the way in which religious interest or belief enters directly into the mainstream of political controversy.[2]

Psychologist Peter L. Benson says that "Until now, political scientists have not taken religion seriously either in theory or in research."[3]

Sociologists Peter L. Berger and Richard John Neuhaus believe that "there is a profoundly antidemocratic prejudice in public policy discourse that ignores the role of religious institutions in the lives of most Americans."[4]

1

Theologian Michael Novak argues that "There is a hidden religious power base in American culture, which our secular biases prevent many of us from noticing."[5]

Obviously the study of both the substance and process of American politics is important, but explaining how underlying cultural factors such as theology affect politics is also important. For example, Emile Durkeim has noted that "nearly all the great social institutions have been born in religion. . . . If religion has given birth to all that is essential in society, it is because the idea of society is the soul of religion."[6] And Robert N. Bellah has concluded that "Every movement to make America more fully realize its professed values has grown out of some form of public theology."[7]

The substantial media attention devoted to the emergence of the "religious right" and the assertion and opposition of the "religious left" on such policy issues as nuclear disarmament, abortion and school prayer also indicates that this is a subject ripe for inquiry and understanding. Such questions as these warrant attention:

- Are Jerry Falwell and the Moral Majority a passing fancy or do they represent some enduring values in the American political tradition?
- Is the National Council of Churches a legitimate representative of American churches or does it misrepresent the people it claims to represent?
- Is there any significance to the fact that Presidents Carter and Reagan claim to have been "born again"?
- Does the Moral Majority or the National Council of Churches have a better claim to the religious heritage of American Protestants?
- Who is a more legitimate representative of the Roman Catholic tradition in American politics, liberal pacifist bishops opposed to nuclear development or conservative Roman Catholics like William F. Buckley?
- Among Jews, should conservative or liberal Protestants be trusted more with respect to support of Israel on Middle East issues?
- Is "secular humanism" a myth conjured up by the "new right" or a form of theology that significantly influences public policy?
- Do religion and theology significantly affect presidential leadership or are they merely symbols manipulated by presidents to pacify the religious among the electorate?
- Is America a Christian nation as conservatives argue or a secular state as liberals contend?
- Are theological and religious interest groups generally only interested in volatile and emotional issues like abortion and nuclear development and content to let other groups dominate debate about less dramatic concerns?

- Who is more successful at influencing public policy, conservative or liberal theological groups?
- Book burnings — why do both conservatives and liberals burn books in the name of theology?

Each of these and a veritable host of other questions engage countless biases and incur heated debates. Yet, they are significant questions that merit seasoned answers.

Theology and politics are uncomfortable subjects for many, and like oil and water, they do not mix in the minds of others. Meanwhile, like "old man river" who just keeps rolling along, they indelibly mark the landscape of political discourse. Not only has the mythical common man frequently avoided discussing the two, scholars, journalists and others have all too often avoided anything more than superficial writing about the relationship between the subjects.

Major political events like the founding of America, the Civil War and the New Deal do not just happen. These epochs have a long prelude that may include economic, ideological, legal, and military preparation. While much has been written about these and other parts of the prelude to epochal political changes in America, surprisingly little has been written about the theological component.[8]

Ironically, political science and theology were once closely linked in the study of political thought by Augustine and others, but modern political science has generally limited its attention to such relationships as the impact of religious affiliation on party loyalty and voting behavior. In American government textbooks, major turning points in American politics and party affiliation are normally explained by the presence of a catalytic event, such as the Civil War or the Great Depression. Not to belittle the importance of this analysis, but to ask two important questions is our purpose here.

First, did theology serve as a cradle helping to nurture public opinion with respect to these major political changes in the decades prior to the catalytic event? Second, since there has been no catalytic event in recent years comparable either to the Civil War or the Great Depression, is it plausible to think that another major turning point in American politics could be in progress without such a catalyst?

To provide a framework for discussing the relationships between theology and American politics, Figure 1.1 presents a time line of the major eras of theological tension and subsequent American political epochs, and Figure 1.2 presents a paradigm of 24 different directions, emphases, and tendencies of belief between conservative and liberal theology. As a typology, of course, the latter represents degrees of differences rather than absolute differences.

With respect to Figure 1.1, we can see that prior to each major change in American politics, tension has existed between conservative and liberal theology.

FIGURE 1.1. Time Line of Theological Tension Eras and American Political Epochs: 1700s-1980s

Tension: 1700-1775	*Tension: 1800-1860*	*Tension: 1900-1930*	*Tension: 1940-1960*
Deism	Unitarianism/ Transcendentalism	Social Gospel/ Neo-Orthodoxy	Humanism
Conservatism	Conservatism	Conservatism	Conservatism
Epoch 1	*Epoch 2*	*Epoch 3*	*Epoch 4*
Declaration of Independence Revolutionary War Constitution	Civil War	New Deal	Social Turmoil: 1960s-80s Post New Deal Era New Federalism

FIGURE 1.2. Paradigm/Comparison of Conservative and Liberal Theology*

Direction/Tendency of Belief

Liberal		Conservative
Nature, Reason	Ultimate Source of Knowledge	Bible
Fallible	Bible	Infallible
More Symbolic	Biblical Interpretation	More Literal
Relative/Situational	Moral Standards	Absolute
Man	Relative Emphasis	God
Remote/Impersonal	Conception of God	Sovereign/Personal
Evolution	Creation of Man	God's Direct Act
Good	Human Nature	Evil
Social	Moral Emphasis	Personal
Rights	Relative Importance to Man	Responsibilities
Unjust Social Systems	Origin of Evil	Satan and Fall of Man
Good Works	Basis of Salvation	Grace/Faith
Earth	Relative Focus	Heaven
Man	Locus of Government Power	God
To Man	Accountability of Government	To God
More Unlimited	Role of Government	More Limited
Equality	Relative Importance	Liberty
Make Society Just	Primary Citizen Duty	Seek Salvation of Souls
Governmental Reform	Justice Achieved By	Spiritual Regeneration
National	Preferred Government	State/Local
Internationalist	Direction of Sentiment	Nationalist
Direct	Primary Method of Government Influence	Indirect
More Socialist	Economic Tendency	More Capitalist
Faster, within or outside existing institutions	Preferred Rate/Type of Change	Slower, within existing institutions

*Developed from content analysis of major theological and political documents from the late 1700s to early 1980s.

Deist theology contested with conservative theology prior to the founding of American government. Unitarian and transcendental theology challenged conservative theology prior to the Civil War. Social gospel and neo-orthodox theology competed with conservative theology prior to the New Deal. And today humanist, liberation, and prophetic politics theologies together with the remnants of social gospel and neo-orthodox theology conflict with conservative theology. Each era of theological tension has generally occurred over several decades prior to each political epoch.

To understand the political implications of each form of theology, the book contains a selection of documents and analyses that illustrate and critique the respective conservative and liberal theological perspectives.

Among the reasons for utilizing a representative selection of sources are (1) to provide a balanced presentation of a subject matter on issues that are often emotion-charged and lacking in a clear understanding of the contending points of view, and (2) to provide primary source justification for the paradigm in Figure 1.2.

The comparison of directions, emphases and tendencies of belief in Figure 1.2 not only provides a convenient way to distinguish between conservative and liberal theology, recognizing that not all theologians or brands of theology fully conform to either, but it also helps to explain how theology has affected American politics in the four major eras of theological tension and subsequent political epochs. For example, generally conservative theology as compared with liberal theology has been (1) historically less concerned with government for the achievement of its objectives, (2) more nationalistic, especially in this century, (3) relatively more concerned with liberty than equality, (4) more partial to state government, and (5) more desirous of a generally limited role for government.

Former U.S. Senator George McGovern offers a striking illustration of some of the typological differences between conservative and liberal theology:

> The study of these men (Hegel and Marx) forced me to think seriously about the political process, but neither of them captured my interest with anything approaching the enthusiasm I experienced in discovering 'the Social Gospel.' This effort to find in the New Testament and the Hebrew prophets an ethical imperative for a just social order strongly appealed to me. To know that long years of familiarity with the Bible and the idealism nurtured in my public-school years were resources that I could direct to humane political and economic ends was a satisfying discovery. *Religion was more than a search for personal salvation, more than an instantaneous expression of God's grace; it could be the essential moral underpinning for a life devoted to the service of one's time. Indeed, one's own salvation depended upon service to others.*[9] (Emphasis added)

Figure 1.2 also shows a relationship between theological beliefs and political or ideological convictions about the role of government. If a person holds to conservative theological beliefs, generally he would be expected to have conservative ideological convictions about the role of government. The same would be expected of a person with liberal theological tendencies. Of course, someone might hold political or ideological convictions contrary to his theological beliefs as was the case with three-time presidential candidate William Jennings Bryan, a conservative theologically, but a liberal politically.

Figure 1.3 sets forth quadrants into which persons may be categorized based upon their theological beliefs and political or ideological convictions. The horizontal line represents the theological division between conservative and liberal while the vertical line represents the political or ideological division between conservative and liberal. Several well known contemporary political figures help illustrate the utility of these quadrants:

> conservative theologically, but liberal politically, former U.S. Representative John Anderson (R Illionois), U.S. Senator Mark Hatfield (R Oregon), and former U.S. Senator Harold Hughes (D Iowa);

FIGURE 1.3.   Theological and Political/Ideological Relationships

	Liberal Political Ideology	
Gary Hart Jesse Jackson Ted Kennedy George McGovern Walter Mondale		John Anderson Mark Hatfield Harold Hughes
Liberal Theology		Conservative Theology
George Bush Barry Goldwater		Ronald Reagan Jesse Helms Strom Thurmond William F. Buckley
	Conservative Political Ideology	

conservative theologically, politically, and ideologically are U.S. Senators Jesse Helms (R N.C.) and Strom Thurmond (R S.C.), political commentator and author William F. Buckley, and President Ronald Reagan.

liberal theologically, but conservative politically and ideologically, are Vice President George Bush and U.S. Senator Barry Goldwater (R Arizona); and

liberal theologically, politically, and ideologically are Black civil rights leader Jesse Jackson, former U.S. Senator and Vice President Walter Mondale (D Minn.), U.S. Senators Ted Kennedy (D Mass.) and Gary Hart (D Col.), and former U.S. Senator George McGovern (D S.D.).

The importance of establishing these and other relationships between theology and politics are quite apparent. Academically, James V. Schall notes that the "severing of much connection of political theory from religion and theology . . . has unfortunately served to separate them precisely at a moment when religion . . . is gaining an unprecedented political influence."[10] Practically, theological activism has become a hallmark of American politics. While liberal Jews, Protestants, and Roman Catholics have fought for a nuclear freeze and other political objectives, their conservative counterparts have sought such political goals as school prayer and an end to abortion. Without the liberal theological force, support for a nuclear freeze in 1983 would have lost most of its strength just as the anti-abortion, school prayer and other conservative crusades would have been sapped of their fervor minus the conservative theological force.

Meanwhile, political leaders, aware of these and other theological landmines on the political battlefield, step carefully to avoid political fatality. For example, President Carter, personally opposed to abortion, refused to attack the Democratic Party's position in favor of abortion while President Reagan, personally supportive of tax exempt status for parochial schools that discriminate for religious reasons, backed down from his position when opponents charged his position aided the cause of racism. Whether academically or practically, it is important to develop an understanding of how theology affects American politics.

Figures 1.1, 1.2, and 1.3 provide the organizational structure of the book. Chapters 2-5 consider the four principal political epochs shown in Figure 1.1. Chapter 6 develops the relationships between theology and presidential leadership as set forth in Figure 1.3. Chapter 7 sets forth a theory of relationships between theology and politics, particularly with respect to differences between conservative and liberal theology as identified in Figure 1.2.

NOTES

1. Robert N. Bellah, *The Broken Covenant: American Civil Religion in Time of Trial* (New York: Seabury Press, 1975), p. ix.

2. Robert Lee and Martin E. Marty, eds., *Religion and Social Conflict* (New York: Oxford University Press, 1964), p. 70.

3. Peter L. Benson, "Religion on Capitol Hill: How Beliefs Affect Voting Behavior," *Psychology Today* 15 (1981): 57.

4. Peter L. Berger and Richard John Neuhaus, *To Empower the People* (Washington, D.C.: American Enterprise Institute, 1977), p. 28.

5. Betty Glad, *Jimmy Carter* (New York: Norton, 1980), p. 337.

6. Robert N. Bellah, *On Morality and Society* (Chicago: University of Chicago Press, 1973), p. 191.

7. Robert N. Bellah, "Religion and Legitimation in the American Republic," *Transaction* 15 (1978): 21.

8. Two books treating the subject limit their focus principally to the theological aspects of the issues rather than the relationships between the theological and the political. They are: William G. McLoughlin, *Revivals, Awakenings and Reform* (Chicago: University of Chicago Press, 1978) and C. Gregg Singer, *A Theological Interpretation of American History* (Philadelphia: Presbyterian and Reformed Publishing Company, 1964).

9. George McGovern, *Grassroots* (New York: Random House, 1977), p. 34.

10. James V. Schall, "Political Theory: The Place of Christianity," *Modern Age* 25 (Winter 1981), p. 31.

2 | THEOLOGICAL TENSION AND THE FOUNDING OF AMERICAN GOVERNMENT

At the core of [America's] founding and history is a moral and political tradition representing what Walter Lippmann has called 'the forgotten foundations of democracy.' But if the foundations have been forgotten, they have never been lost. Moreover, they affect foreign policy, for as the brilliant diplomatic columnist James Reston has pointed out, 'The liberties which all the spokesmen at the White House, the State Department and the Pentagon talk about defending today, after all, were established by that remarkable group of eighteenth century American political leaders who took their conception of man from the central religious tradition of Western civilization.'[1]

KENNETH W. THOMPSON

In origin, was America a secular state as liberals contend or a Christian nation as conservatives argue? Today most scholars see the founding of American government from a liberal or deist point of view, contending among other things that:

1. The Federalist Papers, the fundamental explanation of the government established, contain no references to God or to the Bible.
2. The only person of major significance during the Founding era to refer to the Bible, Thomas Paine, was obviously not a Christian.
3. James Madison and Thomas Jefferson, leading architects of America's founding, generally refrained from invoking the Bible in their writings.

4. The U.S. Constitution contains no references to deity while the Declaration of Independence contains only limited references.
5. The Founding Fathers generally emphasized "natural law" rather than "divine law," believing that man has rights just because he is man and not because he is a creature of God.

Convinced that today's dominant liberal explanation of the Founding era is deficient, conservatives argue among other things that:

1. Men like John Jay, one of the three authors of *The Federalist Papers*, were of ardent conservative Christian convictions and that other prominent Founders like James Madison received strongly conservative theological educations which influenced how they perceived government.
2. Conservative theology significantly influenced leading deists of the day, such as Thomas Jefferson and Benjamin Franklin, who recognized and responded to the dominant conservative theological influences during the Founding era.
3. The term, "law of nature" or "natural law," used by Jefferson in the Declaration of Independence, was taken from *Blackstone's Commentaries* where the term clearly referred to laws of God and was not intended to be distinct from "divine law".
4. Today's scholars, generally either of liberal theological persuasion or none at all, understandably explain the Founding era from their own set of biases.
5. Scholars in the last century tended to look upon America's founding more from a conservative theological point of view.

Some try to take a middle position on the issue in one of two ways. First is the view that the Declaration of Independence, written by deist Thomas Jefferson and strongly influenced by other deists like Samuel Adams and Thomas Paine, reflects a liberal origin, while the U.S. Constitutional Convention, attended by delegates almost uniformly of conservative Christian theological convictions, reflects a conservative origin. Second is the view that the Declaration of Independence, possessing several references to deity, affirms a conservative theological heritage, while the U.S. Constitution, absent of any references to deity or the Bible, confirms a liberal theological heritage.

Regardless of the position taken, the issue is exceedingly important. If America is a Christian nation as conservatives argue, then we have removed ourselves far from the theological and religious precedents of the Founding, and in the process, we have created a government decidedly contrary to the Founders' intentions. If, on the other hand, America is a secular state as liberals contend, perhaps undue deference has been given to religious issues and too much protection to religious causes.

ORIGINS OF TENSION

Sociologist Robert N. Bellah states: "The Bible was the one book that literate Americans in the 17th, 18th, and 19th centuries could be expected to know well. Biblical imagery provided the basic framework for imaginative thought in America up until quite recent times and, unconsciously, its control is still formidable."[2]

Historian Richard Hofstadter indicates a link between theology and the fundamental political decisions of the Founders, such as the U.S. Constitution.

> To them a human being was an atom of self-interest. They did not
> believe in man, but they did believe in the power of a good political
> constitution to control him. . . . From a humanistic standpoint there
> is a serious dilemma in the philosophy of the Fathers, which derives
> from their conception of man. They thought man was a creature of
> rapacious self-interest, yet they wanted him to be free — free, in essence,
> to contend, to engage in an umpired strife. . . . They had no hope
> and they offered none for any ultimate organic change in the way men
> conduct themselves. The result was that while they thought self-inter-
> est the most dangerous and unbrookable quality of man, they neces-
> sarily underwrote it in trying to control it.[3]

James Madison refers to the "degree of depravity in mankind which requires a certain degree of circumspection and distrust,"[4] the "caprice and wickedness of man,"[5] and to the "infirmities and depravities of the human character."[6] Alexander Hamilton spoke of the "folly and wickedness of mankind"[7] while John Jay saw man as governed by "dictates of personal interest."[8] Even the deist Thomas Jefferson said: "Free government is founded on jealousy, not in confidence; it is jealousy and not confidence which prescribes limited constitutions, to bind those we are obligated to trust with power. In questions of power, let no more be heard of confidence in man but bind him down from mischief by the chains of the constitution."[9]

This very strongly held biblical view of the nature of man, it may be argued, helped influence the type of government they established: one limited by checks and balances of power among the several branches and protection of the individual from capricious exercise of governmental power through a Bill of Rights. Their distrust of the nature of man helped lead them to create a government in which the people directly elected only the members of the House of Representatives with membership in the Senate, the Courts, and the president being indirectly elected by the people. Summarizing this relationship between theology and public policy, Alexis de Tocqueville said:

> The greatest part of British America was peopled by men who, after
> having shaken off the authority of the Pope, acknowledged no other

religious supremacy: They brought with them into the New World a form of Christianity which I cannot better describe than by styling it a democratic and republican religion.[10]

The Congressional Thanksgiving Day Proclamations of 1780 and 1782 reveal the prevailing strength of conservative protestant thought in a nation that then had very little Roman Catholic and Jewish influence. In 1780, the Congress proclaimed the desire to "cause the knowledge of Christianity to spread over the earth," and in 1782 "that the religion of our divine Redeemer, with all its divine influences, may cover the earth as the waters cover the seas."

From a conservative protestant perspective, the U.S. Constitution and the Bill of Rights were "negative" documents designed to protect the populace from undue governmental interference in their lives. The First Amendment, for example, was designed to prevent a "state church" from being established that would be superior to other churches. The Founders strenuously resisted the idea of an Anglican or Roman Catholic state church. To them, the separation of church and state did not mean that prayer and Bible reading could be excluded from the public schools; indeed, they encouraged both in many ways. For example, during early American history, 75 percent or more of public school education centered around the Bible. It was only later through the influence of such men as Unitarian Horace Mann in the nineteenth century and humanist John Dewey in the twentieth century that biblically based education declined from its zenith in the days of the McGuffey Readers.

Liberal protestant deist theology, although more liberal than the prevailing conservative protestant theology during the Founding era, was geographically isolated in the northeastern United States and was hardly the theology of the general populace. It differed from conservative theology principally on the matter of the deity of Christ. With respect to God, however, deist and conservative theology had much in common with a view that God acts directly in the affairs of men. For example, the principal deist political leaders, Thomas Jefferson and Benjamin Franklin, held this view. Franklin said: "I never doubted, for instance, the existence of the Deity; that He made the world and govern'd it by His Providence; that the most acceptable service of God was the doing of good to men; that our souls are immortal; and that crime will be punished, and virtue rewarded either here or hereafter."[11] And Thomas Jefferson declared: "Can the liberties of a nation be thought secure, when we have removed their only firm basis, a conviction in the minds of the people that these liberties are the gift of God? That they are not to be violated but by His wrath? Indeed, I tremble for my country when I reflect that God is just; that His justice cannot sleep forever."[12]

The covenant idea of conservative theology also significantly influenced governmental structures during the founding of American government as illustrated in the Mayflower Compact which reads: "We . . . do by Presents, solemnly and mutually in the Presence of God and one another, covenant and combine ourselves together into a civil Body Politick." Based upon the biblical concept of God's covenant with man, governments were to reflect the idea of the people covenanting together under God to form a government responsible to God and His law. As Daniel Elazar has pointed out:

> The constitutions of the American states in the founding era were perhaps the greatest products of the American covenant tradition. But just as they were not the first expressions of this tradition, they were by no means the last. *The creation of new states, even new towns, across the United States throughout the 19th century reflected the covenanting impulse.*
> As a consequence of these many uses of covenant, the American 'instinct' for federalism was extended into most areas of human relationships, shaping Americans' notions of individualism, human rights and obligations, business organization, civil association, and church structure as well as their notions of politics. While there were different interpretations of the covenant principle across the country's various regions and from generation to generation, there was also a broad area of agreement which unified those who subscribe to the principle and which set them and their doctrine apart within the larger realm of political theory. *All agreed on the importance of popular or republican government, the necessity to diffuse power, and the importance of individual rights and dignity as the foundation of any good political system.* At the same time, all agreed that the existence of inalienable rights was not an excuse for anarchy just as the existence of ineradicable human passions was not an excuse for tyranny. *For Americans, covenant provided a means for a free people to form political communities without sacrificing their essential freedom and without making energetic government possible.*[13] (emphasis added)

Social contract or compact thought, although having a liberal theological base of support and origin with such writers as John Locke, provided a natural basis for compromise between the two theological perspectives, based upon their mutual concern for the protection of individual rights and preference for limited government. Thus, even though theological tension existed, the ideas of social contract and covenant theology did not clash extensively. Federalism and protection of the rights of man fit both well.

Viewing the contribution of conservative theology to the founding of America, Harvard University historian Samuel Eliot Morison noted their important connection:

> Puritanism was a cutting edge which hewed liberty, democracy, humanitarianism, and universal education out of the black forest of feudal Europe and the American wilderness.

Puritan doctrine taught each person to consider himself a significant if sinful unit to whom God had given a particular place and duty, and that he must help his fellow men.

Puritanism is an American heritage to be grateful for and not to be sneered at because it required everyone to attend divine worship and maintained a strict code of moral ethics.[14]

Also significant to this era was the founding and growth of theologically conservative schools like Harvard and Yale which helped provide essential leadership. Michael Novak has pointed out:

Schools in the colonies were founded around the same purpose. Even the great universities, which subsequently were secularized, had evangelistic roots. Harvard College, founded in 1636 to train ministers of the gospel, adopted as one of the rules and precepts for students: 'Everyone shall consider the main end of his life and studies to know God and Jesus Christ, which is eternal life.'

Yale was constituted in 1701 in recognition of the fact that the colonies had been established 'both to plant and under the Divine Blessing to propagate in this wilderness, the blessed reformed Protestant religion, in the purity of its order and worship, not only to their posterity, but also to the barbarous natives.'[15]

Distinguishing yet another difference between liberal and conservative theology at the founding, Robert Bellah points out that:

neutral deistic language warmed the hearts of none and by itself and unaided, it could hardly have provided the imaginative basis of a national consciousness without which the new nation could easily have shattered into the divisions and fragments that continually threatened it. What civil religion unaided could not accomplish became possible with the help of a burgeoning revivalism. Cold external forms could be filled with a warm inner life, appropriated and impressed into the imaginative life of the people.[16]

Bellah's view is that the foundation for the civil religion of today was largely laid by the deists during the founding. Civil religion, of course, seeks to unify all people, Protestant, Catholic, and Jew, around religious words and symbols that are inoffensive, such as neutral references to God and prayer. Conservative theology, on the other hand, provided the spirit of nationalism that also helped to unify the country. For example, the deist Thomas Jefferson in his second inaugural address reveals the theological impulse of nationalism by likening America to biblical Israel when he said that he would need "the favor of that Being in whose hands we are, who led our forefathers, as Israel of Old, from their native land and planted them in a country flowing with all the necessaries and comforts of life, who has covered our infancy with His providence and our riper years with His wisdom and power."[17]

The strongly separatist theology of the Old and New Testaments, it may be contended, may have helped to mold the nationalistic and separatist character of American foreign policy for many generations. Israel, for example, was always blessed in the Old Testament so long as she did not succumb to the alien influences of foreign nations and religions. In the New Testament, the influential themes were "what fellowship hath light with darkness," and "ye are the light of the world." As a nation, our foreign policy came to be distinguished by an aversion to entangling alliances, but with a "white man's burden" to export our religious, social and governmental heritage to the world. The controlling and prevailing indirect influence that Christianity exercised over the American mind and public policy before, during and after the founding of American government is revealed in two comments by Alexis de Tocqueville in the late 1840s.

> In the United States religion exercises little influence upon the laws and upon the details of public opinion; but it directs the customs of the community, and by regulating domestic life, it regulates the state.[18]

> It was religion that gave birth to the English colonies in America. One must never forget that. In the United States religion is mingled with all the national customs and all those feelings which the word evokes. For that reason it has a peculiar power . . . Christianity has kept a strong hold over the minds of Americans, and . . . its power is not just that of a philosophy which has been examined and accepted, but that of a religion believed in without discussion . . . Christianity itself is an established and irresistible fact which no one seeks to attack or to defend.[19]

The theological prelude to the founding of American government occurred during the Great Awakening from about 1720-1760. This religious event helped crystallize both a religious and a political unity among the colonists that paved the way for the successful writing and acceptance of the Declaration of Independence that although written by Jefferson, a deist, was carefully weighed by John Adams, a theological conservative, and was signed by persons of conservative theological convictions. Even though commonly styled the Revolutionary War, the original intent of most, if not all, of the Founders was perhaps not so much to revolt from the mother country, England, as to secure their rights as Englishmen. The Founders resented taxation by Parliament without representation in Parliament. For example, Samuel Langdon proclaimed to the Congress of Massachusetts in 1775: "Because we refuse submission to the despotic power of a ministerial Parliament, our own sovereign, to whom we have been always ready to swear allegiance — whose authority we never meant to cast off . . . has given us up to the rage of his ministers."[20]

From a conservative theological perspective, the burden of the Declaration of Independence was to demonstrate that the colonists under God had rights that English Parliamentary tyranny had abridged; that is, "All men are created equal, that they are endowed by their Creator with certain unalienable rights." Had the God-given rights of the colonists not been abridged by a tyrannical Parliament, then the colonists had no other stipulated reason for revolt. Even with the abridgement of their rights, many colonists (the Tories) remained loyal to the mother country.

The Revolutionary War, therefore, may be interpreted in part as a conservative theological undertaking premised upon the colonists' biblical understanding that a people have no right to revolt against established government unless that government violates their divinely endowed rights. As stated in the Declaration of Independence, "whenever any form of government becomes destructive to these ends, it is the Right of the People to alter or to abolish it, and to institute new government."

The liberal deist pen of Jefferson, though evident in the Declaration of Independence, seems to have bowed to the prevailing conservative theological convictions of John Adams and other American colonists. Indeed, at their insistence, Jefferson added several references to God in the Declaration of Independence. His states' rights political party, the Jeffersonian-Republicans, provide even further evidence of this conservative theological consciousness and also a touch of irony that the deist Jefferson led a party substantially populated by persons of conservative theological convictions, who supported states' rights within the federal system. Jefferson's deism, like that of the relatively few American deists then, was mild by comparison with European deism of the day and generally did not conflict with the prevailing conservative theology on political matters that began to dominate the national mind through the Great Awakening prior to the Declaration of Independence and the Revolutionary War.

Both the political and religious rights of the colonists were perceived to be in jeopardy through parliamentary tyranny that not only imposed taxation without representation, but also threatened the loss of their religious liberty. Joseph Emerson, a Congregational minister, stated in 1776: "For they [the colonial leaders] saw, while our civil liberties were openly threatened, our religious shook; after taking away the liberty of our taxing ourselves, and breaking in upon our charters, they feared the breaking in upon the act of toleration, the taking away of liberty to choose our own ministers, and then imposing whom they [Parliament] pleased upon us for spiritual guides, largely taxing us to support the pride and vanity of diocesan Bishops."[21]

Later when the Founders adjourned the 1787 Constitutional Convention in Philadelphia without incorporating a Bill of Rights, especially the right to freedom of religion, it is easy to understand why both conservative and liberal theological forces insisted that a Bill of Rights be added.

AN ENDURING TENSION

The documents that follow reveal that while deism was evident before and during America's first political epoch, conservative Christian theology generally dominated the public mind with respect to the nation's legal system. Certainly this was true in *The Mayflower Compact* (1620), the *Fundamental Orders of Connecticut* (1638-39) and the *Massachusetts Body of Liberties* (1641). The *Virginia Bill of Rights* (1776) on the other hand, while not using as much biblical terminology, does state that "it is the mutual duty of all to practice Christian forebearance, love, and charity towards each other." Besides a language difference, the Virginia Bill of Rights also seems to evidence more of the influence of social contract thought as contrasted with the biblical covenant thought of the former. Moreover, the Virginia Bill of Rights both in title and content exhibit more concern for individual rights as contrasted with individual liberties. As a result equality as a concept is relatively more important in the Virginia Bill of Rights. The selections from Yale University President Timothy Dwight and Thomas Jefferson show clearly the theological conflict between conservative Christian theology and deism that worked its way into political discourse.

The principal political issues of the American founding, the Declaration of Independence, the Revolutionary War, the U.S. Constitution, and the Bill of Rights, had their roots deeply embedded in the political philosophy of conservative theology that generally coincided with a mild American brand of deism held by a small minority of men like Franklin and Jefferson.

From these two theological roots have emerged an increasingly more hostile tension during the rest of American history, particularly during the remaining three public-policy epochs, the Civil War, the New Deal, and the Post New Deal era. While the Founders emphasized both liberty and equality, their primary emphasis was on the former. Liberal theology, on the other hand, has increasingly emphasized equality more than liberty, especially in the twentieth century. Thus, the increased tension between the two has generally been prompted by conflicts between liberty and equality and whether America's governmental roots are Christian or secular in origin.

NOTES

1. Kenneth W. Thompson, *The Moral Issue in Statecraft* (Baton Rouge, La.; LSU Press, 1966), p. xii.

2. Robert N. Bellah, *The Broken Covenant: American Civil Religion in Time of Trial* (New York: The Seabury Press, 1975), p. 12.

3. Richard Hofstadter, *The American Political Tradition* (New York: Knopf and Co., 1948), p. 16.

4. *The Federalist* (Rossiter edition), p. 346.

5. Ibid., p. 353.

6. Ibid., p. 231.

7. Ibid., p. 471.

8. Ibid., p. 40.

9. *Resolution Relative to the Alien and Sedition Laws*, 1798.

10. Alexis de Tocqueville, *Democracy in America* (New York: Vintage Books, 1954), p. 311.

11. In Robert N. Bellah, *Beyond Belief: Essays on Religion in a Post-Traditional World* (New York: Harper & Row, 1970), p. 173.

12. In Charles Wallis, ed., *Our American Heritage* (New York: Harper & Row, 1970), p. 51.

13. Daniel J. Elazar, "Political Theory of Covenant: Biblical Origins and Development," Paper presented at 1980 American Political Science Association.

14. In Wallis, p. 53.

15. Michael Novak, *Choosing Our King* (New York: Macmillan, 1974), pp. 114, 115.

16. Bellah, *The Broken Covenant*, p. 45.

17. In Winthrop S. Hudson, *Nationalism and Religion in America* (New York: Harper & Row, 1970), p. 33.

18. In Robert S. Alley, *So Help Me God* (Richmond Va.: John Knox Press, 1972), p. 21.

19. In Ellis Sandoz, "Classical and Christian Dimensions of American Political Thought," *Modern Age* 25:21.

20. In John Wingate Thornton, ed., *The Pulpit of the American Revolution* (New York: Franklin and Co., 1970), p. 21.

21. In Peter N. Carroll, ed., *Religion and the Coming of the American Revolution* (Waltham, Mass.: Ginn-Blaisdell, 1970), pp. 87-88.

THE FOUNDING ERA:
SELECTED POLITICAL AND
THEOLOGICAL DOCUMENTS

1. I *THE MAYFLOWER COMPACT* (1620)

IN the Name of God, Amen. We, whose names are underwritten, the Loyal Subjects of our dread Sovereign Lord King *James*, by the Grace of God, of *Great Britain*, *France*, and *Ireland*, King, *Defender of the Faith*, &c. Having undertaken for the Glory of God, and Advancement of the Christian Faith, and the Honour of our King and Country, a Voyage to plant the first Colony in the northern Parts of *Virginia*; Do by these Presents, solemnly and mutually, in the Presence of God and one another, covenant and combine ourselves together into a civil Body Politick, for our better Ordering and Preservation, and Furtherance of the Ends aforesaid: And by Virtue hereof do enact, constitute, and frame, such just and equal Laws, Ordinances, Acts, Constitutions, and Officers, from time to time, as shall be thought most meet and convenient for the general Good of the Colony; unto which we promise all due Submission and Obedience. IN WITNESS whereof we have hereunto subscribed our names at *Cape-Cod* the eleventh of *November*, in the Reign of our Sovereign Lord King *James*, of *England*, *France*, and *Ireland*, the eighteenth, and of *Scotland*, the fifty-fourth, *Anno Domini*, 1620.

Source: Benjamin Perley Poore (ed.), *The Federal and State Constitutions, Colonial Charters and other Organic Laws of the United States* (Washington, D.C.: U.S. Government Printing Office, 1877).

2. | *FUNDAMENTAL ORDERS OF CONNECTICUT* (1638-39)

Forasmuch as it hath pleased the Almighty God by the wise disposition of his divine providence so to Order and dispose of things that we the Inhabitants and Residents of Windsor, Hartford and Wethersfield are now cohabiting and dwelling in and upon the River of Connecticut and the Lands thereunto adjoining; And well knowing where a people are gathered together the word of God requires that to maintain the peace and union of such a people there should be an orderly and decent Government established according to God, to order and dispose of the affairs of the people at all seasons as occasion shall require; do therefore associate and conjoin ourselves to be as one public State or Comonwelth; and do, for ourselves and our Successors and such as shall be adjoined to us at any time hereafter, enter into Combination and Confederation together, to maintain and pursue the liberty and purity of the gospel of our Lord Jesus which we now profess, as also the discipline of the Churches, which according to the truth of the said gospel is now practised amongst us; As also in our Civil Affaires to be guided and governed according to such Laws, Rules, Orders and decrees as shall be made, ordered & decreed, as followeth:—

Source: Benjamin Perley Poore, op. cit.

3. | *THE MASSACHUSETTS BODY OF LIBERTIES* (1641)

The free fruition of such liberties, Immunities and privileges as humanity, Civility, and Christianity call for as due to every man in his place and proportion without impeachment and infringement hath ever been and ever will be the tranquility and Stability of Churches and Commonwealths. And the denial or deprival thereof, the disturbance if not the ruin of both.

We hold it therefore our duty and safety whilst we are about the further establishing of this Government to collect and express all such freedoms as for present we foresee may concern us, and our posterity after us, And to ratify them with our solemn consent. We do therefore this day religiously and unanimously decree and confirm these following Rites, liberties and privileges concerning our Churches, and Civil State to be respectively impartial and inviolably enjoyed and observed throughout our Jurisdiction for ever.

No man's life shall be taken away, no man's honour or good name shall be stained, no man's person shall be arrested, restrained, banished, dismembered, nor any way punished, no man shall be deprived of his wife or children, no man's goods or estate shall be taken away from him, nor any way indammaged under color of law or Countenance of Authority, unless it be by virtue or equity of some express law of the Country warranting the same, established by a general Court and sufficiently published, or in case of the defect of a law in any particular case by the word of god. And in Capital cases, or in cases concerning dismembering or banishment, according to that word to be judged by the General Court.

Liberties of Foreigners and Strangers

If any people of other Nations professing the true Christian religion shall flee to us from the Tyranny or oppression of their persecutors, or from famine, wars or the like necessary and compulsory cause, They shall be entertained and succoured amongst us, according to that power and prudence god shall give us.

Capital Laws

1.
If any man after legal conviction shall have or worship any other god, but the lord god, he shall be put to death.

2.
If any man or woman be a witch, (that is hath or consulteth with a familiar spirit,) They shall be put to death.

3.
If any man shall Blaspheme the name of God, the father, Son or Holy ghost, with direct, express, presumptuous or high handed blasphemy, or shall curse god in the like manner, he shall be put to death.

4.
If any person commit any willful murder, which is manslaughter, committed upon premeditated mailice, hatred or Cruelty, not in a man's necessary and just defense, nor by mere casualty against his will, he shall be put to death.

5.
If any person slayeth an other suddenly in his anger or Cruelty of passion, he shall be put to death.

6.
If any person shall slay an other through guile, either by poisioning or other such devilish practice, he shall be put to death.

7.
If any man or woman shall lie with any beast or brute creature by Carnal Copulation, They shall surely be put to death. And the beast shall be slain and buried and not eaten.

8.
If any man lieth with mankind as he lieth with a woman, both of them have committed abomination, they both shall surely be put to death.

9.
If any person committeth Adultery with a married or espoused wife, the Adulterer and Adulteress shall surely be put to death.

10.

If any man stealeth a man or mankind, he shall surely be put to death.

11.

If any man rise up by false witness, wittingly and of purpose to take away any man's life, he shall be put to death.

12.

If any man shall conspire and attempt any invasion, insurrection, or public rebellion against our commonwealth, or shall indeavour to surprise any Town or Towns, fort or forts therein, or shall treacherously and perfidiously attempt the alteration and subversion of our frame of politics or Government fundamentals he shall be put to death.

Lastly because our duty and desire is to do nothing suddenly which fundamentally concern us, we decree that these rites and liberties, shall be Audably read and deliberately weighed at every General court that shall be held, within three years next insueing, And such of them as shall not be altered or repealed they shall stand so ratified, That no man shall infringe them without due punishment.

And if any General Court within these next three years shall fail or forget to read and consider them as abovesaid, The Governor and Deputy Governor for the time being, and every Assistant present at such Courts shall forfeit 20sh, a man, and every Deputy 10sh, a man for each neglect, which shall be paid out of their proper estate, and not by the Country or the Towns which choose them, and whensoever there shall arise any question in any Court among the Assistants and Associates thereof about the explanation of these Rites and liberties, The General Court only shall have power to interpret them.

Source: *Colonial Laws of Massachusetts*, compiled by Order of the City Council of Boston under the direction of Mr. S. Whitmore, 1889. Text partial.

4. I *VIRGINIA BILL OF RIGHTS* (1776)

A declaration of rights made by the representatives of the good people of Virginia, assembled in full and free convention; which rights do pertain to them and their posterity, as the basis and foundation of government.

Section 1. That all men are by nature equally free and independent, and have certain inherent rights, of which, when they enter into a state of society, they cannot, by any compact, deprive or divest their posterity; namely, the enjoyment of life and liberty, with the means of acquiring and possessing property, and pursuing and obtaining happiness and safety.

Sec. 2. That all power is vested in, and consequently derived from the people; that magistrates are their trustees and servants, and at all times amenable to them.

Sec. 3. That government is, or ought to be, instituted for the common benefit, protection, and security of the people, nation, or community; of all the various modes and forms of government, that is best which is capable of producing the greatest degree of happiness and safety, and is most effectually secured against the danger of maladministration; and that, when any government shall be found inadequate or contrary to these purposes, a majority of the community hath an indubitable, inalienable, and indefeasible right to reform, alter, or abolish it, in such manner as shall be judged most conducive to the public weal.

Sec. 4. That no man, or set of men, are entitled to exclusive or separate emoluments or privileges from the community, but in consideration of public services; which, not being descendible, neither ought the offices of magistrate, legislator, or judge to be hereditary.

Sec. 5. That the legislative and executive powers of the State should be separate and distinct from the judiciary; and that the members of the two first may be restrained from oppression, by feeling and participating the burdens of the people, they should, at fixed periods, be reduced to a private station, return into that body from which they were originally taken, and the vacancies be supplied by frequent, certain, and regular elections, in which all, or any part of the former members, to be again eligible, or ineligible, as the laws shall direct.

Sec. 6. That elections of members to serve as representatives of the people, in assembly, ought to be free; and that all men, having sufficient evidence of permanent common interest with, and attachment to, the community, have the right of suffrage, and cannot be taxed or deprived of their property for public uses, without their own consent, or that of their representatives so elected, nor bound by any law to which they have not, in like manner, assented, for the public good.

Sec. 7. That all power of suspending laws, or the execution of laws, by any authority, without consent of the representatives of the people, is injurious to their rights, and ought not to be exercised.

Sec. 8. That in all capital or criminal prosecutions a man hath a right to demand the cause and nature of his accusation, to be confronted with the accusers and witnesses, to call for evidence in his favor, and to a speedy trial by an impartial jury of twelve men of his vicinage, without whose unanimous consent he cannot be found guilty; nor can he be compelled to give evidence against himself; that no man be deprived of his liberty, except by the law of the land or the judgment of his peers.

Sec. 9. That excessive bail ought not to be required, nor excessive fines imposed, nor cruel and unusual punishments inflicted.

Sec. 10. That general warrants, whereby an officer or messenger may be commanded to search suspected places without evidence of a fact committed, or to seize any person or persons not named, or whose offence is not particularly described and supported by evidence, are grievous and oppressive, and ought not to be granted.

Sec. 11. That in controversies respecting property, and in suits between man and man, the ancient trial by jury is preferable to any other, and ought to be held sacred.

Sec. 12. That the freedom of the press is one of the great bulwarks of liberty, and can never be restrained but by despotic governments.

Sec. 13. That a well-regulated militia, composed of the body of the people, trained to arms, is the proper, natural, and safe defence of a free State; that standing armies, in time of peace, should be avoided, as dangerous to liberty; and that in all cases the military should be under strict subordination to, and governed by, the civil power.

Sec. 14. That the people have a right to uniform government; and, therefore, that no government separate from, or independent of the government of Virginia, ought to be erected or established within the limits thereof.

Sec. 15. That no free government, or the blessings of liberty, can be preserved to any people, but by a firm adherence to justice, moderation, temperance, frugality, and virtue, and by frequent recurrence to fundamental principles.

Sec. 16. That religion, or the duty which we owe to our Creator, and the manner of discharging it, can be directed only by reason and conviction, not by force or violence; and therefore all men are equally entitled to the free exercise of religion, according to the dictates of conscience; and that it is the mutual duty of all to practise Christian forbearance, love, and charity towards each other.

Source: Poore, op. cit.

5. | "THEOLOGY EXPLAINED AND DEFENDED" (1801)

Timothy Dwight, President of Yale University

It ought, here, and forever, to be remembered with peculiar gratitude, that God has, during the past Century, often and wonderfully interposed in our behalf, and snatched us from the jaws of approaching destruction. The instances of this interposition are too numerous to be now recounted, and are happily too extraordinary to be either unknown or forgotten. We have been frequently on the brink of destruction; but although cast down, we have not been destroyed. Perhaps we have so often been, and are still, suffered to stand on this precipice, that we may see, and feel, and acknowledge, the hand of our Preserver. . . .

In the mean time, let me solemnly warn you, that if you intend to accomplish anything, if you mean not to labour in vain, and to spend your strength for nought, you must take your side. There can be here no halting between two opinions. You must marshal yourselves, finally, in your own defense, and in the defense of all that is dear to you. You must meet face to face the bands of disorder, of falshood, and of sin. Between them and you there is, there can be, no natural, real, or lasting harmony. What communion hath light with darkness? what concord hath Christ with Belial? or what part hath he that believeth with an Infidel? From a connection with them what can you gain? What will you not lose? Their neighbourhood is contagious; their friendship is a blast; their communion is death. Will you imbibe their principles? Will you copy their practices? Will you teach your children, that death is an eternal sleep; that the end sanctifies the means? that moral obligation is a dream? Religion a farce? and your Saviour the spurious offspring of pollution? Will you send your daughters abroad in the attire of a female Greek? Will you enroll your sons as conscripts for plunder and butchery? Will you make marriage the mockery of a registers' office? Will you become the rulers of Sodom, and the people of Gomorrha? Shall your love to man vanish in a word, and evaporate on the tongue? Shall it be lost in a tear, and perish in a sigh? Will you enthrone a Goddess of Reason before the table of Christ? Will you burn your Bibles? Will you crucify anew your Redeemer? Will you deny your God?

COME out, therefore, from among them, and be ye separate, saith the Lord, and touch not the unclean thing; and I will receive you, and will be a father to you: And ye shall be my sons and daughters, saith the Lord Almighty.

To this end you must coolly, firmly, and irrevocably make your determination, and resolve, that Jehovah is your God, and that you will serve him only. His enemies are the enemies of yourselves, and of your children; of your peace, liberty, and happiness; of your religion, virtue, and salvation. —Their principles abhor; their practices detest. Before your steady indignation, and firm contempt, they will fall of course. No falshood can bear the sunbeams of truth; no vice can withstand the steady current of virtue. The motives to this opposition are infinite. Your all, your children's all, is at stake. If you contend manfully, you will be more than conquerors; if you yield, both you and they are undone. You are endeared by a thousand ties. Your common country is a land of milk and honey: In it a thousand churches are vocal with the praise of your Creator; and four thousand schools receive your children to their bosom, and nurse them to wisdom and piety. In this country you all sprang from one stock, speak one language, have one system of manners, profess one religion, and wear one character. Your laws, your institutions, your interests, are one. No mixture weakens, no strangers divide, you. You have fought and bled, your fathers have fought and died, together. Together they worshipped God; together they sate around the table of the Redeemer; together they ascended to heaven; and together they now unite in the glorious concert of eternal praise. With such an interest at hazard, with such bonds of union, with such examples, you cannot separate; you cannot fear.

Let me at the same time warn you, that your enemies are numerous, industrious, and daring, full of subtlety, and full of zeal. Nay, some of them are your own brethren, and endeared to you by all the ties of nature. The contest is, therefore, fraught with hazard and alarm. Were it a war of arms, you would have little to dread. It is a war of arts; of temptations; of enchantments; a war against the magicians of Egypt; in which no weapons will avail, but "the rod of God." In this contest you may be left alone. Fear not; "they that be for you will even then be more than they that are against you." Almighty power will protect, Infinite wisdom will guide, and Unchangeable goodness will prosper, you. The Christian world rises daily in prayer to heaven for your faithfulness and success; the host of sleeping saints calls to you from the grave, and bids you God speed. The spirits of your fathers lean from yonder skies to survey the conflict, and your children of many generations, will rise up, and call you blessed.

Source: Timothy Dwight, *A Discourse, on Some Events of the Last Century*, delivered in the Brick Church in New Haven, Wednesday, January 7, 1801 (New Haven, 1801), pp. 17-23, 28-30, 32-34, 45-47.

6. | "LETTER TO DR. BENJAMIN WATERHOUSE" (1822)

Thomas Jefferson

Dear Sir,—

I have received and read with thankfulness and pleasure your denunciation of the abuses of tobacco and wine. Yet, however sound in its principles, I expect it will be but a sermon to the wind. You will find it is as difficult to inculcate these sanative precepts on the sensualities of the present day, as to convince an Athanasian that there is but one God. I wish success to both attempts, and am happy to learn from you that the latter, at least, is making progress, and the more rapidly in proportion as our Platonizing Christians make more stir and noise about it. The doctrines of Jesus are simple, and tend all to the happiness of man.

1. That there is one only God, and He all perfect.
2. That there is a future state of rewards and punishments.
3. That to love God with all thy heart and thy neighbor as thyself, is the sum of religion.

These are the great points on which He endeavored to reform the religion of the Jews. But compare with these the demoralizing dogmas of Calvin.

1. That there are three Gods.
2. That good works, or the love of our neighbor, are nothing.
3. That faith is everything, and the more incomprehensible the proposition, the more merit in its faith.
4. That reason in religion is of unlawful use.
5. That God, from the beginning, elected certain individuals to be saved, and certain others to be damned; and that no crimes of the former can damn them; no virtues of the latter save.

Now, which of these is the true and charitable Christian? He who believes and acts on the simple doctrines of Jesus? Or the impious dogmatists, as Athanasius and Calvin? Verily I say these are the false shepherds foretold as to enter not by the door into the sheepfold, but to climb up some other way. They are mere usurpers of the Christian name, teaching a counter-religion made up of the *deliria* of crazy imaginations, as foreign from Christianity as is that of Mahomet. Their blasphemies have driven thinking men into infidelity, who have too hastily rejected the supposed Author himself, with the horrors so falsely imputed to Him. Had the doctrines of Jesus been preached always as pure as they came from his lips, the whole civilized world would now have been Christian. I rejoice that in this blessed country of free inquiry and belief, which has surrendered its creed and conscience to neither kings nor priests, the genuine doctrine of one only God is reviving, and I trust that there is not a *young man* now living in the United States who will not die an Unitarian.

But much I fear, that when this great truth shall be reestablished, its votaries will fall into the fatal error of fabricating formulas of creed and confessions of faith, the engines which so soon destroyed the religion of Jesus, and made of Christendom a mere Aceldama; that they will give up morals for mysteries, and Jesus for Plato. How much wiser are the Quakers, who, agreeing in the fundamental doctrines of the Gospel, schismatize about no mysteries, and, keeping within the pale of common sense, suffer no speculative differences of opinion, any more than of feature, to impair the love of their brethren. Be this the wisdom of Unitarians, this the holy mantle which shall cover within its charitable circumference all who believe in one God, and who love their neighbor! I conclude my sermon with sincere assurances of my friendly esteem and respect.

Source: Albert E. Bergh, ed., *The Writings of Thomas Jefferson* (Memorial edition, 20 vols., Washington, 1903-4), XV, pp. 383-85.

3 | *THEOLOGICAL TENSION AND THE CIVIL WAR*

The transformation of American theology in the first quarter of the nineteenth century released the very forces of romantic perfectionism that conservatives most feared. . . . As it spread, perfectionism swept across denominational barriers and penetrated even secular thought.[1]

JOHN L. THOMAS

Great persons and great ideas mold history. Or at least they reflect in their greatness the transformation of history and a bridge to the future. Why has American government grown substantially in size and power during the twentieth century? The answer fundamentally rests with what happened prior to the Civil War in the lives of certain individuals and their ideas about equality. Why did liberal theological interest groups, such as the National Council of Churches and other liberal denomination church organizations, establish their presence earlier in the twentieth century than conservative theological groups like the Moral Majority? Once again, the answer fundamentally resides in pre-Civil War History. The beachheads of American theological warfare were rather clearly defined during the Civil War epoch.

CONSERVATIVE AND LIBERAL BEACHHEADS

Where liberty and limited government were hallmarks of the theological ferment prior to the founding of American government, equality and social reform became hallmarks of the new "perfectionist" emphasis of conservative theology and of transcendental and unitarian theology prior to the Civil War.

While still holding to the essential features of conservative theology, leading conservative theologians and preachers like Charles Finney of Oberlin College began to emphasize the sanctification or perfection of man after salvation. Finney and others, such as William Lloyd Garrison, provided much of the leadership in the cause of slavery's abolition. There was a distinct difference between their approaches, however, as Finney, who brought Garrison into the limelight of the abolition movement, later split with him on the issue of whether the abolitionists should lobby government as an interest group to curtail slavery or whether they should rely upon the salvation and sanctification of man in response to the preaching of the gospel to terminate slavery.

To Finney, governmental reform would be of no avail unless there was regeneration of the heart, but Garrison believed that direct action should be taken to pressure the government to abolish slavery while the gospel message of regeneration was preached.

Garrison asserted: "I shall strenuously contend for the immediate enfranchisement of our slave population. . . . I will be as harsh as truth, and as uncompromising as justice. On this subject, I do not wish to think, or speak, or write, with moderation. . . ."[2] Finney, however, said: "If abolition can be made an appendage of general revival, all is well. I fear no other form of carrying this question will save our country or the liberty or soul of the slave."[3]

Although Garrison has received greater notice in history textbooks in the abolitionist fight, primarily due to his aggressive methods, Finney preached against slavery to hundreds of thousands of persons in his mammoth crusades, and trained anti-slavery leadership through his Oberlin College position. In the final analysis, perhaps both the direct and indirect approaches were necessary to condition the public mind about the institution.

Transcendentalists, far more liberal than either the deists of the founding or the 18th century Unitarians, were also a major force in advocating slavery's abolition. Transcendental theology (1) stressed the presence of the divine within man as a source of truth and a guide to action, (2) denied the biblical doctrine of sin, (3) looked upon man as innately good, (4) optimistically viewed the future of man, and (5) generally believed in eliminating restrictions on man's freedom.

Herein is an irony of liberal transcendental theology. Their leaders, such as Ralph Waldo Emerson and Henry Thoreau, emphasized the freedom of man from coercion, but as the abolitionist cause developed, they believed that coercive governmental action would be necessary to achieve this reform. Contrast Emerson's dilemma on this matter in these quotations:

> The root and seed of democracy is the doctrine, Judge for yourself. Reverence thyself. It is the inevitable effect of the doctrine, where it has any effect (which is rare), to insulate the partisan, to make each man a state.[4]

Democracy, Freedom, has its root in the sacred truth that every man hath in him the divine Reason, or that, though few men since the creation of the world live according to the dictates of Reason, yet all men are created capable of so doing. That is the equality and the only equality of all men. To this truth we look when we say, Reverence thyself; be true to thyself.[5]

I waked at night [he recorded in his journal] and bemoaned myself, because I had not thrown myself into this deplorable question of Slavery, which seems to want nothing so much as a few assured voices. But then, in hours of sanity, I recover myself, and say, 'God must govern his own world, and knows his own way out of this pit, without my desertion of my post, which has none to guard it but me. I have quite other slaves to free than those negroes, to wit, imprisoned spirits, imprisoned thoughts, far back in the brain of man—far retired in the heaven of invention, and which, important to the republic of Man, have no other watchman, or lover, or defender, but I.'[6]

Just as transcendentalists sometimes had difficulty reconciling their emphasis on freedom from coercion with taking direct action to abolish slavery, so too not all of conservative theology opposed slavery, especially in the South. However, where the conservative theological current in the North was generally a prime mover in shaping public policy on this issue, in the South it was more of a reinforcer of the institution of slavery. While the South had much in common with the dominant conservative theological tendencies of the North and Midwest, it refused to allow the "perfectionist" emphasis of Finney and other theologians to challenge the position of slavery or other governmental and social traditions of the region.

BEACHHEAD STRATEGIES AND STRENGTHS

What then can be said about the impact of theological tension during this second public policy epoch?

First, without the voices of Finney, Garrison, and others in conservative theological circles and Emerson, Thoreau, and Theodore Parker in the liberal theological circles of transcendentalism and unitarianism, the abolitionist movement would most likely have fizzled and the political base for abolition and the public consciousness of slavery might have been irreparably damaged.

Second, social reform through the use of governmental power began to emerge as a tool for theological action. In the twentieth century, liberal theology has increasingly built upon this foundation of direct governmental action in the interest of social reform as will be shown in Chapter 4.

Third, conservative theology in the twentieth century, especially until the late 1970s, has generally followed the Finney model of trying to influence public policy indirectly through preaching the salvation and regeneration of man. The conversion and regeneration of man, he argued, would thereby bring about social reform.

Fourth, as can be gleaned from the second and third conclusions, the theological tension of this epoch laid the foundation for direct influence on government by liberal theology and the continued emphasis by conservative theology on indirect influence. As a result during the twentieth century until the late 1970s, the principal church lobbies in Washington were those of liberal theological persuasion, such as the National Council of Churches, and others from mainline and liberal denominations like the Methodist and Presbyterian.

Fifth, the church began to be transformed, especially in liberal theological circles, from predominantly a spiritual institution to a more secular organization, acquiring characteristics of an interest group that competed with other groups to influence public policy. Rather than functioning separately from the interest group conflict, it began to function on an equal footing with other interest groups in seeking to influence public policy. To conservative theologians, this trend that was greatly accentuated during the twentieth century, removed the church from its prophetic pinnacle and reduced its political power. Alexis de Tocqueville's observation that although the church in the late 1700s and early 1800s exercised little direct influence upon public policy, it did direct "the customs of the community, and by regulating domestic life, it regulates the state"[7] reveals the significance of the conservative point of view. Namely, the church has more political power when it is less political.

Sixth, this was the last time in American history that conservative and liberal theology had significant and common public policy aims. Despite theological tension between them during the founding and Civil War epochs, they could agree on certain major common goals except in the South. But in the twentieth century, as liberal theology departed more from its roots in conservative theology, there has been little if any common agreement on either the means or the ends of public policy.

Seventh, the emphasis of liberal theology on direct influence may also help to explain why liberal protestant denominations are now better represented in government, such as in the U.S. Congress. In conservative theological circles, the call to preach has customarily been considered a higher calling than the call to a political vocation while laymen in liberal theological circles have been encouraged to engage more in politics as a vocation.

Eighth, by raising the concepts of equality and social reform, this epoch provided substantial impetus to the later growth of big government as political party platforms began to emphasize social reform and the equal protection clause of the Fourteenth Amendment began to be used to justify governmental action in domestic, social, and economic life. Much of the reason for twentieth century governmental expansion may rest at the doorstep of the theological fermentation prior to the Civil War. As Harvey Mansfield points out: "A society of natural equals then needs government of unlimited scope, that is, an enormous inequality of political power, in order to protect its equality."[8] Although equality was raised during the founding period, particularly in the Declaration of Independence, it was relatively less important than liberty and was not associated with the concept of social reform as during the second epoch which thereby set the stage for a continuing twentieth century tension between the concepts of liberty and equality in the making of public policy.

Ninth, this era's theological emphasis on economic, social and governmental reform helped pave the way for political party platforms to emphasize the same. Prior to then, party platforms were generally lacking in clarion calls for reform that later punctuated the platforms of such third parties as the Populist and Progressive as well as the two major parties.

Tenth, where the preservation of constitutional government has been the hallmark of conservative theology throughout the twentieth century, the call for democratic action in the interest of economic, social and political reform became the hallmark of liberal theology through the legacy of the pre-Civil War era. Indeed, during this century, many persons of liberal theological persuasion have come to view the checks and balances and division of power within the American constitutional system as unnecessary obstacles to democratic action, as will be shown in Chapter 4.

Eleventh, probably without the catalyst of the slavery crisis, liberal theology would never have had the success that it later achieved in the twentieth century. Slavery provided a point of protest that prompted the promulgation of liberal theology. Then in the twentieth century, the Great Depression provided even further opportunity for liberal theology to influence public policy through rallying behind economic, political and social reforms.

Twelfth, the prelude to the influence of Jewish and Roman Catholic theology in American public policy occurred during the pre-Civil War era with the immigration of large numbers of both groups, especially German Jews and Irish Catholics. The fountainhead not only of protestant liberalism, but also Jewish liberalism, was in Germany; hence, the influx of German Jews brought a natural tie to liberal economic, ideological, political, and social movements in America. Roman Catholic theology, on the other hand, has generally adapted to the social and political realities of the culture in which it finds itself; thus, the bulk of the Roman Catholic immigrant group, generally less well off economically, and big city residents, gradually began to identify more with the Democratic Party and labor unions during the twentieth century.

Thirteenth, emancipation of the American Negro during this era paved the way for their identification first with the Republican Party or Party of Lincoln, but then to transfer their allegiance to the Democratic Party of Franklin Roosevelt whose social and economic policies and big government tendencies benefited them more.

HERITAGE OF BATTLE

The optimistic theological spirit of the age that later influenced so much of twentieth century thought and action is evidenced in Charles Finney's observation that "The world is not growing worse but better."[9] This optimism helped fuel the fire of the League of Nations, the United Nations, the New Deal, and many other economic, political and social programs. Government which became the key instrument to achieve these goals naturally grew in response to the pressure placed upon it. Not until the 1970s did this spirit of optimism come crashing down as the programs designed to usher in a better world lost their luster in the ashes of dissent and discontent about their actual achievements.

The following documents reveal the fundamental issues of theological debate prior to the Civil War. The respective sides of the slavery issue are taken by the northern Presbyterian Church in their 1818 General Assembly and by Roman Catholic Bishop John England in his 1840 letter on the subject. The broader theological debate of liberal versus conservative theology is developed in selections from Ralph Waldo Emerson's address to the Harvard Divinity School in 1838 and from Oberlin College President Asa Mahan's writings in 1839.

NOTES

1. John L. Thomas, "Romantic Reform in America," *American Quarterly* 17 (1965), p. 658.
2. In Vernon L. Parrington, *Main Currents in American Thought: 1800-1860*, Volume II (New York: Harcourt, Brace and Co., 1930), p. 354.
3. In William G. McLoughlin, *Revivals, Awakenings and Reform* (Chicago: University of Chicago Press, 1978), p. 130.
4. In Parrington, p. 392.
5. Ibid.
6. Ibid., p. 399
7. In Robert S. Alley, *So Help Me God* (Richmond, Va.: John Knox Press, 1972), p. 21.
8. Harvey C. Mansfield, *The Spirit of Liberalism* (Cambridge, Mass.: Harvard University Press, 1978), p. 39.
9. In McLoughlin, p. 130.

THE CIVIL WAR ERA:
SELECTED POLITICAL AND
THEOLOGICAL DOCUMENTS

1. "Extracts" from the Minutes of the General Assembly
   of the Presbyterian Church in the United States of
   America (1818)
2. *Letters* (1840) by Roman Catholic Bishop John
   England
3. "Manifesto" (1838) by Ralph Waldo Emerson
4. *Scripture Doctrine of Christian Perfection* (1839) by
   Asa Mahan, President of Oberlin College

1. ∣ "EXTRACTS" FROM THE MINUTES OF
THE GENERAL ASSEMBLY OF THE PRESBYTERIAN CHURCH
IN THE UNITED STATES OF AMERICA (1818)

The General Assembly of the Presbyterian Church, having taken into consideration the subject of SLAVERY, think proper to make known their sentiments upon it to the churches and people under their care.

We consider the voluntary enslaving of one part of the human race by another, as a gross violation of the most precious and sacred rights of human nature; as utterly inconsistent with the law of God, which requires us to love our neighbour as ourselves; and as totally irreconcilable with the spirit and principles of the Gospel of Christ, which enjoin that, "all things whatsoever ye would that men should do to you, do ye even so to them." Slavery creates a paradox in the moral system—it exhibits rational, accountable, and immortal beings, in such circumstances as scarcely to leave them the power of moral action. It exhibits them as dependent on the will of others, whether they shall receive religious instruction; whether they shall know and worship the true God; whether they shall enjoy the ordinances of the Gospel; whether they shall perform the duties and cherish the endearments of husbands and wives, parents and children, neighbours and friends; whether they shall preserve their chastity and purity, or regard the dictates of justice and humanity. Such are some of the consequences of Slavery—consequences not imaginary—but which connect themselves with its very existence. The evils to which the slave is *always* exposed, often take place in fact, and in their very worst degree and form: and where all of them do not take place, as we rejoice to say that in many instances, through the influence of the principles of humanity and religion on the minds of masters, they do not—still the slave is deprived of his natural right, degraded as a human being, and exposed to the danger of passing into the hands of a master who may inflict upon him all the hardships and injuries which inhumanity and avarice may suggest.

From this view of the consequences resulting from the practice into which christian people have most inconsistently fallen, of enslaving a portion of their *brethren* of mankind—for "God hath made of one blood all nations of men to dwell on the face of the earth"—it is manifestly the duty of all christians who enjoy the light of the present day, when the inconsistency of slavery, both with the dictates of humanity and religion, has been demonstrated, and is generally seen and acknowledged, to use their honest, earnest, and unwearied endeavours, to correct the errors of former times, and as speedily as possible to efface this blot on our holy religion, and to obtain the complete abolition of slavery throughout christendom, and if possible throughout the world.

We rejoice that the church to which we belong commenced, as early as any other in this country, the good work of endeavouring to put an end to slavery,* and that in the same work, many of its members have ever since been, and now are, among the most active, vigorous, and efficient labourers. We do, indeed, tenderly sympathize with those portions of our church and our country, where the evil of slavery has been entailed upon them; where a *great*, and *the most virtuous part* of the *community* abhor slavery, and wish its extermination, as sincerely as any others—but where the number of slaves, their ignorance, and their vicious habits generally, render an immediate and universal emancipation inconsistent, alike, with the safety and happiness of the master and the

---

*In the minutes of the Synod of New York and Philadelphia, for the year 1787, before the General Assembly was constituted, we find the following, viz.

"The Synod of New York and Philadelphia, do highly approve of the general principles, in favor of universal liberty, that prevail in America; and of the interest which many of the states have taken in promoting the abolition of slavery; yet, inasmuch as men, introduced from a servile state to a participation of all the privileges of civil society, without a proper education, and without previous habits of industry, may be, in many respects, dangerous to the community: Therefore, they earnestly recommend it to all the members belonging to their communion, to give those persons who are, at present, held in servitude, such good education as may prepare them for the better enjoyment of freedom. And they, moreover, recommend, that masters, whenever they find servants disposed to make a proper improvement of the privilege, would give them some share of property to begin with; or grant them sufficient time and sufficient means of procuring, by industry, their own liberty, at a moderate rate; that they may, thereby, be brought into society with those habits of industry, that may render them useful citizens: —And finally, they recommend it to all the people under their care, to use the most prudent measures consistent with the interest and the state of civil society, in the parts where they live, to procure eventually, the final abolition of slavery in America." [The Minutes]

slave. With those who are thus circumstanced, we repeat that we tenderly sympathize. —At the same time, we earnestly exhort them to continue, and, if possible, to increase their exertions to effect a total abolition of slavery. —We exhort them to suffer no greater delay to take place in this most interesting concern, than a regard to the public welfare *truly* and *indispensably* demands.

Source: "Extracts" from the Minutes of the General Assembly of the Presbyterian Church, in the United States of America: A.D. 1818 (Phila., 1818), pp. 28-33.

2. ⏐ *LETTERS* (1840)

Roman Catholic Bishop John England

In the New Testament we find instances of pious and good men having slaves, and in no case do we find the Saviour imputing it to them as a crime, or requiring their servants' emancipation. —In chap. viii, of St. Matthew, we read of a centurion, who addressing the Lord Jesus, said, v. 9, "For I also am a man under authority, having soldiers under me, and I say to this man, go, and he goeth; and to another, come, and he cometh: and to my servant, do this and he doeth it." v. 10. "And Jesus hearing this wondered, and said to those that followed him: Amen, I say to you, I have not found so great faith in Israel." v. 13. ["] And Jesus said to the centurion, go, and as thou hast believed, so be it done to thee. And the servant was healed at the same hour." St. Luke, in ch. vii, relates also the testimony which the ancients of Israel gave of this stranger's virtue, and how he loved their nation, and built a synagogue for them.

In many of his parables, the Saviour describes the master and his servants in a variety of ways, without any condemnation or censure of slavery. In Luke xvii, he describes the usual mode of acting towards slaves as the very basis upon which he teaches one of the most useful lessons of Christian virtue, v. 7. "But which of you having a servant ploughing or feeding cattle, will say to him, when he is come from the field, immediately, go sit down." 8. "And will not rather say to him, make ready my supper, and gird thyself, and serve me while I eat and drink, and afterwards, thou shalt eat and drink?" 9. "Doth he thank that servant because he did the things that were commanded him?" 10. "I think not. So you also, when you shall have done all the things that are commanded you, say: we are unprofitable servants, we have done that which we ought to do."

After the promulgation of the Christian religion by the apostles, the slave was not told by them that he was in a state of unchristian durance. I. Cor. vii, 20. "Let every man abide in the same calling in which he was called." 21. "Art thou called being a bond-man? Care not for it; but if thou mayest be made free, use it rather." 22. "For he that is called in the Lord, being a bond-man, is the free-man of the Lord. Likewise he that is called being free, is the bond-man of

Christ." 23. "You are bought with a price, be not made the bond-slaves of men." 24. "Brethren, let every man, wherein he was called, therein abide with God." Thus a man by becoming a Christian was not either made free nor told that he was free, but he was advised, if he could lawfully procure his freedom, to prefer it to slavery. The 23d verse has exactly that meaning which we find expressed also in chap. vi, v. 20. "For you are bought with a great price, glorify and bear God in your body," which is addressed to the free as well as to the slave: all are the servants of God, and should not be drawn from his service by the devices of men, but should "walk worthy of the vocation in which they are called." Eph. iv. i. and the price by which their souls, (not their bodies) were redeemed, is also described by St. Peter I, c. i, 10. "Knowing that you were not redeemed with corruptible gold or silver from your vain conversation of the tradition of your fathers." 19. "But with the precious blood of Christ, as of a lamb unspotted and undefiled." —That it was a spiritual redemption and a spiritual service, St. Paul again shows, Heb. ix, 14. "How much more shall the blood of Christ, who through the Holy Ghost, offered himself without spot to God, cleanse our conscience from dead works to serve the living God?" It is then a spiritual equality as was before remarked, in the words of St. Paul, I Cor. xii, 13. "For in one spirit we are baptized into one body, whether Jews or Gentiles, whether bond or free." And in the same chapter he expatiates to show that though all members of the one mystical body, their places, their duties, their gifts are various and different. And in his epistle to the Galatians, chap. iv. he exhibits the great truth which he desires to inculcate by an illustration taken from the institutions of slavery, and without a single expression of their censure.

Nor did the apostles consider the Christian master obliged to liberate his Christian servant. St. Paul in his epistle to Philemon acknowledges the right of the master to the services of his slave for whom however he asks, as a special favor, pardon for having deserted his owner. 10. "I beseech thee for my son Onesimus whom I have begotten in my chains." 11. "Who was heretofore unprofitable to thee, but now profitable both to thee and to thee [sic]." 12. "Whom I have sent back to thee. And do thou receive him as my own bowels." Thus a runaway slave still belonged to his master, and though having become a Christian, so far from being thereby liberated from service, he was bound to return thereto and submit himself to his owner. . . .

Again it is manifest from the Epistle of St. Paul to Timothy that the title of the master continued good to his slave though both should be Christians, c. vii. "Whosoever are servants under the yoke, let them count their masters worthy of all honor, lest the name and doctrine of the Lord be blasphemed." 2. "But they who have believing masters, let them not despise them because they are brethren, but serve them the rather, because they are faithful and beloved, who are partakers of the benefit. These things exhort and teach." And in the subsequent part he declares the contrary teaching to be against the sound words of Jesus Christ, and to spring from ignorant pride. . . .

It will now fully establish what will be necessary to perfect the view which I desire to give, if I can show that masters who were Christians were not required to emancipate their slaves, but had pointed out the duties which they were bound as masters to perform, because this will show under the Christian dispensation the legal, moral and religious existence of slave and master.

The apostle, as we have previously seen, I Tim. vi, 2, wrote of slaves who had believing or Christian masters. The inspired penman did not address his instructions and exhortations to masters who were not of the household of the Faith. I Cor. v, 12. "For what have I to do, to judge them that are without?" 13. "For them that are without, God will judge; take away the evil one from amongst yourselves." Thus when he addresses masters; they are Christian masters. Ephes. vi, 9. "And you, masters, do the same things to them (servants) forbearing threatenings, knowing that the Lord both of them and you is in heaven: and there is no respect of persons with him,"—and again, Colos. iv, i, "Masters do to your servants that which is just and equal: knowing that you also have a master in heaven."

We have then in the teaching of the apostles nothing which contradicts the law of Moses, but we have much which corrects the cruelty of the Pagan practice. The exhibition which is presented to us is one of a cheering and of an elevated character. It is true that the state of slavery is continued under the legal sanction, but the slave is taught from the most powerful motives to be faithful, patient, obedient and contented, and the master is taught that though despotism may pass unpunished on earth it will be examined into at the bar of heaven: and though the slave owes him bodily service, yet that the soul of this drudge, having been purchased at the same price as his own, and sanctified by the same law of regeneration, he who is his slave according to the flesh, is his brother according to the spirit. —His humanity, his charity, his affection are enlisted and interested, and he feels that his own father is also, the father of his slave, hence though the servant must readily and cheerfully pay him homage and perform his behests on earth, yet, they may be on an equality in heaven. . . .

To the Christian slave was exhibited the humiliation of an incarnate God, the suffering of an unoffending victim, the invitation of this model of perfection to that meekness, that humility, that peaceful spirit, that charity and forgiveness of injuries which constitute the glorious beatitudes. He was shown the advantage of suffering, the reward of patience, and the narrow road along whose rugged ascents he was to bear the cross, walking in the footsteps of his Saviour. The curtains which divide both worlds were raised as he advanced, and he beheld Lazarus in the bosom of Abraham, whilst the rich man vainly cried to have this once miserable beggar allowed to dip the tip of his finger in water and touch it to his tongue, for he was tormented in that flame.

Thus, sir, did the legislator of Christianity, whilst he admitted the legality of slavery, render the master merciful, and the slave faithful, obedient and religious, looking for his freedom in that region, where alone true and lasting enjoyment can be found.

Source: Letters of the Late Bishop England to the Hon. John Forsyth, on the Subject of Domestic Slavery (Baltimore, 1844), pp. 34-39.

3. | "MANIFESTO" (1838)

Ralph Waldo Emerson

Truly speaking it is not instruction, but provocation, that I can receive from another soul. What he announces, I must find true in me, or reject; and on his word, or as his second, be he who he may, I can accept nothing. On the contrary, the absence of this primary faith is the presence of degradation. As is the flood, so is the ebb. Let this faith depart, and the very words it spake and the things it made become false and hurtful. Then falls the church, the state, art, letters, life. The doctrine of the divine nature being forgotten, a sickness infects and dwarfs the constitution. Once man was all; now he is an appendage, a nuisance. And because the indwelling Supreme Spirit cannot wholly be got rid of, the doctrine of it suffers this perversion, that the divine nature is attributed to one or two persons, and denied to all the rest, and denied with fury. The doctrine of inspiration is lost; the base doctrine of the majority of voices usurps the place of the doctrine of the soul. Miracles, prophecy, poetry, the ideal life, the holy life, exist as ancient history merely; they are not in the belief, nor in the aspiration of society; but, when suggested, seem ridiculous. Life is comic or pitiful as soon as the high ends of being fade out of sight, and man becomes near-sighted, and can only attend to what addresses the senses. . . .

Jesus Christ belonged to the true race of prophets. He saw with open eye the mystery of the soul. Drawn by its severe harmony, ravished with its beauty, he lived in it, and had his being there. Alone in all history he estimated the greatness of man. One man was true to what is in you and me. He saw that God incarnates himself in man, and evermore goes forth anew to take possession of his World. He said, in this jubilee of sublime emotion, 'I am divine. Through me, God acts; through me, speaks. Would you see God, see me; or see thee, when thou also thinkest as I now think.' But what a distortion did his doctrine and memory suffer in the same, in the next, and the following ages! There is no doctrine of the Reason which will bear to be taught by the Understanding. The understanding caught this high chant from the poet's lips, and said, in the next age, 'This was Jehovah come down out of heaven. I will kill you, if you say he was a man.' The idioms of his language and the figures of his rhetoric have usurped the place of his truth; and churches are not built on his principles, but on his tropes. Christianity became a Mythus, as the poetic teaching of Greece and of Egypt, before. He spoke of miracles; for he felt that man's life was a miracle, and all that man doeth, and he knew that this daily miracle shines as the character ascends. But the word Miracle, as pronounced by Christian churches, gives a false impression; it is Monster. It is not one with the blowing clover and the falling rain.

He felt respect for Moses and the prophets, but no unfit tenderness at postponing their initial revelations to the hour and the man that now is; to the eternal revelation in the heart. Thus was he a true man. Having seen that the law in us is commanding, he would not suffer it to be commanded. Boldly, with hand, and heart, and life, he declared it was God. Thus is he, as I think, the only soul in history who has appreciated the worth of man.

1. In this point of view we become sensible of the first defect of historical Christianity. Historical Christianity has fallen into the error that corrupts all attempts to communicate religion. As it appears to us, and as it has appeared for ages, it is not the doctrine of the soul, but an exaggeration of the personal, the positive, the ritual. It has dwelt, it dwells, with noxious exaggeration about the *person* of Jesus. The soul knows no persons. It invites every man to expand to the full circle of the universe, and will have no preferences but those of spontaneous love. . . .

   That is always best which gives me to myself. The sublime is excited in me by the great stoical doctrine, Obey thyself. That which shows God in me, fortifies me. That which shows God out of me, makes me a wart and a wen. There is no longer a necessary reason for my being. Already the long shadows of untimely oblivion creep over me, and I shall decrease forever. . . .

2. The second defect of the traditionary and limited way of using the mind of Christ is a consequence of the first; this, namely; that the Moral Nature, that Law of laws whose revelations introduce greatness—yea, God himself—into the open soul, is not explored as the fountain of the established teaching in society. Men have come to speak of the revelation as somewhat long ago given and done, as if God were dead. The injury to faith throttles the preacher; and the goodliest of institutions becomes an uncertain and inarticulate voice. . . .

The man on whom the soul descends, through whom the soul speaks, alone can teach. Courage, piety, love, wisdom, can teach; and every man can open his door to these angels, and they shall bring him the gift of tongues. But the man who aims to speak as books enable, as synods use, as the fashion guides, and as interest commands, babbles. Let him hush.

Source: Ralph Waldo Emerson, "An Address Delivered Before the Senior Class in Divinity College, Cambridge, Sunday Evening, July 15, 1838," in Edward Waldo Emerson, ed., *The Complete Works of Ralph Waldo Emerson* (12 vols., Boston, 1903-04), I, pp. 127-32, 134-35, 143-47, 149-51.

4. I *SCRIPTURE DOCTRINE OF CHRISTIAN PERFECTION* (1839)

Asa Mahan, President of Oberlin College

To present this subject in a somewhat more distinct and expanded form, the attention to the reader is now invited to a few remarks upon I Thes. v. 23. "And the very God of peace sanctify you wholly: and I pray God your whole spirit and soul and body be preserved blameless unto the coming of our Lord Jesus Christ." . . . In short, the prayer of the apostle is, that all the powers and susceptibilities of our being may not only be purified from all that is unholy, but wholly sanctified and devoted to Christ, and forever preserved in that state. Now, the powers and susceptibilities of our nature are all comprehended in the following enumeration: the will, the intellect, and our mental and physical susceptibilities and propensities. The question to which the special attention of the reader is invited is this: When are we in a perfectly sanctified and blameless state, in respect to the action of all these powers and susceptibilities?

1. That we be in a perfectly sanctified and blameless state in regard to our wills, implies, that the action of all our voluntary powers be in entire conformity to the will of God; that every choice, every preference, and every volition, be controlled by a filial regard to the divine requisitions. The perpetual language of the heart must be, "Lord, what wilt thou have me do?"

2. That we "be preserved blameless" in regard to our intellect, does not imply that we never think of what is evil. If this were so, Christ was not blameless, because he thought of the temptations of Satan. Nor could the Christian repel what is evil, as he is required to do. To repel evil, the evil itself must be before the mind, as an object of thought.

   To be blameless in respect to the action of our intellectual powers, does imply, (1.) That every thought of evil be instantly suppressed and repelled. (2.) That they be constantly employed on the inquiry, what is the truth and will of God, and by what means we may best meet the demands of the great law of love. (3.) That they be employed in the perpetual contemplation of "whatsoever things are true, whatsoever things are honest, whatsoever things are just, whatsoever things are pure, whatsoever things are lovely, whatsoever things are of good report; if there be any virtue, and if there be any praise," in thinking of these things also. When the intellectual powers are thus employed, they are certainly in a blameless state.

3. That our feelings and mental susceptibilities be preserved blameless, does not imply, that they are, at all times and circumstances, in the same intensity of excitement, or in the same identical state. This the powers and laws of our being forbid. Nor, in that case, could we obey the command, "Rejoice with those that do rejoice, and weep with those that weep." Nor does it imply that no feelings can exist in the mind, which, under the circumstances then present, it would be improper to indulge. A Christian, for example, may feel a very strong desire to speak for Christ under circumstances when it would be improper for him to speak. The feeling itself is proper. But we must be guided by wisdom from above in respect to the question, when and where we are to give utterance to our feelings.

   That our feelings and mental susceptibilities be in a blameless state, does imply, (1.) That they all be held in perfect and perpetual subjection to the will of God. (2.) That they be in perfect and perpetual harmony with the truth and will of God as apprehended by the intellect, and thus constituting a spotless mirror, through which there shall be a perfect reflection of whatsoever things are "true," "honest," "just," "pure," "lovely," and of "good report."

4. That our "bodies be preserved blameless," does not, of course, imply that they are free from fatigue, disease, or death. Nor does it imply that no desire be excited through our physical propensities, which, under existing circumstances, it would be unlawful to indulge. The feeling of hunger in Christ, under circumstances in which indulgence was not proper, was not sinful. The consent of the will to gratify the feeling, and not the feeling itself, renders us sinners.

That we be preserved in a sanctified and blameless state in respect to our bodies, does imply, (1.) That we endeavor to acquaint ourselves with all the laws of our physical constitution. (2.) That in regard to food, drink, and dress, and in regard to the indulgence of all our appetites and physical propensities, there be a sacred and undeviating conformity to these laws. (3.) That every unlawful desire be instantly suppressed, and that all our propensities be held in perfect subjection to the will of God. (4.) That our bodies, with all our physical powers and propensities, be "presented to God as a living sacrifice, holy and acceptable," to be employed in his service.

Such is Christian Perfection. It is the consecration of our whole being to Christ, and the perpetual employment of all our powers in his service. It is the perfect assimilation of our entire character to that of Christ, having at all times, and under all circumstances, the "same mind that was also in Christ Jesus." It is, in the language of Mr. Wesley, "In one view, purity of intention, dedicating all the life to God. It is the giving God all the heart; it is one desire and design ruling all our tempers. It is devoting, not a part, but all our soul, body, and substance to God. In another view, it is all the mind that was in Christ Jesus, enabling us to walk as he walked. It is the circumcision of the heart from all filthiness, from all inward as well as outward pollution. It is the renewal of the heart in the whole image of God, the full likeness of him that created it. In yet another, it is loving God with all our heart, and our neighbor as ourselves." . . .*

This doctrine, it is said, is, or in its legitimate tendencies, leads to, Perfectionism. If any individual will point out any thing intrinsic, in the doctrine here maintained, at all allied to *that* error, I, for one, will be among the first to abandon the position which I am now endeavoring to sustain. Perfectionism, technically so called, is, in my judgment, in the native and necessary tendencies of its principles, worse than the worst form of infidelity. The doctrine of holiness, now under consideration, in all its essential features and elements, stands in direct opposition to Perfectionism. It has absolutely nothing in common with it, but a few terms derived from the Bible.

---

*"A Plain Account of Christian Perfection, as Believed and Taught by the Reverend Mr. John Wesley, from the Year 1725, to the Year 1777," *The Works of the Rev. John Wesley* (14 vols., London, 1829), XI, p. 444.

1. Perfectionism, for example, in its fundamental principles, is the abrogation of all law. The doctrine of holiness, as here maintained, is perfect obedience to the precepts of the law. It is the "righteousness of the law fulfilled in us."
2. In abrogating the moral law, as a rule of duty, Perfectionism abrogates all obligation of every kind, and to all beings. The doctrine of holiness, as here maintained, contemplates the Christian as a "debtor to all men," to the full extent of his capacities, and consists in a perfect discharge of all these obligations—of every obligation to God and man.
3. Perfectionism is a "rest" which suspends all efforts and prayer, even, for the salvation of the world. The doctrine of holiness, as here maintained, consists in such a sympathy with the love of Christ, as constrains the subject to consecrate his entire being to the glory of Christ, in the salvation of men.
4. Perfectionism substitutes the direct teaching of the Spirit, falsely called, in the place of the "word." This expects such teachings only in the diligent study of the word, and tries every doctrine by the "law and the testimony," expounded in conformity with the legitimate laws of interpretation.
5. Perfectionism surrenders up the soul to blind impulse, assuming, that every existing desire or impulse is caused by the direct agency of the Spirit, and therefore to be gratified. The doctrine of holiness, as here maintained, consists of the subjection of all our powers and propensities to the revealed will of God.
6. Perfectionism abrogates the Sabbath, and all the ordinances of the gospel, and, in its legitimate tendencies, even marriage itself. The doctrine of holiness, as here maintained, is a state of perfect moral purity, induced and perpetuated by a careful observance of all these ordinances, together with subjection to other influences of the gospel, received by faith.
7. Perfectionism renders, in its fundamental principles, all perfection an impossibility. If, as this system maintains, the Christian is freed from all obligation, is bound by no law—in short, if there is no standard with which to compare his actions, (and there is none), if the moral law, as a rule of action is abrogated—moral perfection can no more be predicted of the Christian than of the horse, the ox, or the ass. The doctrine of holiness, on the other hand, as here maintained, contemplates the moral law as the only rule and standard of the moral conduct, and consists in perfect conformity to the precepts of this law.
8. Perfectionism, in short, in its essential elements, is the perfection of licentiousness. The doctrine of holiness, as here maintained, is the perfect and perpetual harmony of the soul with "whatsoever things are true, whatsoever things are honest," "just," "pure," "lovely," and of "good report," and if there be any virtue, "and if there be any praise," with these things also.

What agreement, then, has the doctrine of holiness, as here maintained with Perfectionism? The same that light has with darkness. A man might, with the same propriety, affirm that I am a Unitarian, because I believe in one God, while I hang my whole eternity upon the doctrine of the Trinity, as to affirm that I am a Perfectionist, because I hold the doctrine of holiness as now presented.

Source: Asa Mahan, *Scripture Doctrine of Christian Perfection: With Other Kindred Subjects, Illustrated and Confirmed in a Series of Discourses Designed to Throw Light on the Way of Holiness* (4th ed., Boston, 1840), pp. 7-13, 71-73.

4 | THEOLOGICAL TENSION AND THE NEW DEAL

During [Roosevelt's] long term in office the churches began the upsurge in theology which came to flower in 'Neo-orthodoxy' under the brilliant leadership of Reinhold Niebuhr and Paul Tillich. By 1940 Niebuhr had become an enthusiastic Roosevelt Democrat. The interplay between FDR's 'brain trust' and Niebuhr is best documented in the statement of George Kennan, who said Niebuhr was 'father to us all.' His realism tempered with the ethic of Jesus undercut the Gospel of Wealth and established the standard of social justice for theologians of the forties and fifties. He became the theologian of the New Deal.[1]

ROBERT S. ALLEY

The New Deal era marked a significant escalation in the conflict between conservative and liberal theology that resulted in (1) clarifying the lines of combat, (2) the marked decline of conservative protestant dominance, (3) the changed role of the church, especially in liberal theological circles, from spiritual interests to secular interest group activism in government and politics and (4) the inclusion of new theological groups with substantial influence on public policy issues. Additionally this era was like a skirmish prior to full-scale warfare between conservative and liberal theology during the last one-third of the twentieth century.

THE LIBERAL ALLIANCE

Early in the twentieth century and long before the New Deal, the social gospel movement began to propose agendas for governmental action on social and economic issues, looking to the government to establish "the kingdom of God on earth." During this period, as liberal theological forces gradually captured control of major denominations, such as the Methodist and Presbyterian, the churches which had had the major role for social welfare prior to the twentieth century began to remove themselves from this function. After the New Deal, of course, social welfare became largely the work of government.

Generally the New Deal is assessed as a response to overwhelming economic and social dislocations, and in the narrow view that is true. But in a much larger and more accurate sense, the social and economic ideas of the New Deal had been hammered out in the halls of liberal theology. For example, as Professors Dulce and Richter have pointed out, "In Wilson's social legislation, the 'social gospel' achieved recognition on a new scale. Here was the birth of the new concept for a new society that eventually found full expression in the programs and philosophy of the New Deal."[2] These professors also note that "In his 1937 Inaugural Roosevelt . . . echoed the fusion of the social gospel and the predominant strain of Wilsonian democracy, declaring, 'The test of our progress is not whether we add more to the abundance of those who have too much; it is whether we provide enough for those who have too little.' He saw 'one-third of a nation ill-housed, ill-clad, ill-nourished.'"[3]

During the pre-New Deal era, both liberal theology and liberal political ideology began to change the generally accepted views of their controlling documents, the Bible, and the Constitution, respectively. Prior to this time the Bible was generally accepted as "the Word of God," meaning that it has no errors, but through the influence of liberal theology, the common view in the leading denominations and seminaries changed to "the Bible contains the Word of God," meaning that it has errors or is only partially God's Word, and that it should be reinterpreted by man in light of new knowledge and a changing society. Gradually, man became more important and God less important, as man became, in effect, judge of what is the Word of God. This erosion of the prevailing view of scripture preceded a similar erosion of the conservative view that the U.S. Constitution contains language with consistent meaning from generation to generation and that it should only be altered by amendment, not reinterpretation of words and concepts hammered out and agreed to by the Founders. Liberal theologians supported both biblical and constitutional reinterpretations.

In inaugural addresses and Thanksgiving proclamations, one detects the shift from conservative to liberal theology as presidents emphasized more the work of man on earth as distinguished from the grace and activity of God in the affairs of men. Contrast, for example, the beginning of George Washington's Thanksgiving Day proclamation with that of Franklin Roosevelt:

Washington: 'Whereas it is the duty of all nations to acknowledge the providence of Almighty God, to obey His will, to be grateful for His benefits, and humbly to implore His protection and favor.'[4]

Roosevelt: 'In traversing a period of national stress our country has been knit together in a closer fellowship of mutual interest and common purpose. We can well be grateful that more and more of our people understand and seek the greater good of the greater number. We can be grateful that selfish purpose of personal gain, at our neighbor's loss, less strongly asserts itself. We can be grateful that peace at home is strengthened by a growing willingness to common counsel. We can be grateful that our peace with other nations continues through recognition of our own peaceful purpose.'[5]

Roosevelt's proclamation is the first to break with Washington's emphasis upon the providence and grace of God and to emphasize the works of man. It also suggests the different view of salvation held by liberal theology as shown below:

	Type of Salvation	*Agent to Achieve Salvation*
Conservative	Spiritual	Spirit of God
Liberal	Secular/Social	State/Government

One of the liberal theological purposes of government became clear during this era, namely to utilize government as the principal tool to bring happiness to humans who could not achieve it on their own.

Although the Founders wanted to strengthen the national government in relation to the states, they still envisioned a national government with limited powers. As James Madison observed in No. 45 of *The Federalist*,

The powers delegated by the proposed Constitution to the federal government are few and defined. Those which are to remain in the state government are numerous and indefinite. The former will be exercised principally on external objects, as war, peace, negotiation, and foreign commerce; with which last the power of taxation will, for the most part, be connected. The powers reserved to the several states will extend to all the objects which, in the ordinary course of affairs, concern the lives, liberties, and properties of the people and the internal order, improvement, and prosperity of the state.[6]

A NEW ATTACK

As an intellectual architect of the New Deal, Rexford Tugwell stated that to reduce liberty and to increase equality in public policy, the New Deal had to undermine the intentions of the Founders by reinterpretation of Constitutional language. He states:

> The intention of the eighteenth and nineteenth century law was to install and protect the principle of conflict; this [principle], if we begin to plan, we shall be changing once for all, and it will require the laying of rough, unholy hands on many a sacred precedent, doubtless calling on an enlarged and nationalized police power for enforcement. We shall also have to give up a distinction of great consequence, and very dear to a legalistic heart, but economically quite absurd, between private and public or quasi-public employments. There is no private business, if by that we mean one of no consequence to anyone but its proprietors; and so none exempt from compulsion to serve a planned public interest.[7]

Some years later, reflecting on delays in achieving this objective, Tugwell remarked: "Organization for these purposes was very inefficient because they were not acknowledged intentions. Much of the lagging reluctance was owed to the constantly reiterated intention that what was being done was in pursuit of the aims embodied in the Constitution of 1787 when obviously it was in contravention of them."[8]

What happened was a change in the meaning of the Constitution's very words. Justice Felix Frankfurter, for example, said that words in the Constitution are "so restricted by their intrinsic meaning or by their history or by tradition or by prior decisions that they leave the individual justice free, if indeed they do not compel him, to gather meaning not from reading the Constitution but from reading life."[9] Justice Oliver Wendell Holmes made much the same point: "When we are dealing with words that also are a constituent act, like the Constitution of the United States, we must realize that they have called into life a being the development of which could not have been foreseen by the most gifted of its begetters."[10] This point of view has led to substantial changes in interpretation which significantly increased the power of the national government in relation to that of the states.

In 1936, the Supreme Court declared that the "general welfare" clause of Article I, Section 8, permitted Congress to appropriate funds for just about any purpose it chose. As the Court put it, "The power of Congress to authorize expenditure of public moneys for public purposes is not limited by the direct grants of legislative power found in the Constitution (*United States* v. *Butler*, 1936).

In 1937, "interstate commerce" (Article I, Section 8) was defined as anything that substantially affected the flow of interstate business, whether or not it actually crossed state lines (*National Labor Relations Board* v. *Jones and Laughlin*, 1937).

In 1942, the Court held that the national government could regulate a product even if the producer did not intend to sell it, because the product could still affect interstate commerce. If a producer keeps what he or she produces, substitute products are not necessary, and interstate commerce is therefore affected (*Wickard* v. *Filburn*, 1942).

More recently, the clauses of the Fourteenth Amendment guaranteeing "equal protection of the laws" and "due process of law" have been used with increasing frequency to establish national regulation in matters dealing with education and criminal law. For more than 100 years these subjects had generally been within the jurisdiction of the states.

SURVEYING THE BATTLEFIELD

When the dust had settled on the battlefield, it was easier to see why the liberal alliance dominated this battle and what the significance of the New Deal battle would be for the future. First, there was not a conservative coalition comparable to the liberal alliance. Given their primary emphasis on the spiritual rather than the material aspects of life, conservative theological leaders generally did not make common cause with their political counterparts; moreover, conservative southern Protestants were yoked with the New Deal program through their solid allegiance to the Democratic Party. Later in the twentieth century conservative southern Protestants began to leave the Democratic Party's fold, thereby allowing conservatives to build substantial strength in a heretofore untapped region.

Second, the liberal churches clearly identified government as the principal agent they needed to influence in the pursuit of their goals, and they organized through the National Council of Churches and denominational interest groups to influence public policy. Conservative theological interests, lacking this organizational interest, were caught short by this liberal theological foray onto the battlefield.

Third, perhaps more than any other single cause, the Great Depression served as a catalytic agent to highlight the liberal view of government. Without this catalyst, it would have been difficult, if not impossible, for the liberal position to have gained dominance. The Great Depression created a problem that liberal theology could utilize in their efforts to enlarge the scope of government into new economic, social, and political areas.

Fourth, since the major denominational seminaries, particularly in the North, were controlled by liberal theological forces, a very important shaper of the public mind, namely the pulpit, which had heretofore been largely in the hands of conservative forces, helped mold public opinion to the side of the liberal view of government's proper role.

Fifth, science and the forces of urbanization and industrialization began to attack the heart of conservative strength. Science challenged biblical teaching about the origins of man and the earth while urbanization and industrialization broke down the rural and farm lifestyle in which conservative theology had been so dominant during the nineteenth century. The big cities helped deemphasize conservative theological convictions and depersonalize American society.

Sixth, with radio and newspaper influence increasing, the leadership of President Roosevelt was enhanced to bring about his New Deal objective. Without these avenues of leadership, the highly ambitious New Deal program probably could not have been achieved. The media provided a way to crystallize public support for the liberal program.

Seventh, the emergence of Roman Catholic, Jewish, and Negro voters in large numbers in the big cities combined with traditional southern protestant support allowed the president sufficient leverage to win both personal victories at the polls and programmatic victories in Congress. Ironically liberal protestant thought could not have won without the overwhelming support of these new groups of voters that were generally alien to their theological influence except as it had political impact.

THE BATTLE'S SIGNIFICANCE

The significance of the liberal theological and political successes was not only in the program adopted, but in other related changes. First, this era presented a clear contrast between conservative and liberal purposes for government. The conservative's religious respect for constitutional government, meaning a limited national government role, versus the liberal's respectful rejection of Constitutional government, meaning a liberal democratic state that emphasized the pragmatic application of political power in the pursuit of liberal political goals and the enlargement of the national government, escalated the stakes for which the two sides were fighting.

Second, the political slogans of the New Deal era, such as New Deal and Fair Deal, revealed a changed emphasis from the responsibilities of man to the rights of man and government's role in securing those rights. These slogans and programs spoke more of what government should do for people rather than what the people should do for themselves.

Third, securing control of the national government and reorienting the goals of government allowed the liberal alliance to maintain effective control over public policy into the 1980s. In the process greater political power was shifted to the national government until challenged by President Reagan's efforts to alter substantially the allocation of governmental power between national and state governments.

Fourth, among the impacts of the New Deal was to raise the concept of equality on a competitive par if not indeed to surpass liberty in importance and in the process to enhance substantially the powers not only of the national government, but also of the presidency. Both the contemporary presidency and the era of cooperative federalism generally mark their genesis with the New Deal.

Fifth, while historically conservative theology has strongly reinforced the concept of nationalism, liberal theology in the twentieth century has had a much more international focus. Social gospel and neo-orthodox theology encouraged internationalism by laying the cornerstones for Wilson's League of Nations and Roosevelt's United Nations. The "real politik" or power politics of Reinhold Niebuhr's neo-orthodox theology also helped to undergird the post-World War II Cold War policies of several administrations.

Sixth, the defeat of prohibition during the New Deal era symbolized not only the weakened conservative protestant position that was now challenged by liberal protestant theology as well as by the masses of Roman Catholic and Jewish voters, but it also foreshadowed a reduced emphasis on this type of personal morality issue in the body politic.

While conservative and liberal theology generally maintained common bonds and goals in public policy during the Founding and Civil War epochs, they were severed during the New Deal, setting the stage for an attempted post-New Deal reassertion of conservative theology and conservative political ideology. The liberal rout of politically lethargic conservative theology during the New Deal epoch perhaps inspired liberal forces to muster more weaponry for even greater victories through the Fair Deal, New Frontier, and Great Society programs. Subsequent efforts to achieve more liberal victories, however, provoked a latent reaction of conservative theology and eclipsed the South's unquestioning loyalty as a member of the liberal alliance. Gradually a conservative coalition of political and theological forces began to form to engage in full scale war with the liberal alliance.

The following sources contrast the major theological and political differences during this era, including (1) a clear statement of historic protestant doctrine in the so-called "Niagara Creed," (2) the emerging social gospel emphasis of liberal protestant theology in "The Social Ideals of the Churches" and the writings of Walter Rauschenbusch, (3) the development of Roman Catholic political involvement in "The Bishops' Program of Social Reconstruction," (4) the origin of neo-orthodoxy with its liberal protestant political emphasis in the writings of H. Richard Niebuhr, and (5) the evolution of Jewish political involvement in the writings of Lawrence Fuchs.

NOTES

1. Robert S. Alley, *So Help Me God* (Richmond, Va.: John Knox Press, 1972), p. 21.

2. Berton Dulce and Edward J. Richter, *Religion and the Presidency* (New York: Macmillan, 1962), p. 63.

3. Ibid., p. 102.

4. John D. Richardson, ed., *A Compilation of Messages and Papers of the President: 1780-1897*, Vol. I. (Washington, D.C.: U.S. Government Printing Office, 1896), p. 64.

5. Samuel I. Rosenman, ed., *The Public Papers and Addresses of Franklin D. Roosevelt*, Vol. IV. (New York: Random House, 1938), p. 449.

6. Henry Cabot Lodge, ed., *The Federal Papers* (New York: G. P. Putnam's, 1902), p. 290.

7. In Howard Zinn, ed., *New Deal Thought* (Indianapolis, Ind.: Bobbs-Merrill, 1966), p. 89.

8. Rexford Guy Tugwell, "Rewriting the Constitution," *The Center Magazine*, I:20.

9. In Carl Brent Swisher, *The Growth of Constitutional Government* (Chicago: University of Chicago Press, 1963), p. 77.

10. In Alpheus T. Mason, *The Supreme Court from Taft to Warren* (New York: Norton, 1964), p. 15.

THE NEW DEAL ERA:
SELECTED POLITICAL AND
THEOLOGICAL DOCUMENTS

1. ∣ "THE FUNDAMENTALS OF THE FAITH" (1878)

The Niagara Bible Conference

So many in the latter times have departed from the faith, giving heed to seducing spirits, and doctrines of devils; so many have turned away their ears from the truth, and turned unto fables, so many are busily engaged in scattering broadcast the seeds of fatal error, directly affecting the honor of our Lord and the destiny of the soul, we are constrained by fidelity to Him to make the following declaration of our doctrinal belief, and to present it as the bond of union with those who wish to be connected with the Niagara Bible Conference.

I

We believe "that all Scripture is given by inspiration of God," by which we understand the whole of the book called the Bible; nor do we take the statement in the sense in which it is sometimes foolishly said that works of human genius are inspired, but in the sense that the Holy Ghost gave the very words of the sacred writings to holy men of old; and that His Divine inspiration is not in different degrees, but extends equally and fully to all parts of these writings, historical, poetical, doctrinal and prophetical, and to the smallest word, and inflection of a word, provided such word is found in the original manuscripts: 2 Tim. 3:16, 17; 2 Pet. 1:21; 1 Cor. 2:13; Mark 12:26, 36; 13:11; Acts 1:16; 2:4.

II

We believe that the Godhead eternally exists in three persons, the Father, the Son, and the Holy Spirit; and that these three are one God, having precisely the same nature, attributes and perfections, and worthy of precisely the same homage, confidence, and obedience: Mark 12:29; John 1:1-4; Matt. 28:19, 20; Acts 5:3, 4; 2 Cor. 13:14; Heb. 1:1-3; Rev. 1:4-6.

III

We believe that man, originally created in the image and after the likeness of God, fell from his high and holy estate by eating the forbidden fruit, and as the consequence of his disobedience the threatened penalty of death was then and there inflicted, so that his moral nature was not only grievously injured by the fall, but he totally lost all spiritual life, becoming dead in trespasses and sins, and subject to the power of the devil: Gen. 1:26; 2:17; John 5:40; 6:53; Ep. 2: 1-3; 1 Tim. 5:6; 1 John 3:8.

IV

We believe that this spiritual death, or total corruption of human nature, has been transmitted to the entire race of man, the man Christ Jesus alone excepted; and hence that every child of Adam is born into the world with a nature which not only possesses no spark of Divine life, but is essentially and unchangeably bad, being in enmity against God, and incapable by any educational process whatever of subjection to His law: Gen. 6:5; Psa. 14:1-3; 51:5; Jer. 17:9; John 3:6; Rom. 5:12-19; 8:6, 7.

V

We believe that, owing to this universal depravity and death in sin, no one can enter the kingdom of God unless born again; and that no degree of reformation however great, no attainment in morality however high, no culture however attractive, no humanitarian and philanthropic schemes and societies however useful, no baptism or other ordinance however administered, can help the sinner to take even one step toward heaven; but a new nature imparted from above, a new life implanted by the Holy Ghost through the Word, is absolutely essential to salvation: Isa. 64:6; John 3:5, 18; Gal. 6:15; Phil. 3:4-9; Tit. 3:5; Jas. 1:18; 1 Pet. 1:23.

VI

We believe that our redemption has been accomplished solely by the blood of our Lord Jesus Christ, who was made to be sin, and made a curse, for us, dying in our room and stead; and that no repentance, no feeling, no faith, no good resolutions, no sincere efforts, no submission to the rules and regulations of any church, or of all the churches that have existed since the days of the Apostles, can add in the very least to the value of that precious blood, or to the merit of that finished work, wrought for us by Him who united in His person true and proper divinity with perfect and sinless humanity: Lev. 17:11; Matt. 26:28; Rom. 5:6-9; 2 Cor. 5:21; Gal. 3:13; Eph. 1:7; 1 Pet. 1:18, 19.

VII

We believe that Christ, in the fulness of the blessings He has secured by His obedience unto death, is received by faith alone, and that the moment we trust in Him as our Saviour we pass out of death into everlasting life, being justified from all things, accepted before the Father according to the measure of His acceptance, loved as He is loved, and having His place and portion, as linked to Him, and one with Him forever: John 5:24; 17:23; Acts 13:39; Rom. 5:1; Eph. 2:4-6, 13; 1 John 4:17; 5:11, 12.

VIII

We believe that it is the privilege, not only of some, but of all who are born again by the Spirit through faith in Christ as revealed in the Scriptures, to be assured of their salvation from the very day they take Him to be their Saviour; and that this assurance is not founded upon any fancied discovery of their own worthiness, but wholly upon the testimony of God in His written Word, exciting within His children filial love, gratitude, and obedience: Luke 10:20; 12:32; John 6:47; Rom. 8:33-39; 2 Cor. 5:1, 6-8; 2 Tim. 1:12; 1 John 5:13.

IX

We believe that all the Scriptures from first to last center about our Lord Jesus Christ, in His person and work, in His first and second coming; and hence that no chapter even of the Old Testament is properly read or understood until it leads to Him; and moreover that all the Scriptures from first to last, including every chapter even of the Old Testament, were designed for our practical instruction: Luke 24:27, 44; John 5:39; Acts 17:2, 3; 18:28; 26:22, 23; 28:23; Rom. 15:4; 1 Cor. 10:11.

X

We believe that the Church is composed of all who are united by the Holy Spirit to the risen and ascended Son of God, that by the same Spirit we are all baptized into one body, whether we be Jews or Gentiles, and thus being members one of another, we are responsible to keep the unity of the Spirit in the bond of peace, rising above all sectarian prejudices and denominational bigotry, and loving one another with a pure heart fervently: Matt. 16:16-18; Acts 2:32-47; Rom. 12:5; 1 Cor. 12:12-27; Eph. 1:20-23; 4:3-10; Col. 3:14, 15.

XI

We believe that the Holy Spirit, not as an influence, but as a Divine Person, the source and power of all acceptable worship and service, is our abiding Comforter and Helper, that He never takes His departure from the Church, nor from the feeblest of the saints, but is ever present to testify of Christ, seeking to occupy us with Him, and not with ourselves nor with our experiences: John 7:38, 39; 14:16, 17; 15:26; 16:13, 14; Acts 1:8; Rom. 8:9; Phil. 3:3.

XII

We believe that we are called with a holy calling to walk, not after the flesh, but after the Spirit, and so to live in the Spirit that we should not fulfill the lusts of the flesh; but the flesh being still in us to the end of our earthly pilgrimage needs to be kept constantly in subjection to Christ, or it will surely manifest its presence to the dishonor of His name: Rom. 8:12, 13; 13:14; Gal. 5:16-25; Eph. 4:22-24; Col. 3:1-10; 1 Pet. 1:14-16; 1 John 3:5-9.

XIII

We believe that the souls of those who have trusted in the Lord Jesus Christ for salvation do at death immediately pass into His presence, and there remain in conscious bliss until the resurrection of the body at His coming, when soul and body reunited shall be associated with Him forever in the glory; but the souls of unbelievers remain after death in conscious misery until the final judgment of the great white throne at the close of the millennium, when soul and body reunited shall be cast into the lake of fire, not to be annihilated, but to be punished with everlasting destruction from the presence of the Lord, and from the glory of His power: Luke 16:19-26; 23:43; 2 Cor. 5:8; Phil. 1:23; 2 Thess. 1:7-9; Jude 6:7; Rev. 20:11-15.

XIV

We believe that the world will not be converted during the present dispensation, but is fast ripening for judgment, while there will be a fearful apostasy in the professing Christian body; and hence that the Lord Jesus will come in person to introduce the millennial age, when Israel shall be restored to their own land, and the earth shall be full of the knowledge of the Lord; and that this personal and premillennial advent is the blessed hope set before us in the Gospel for which we should be constantly looking: Luke 12:35-40; 17:26-30; 18:8; Acts 15:14-17; 2 Thess. 2:3-8; 2 Tim. 3:1-5; Tit. 2:11-15.

Source: "The Fundamentals of the Faith as Expressed in the Articles of Belief of the Niagara Bible Conference" (Chicago: Great Commission Prayer League, n.d.).

2. I "SOCIAL IDEALS OF THE CHURCHES" (1908, 1932)

The Federal Council of Churches

The Churches Should Stand for

1. Practical application of the Christian principle of social well-being to the acquisition and use of wealth, subordination of speculation and the profit motive to the creative and cooperative spirit.

2. Social planning and control of the credit and monetary systems and the economic processes for the common good.

3. The right of all to the opportunity for self-maintenance; a wider and fairer distribution of wealth; a living wage, as a minimum, and above this a just share for the worker in the product of industry and agriculture.

4. Safeguarding of all workers, urban and rural, against harmful conditions of labor and occupational injury and disease.

5. Social insurance against sickness, accident, want in old age and unemployment.

6. Reduction of hours of labor as the general productivity of industry increases; release from employment at least one day in seven, with a shorter working week in prospect.

7. Such special regulation of the conditions of work of women as shall safeguard their welfare and that of the family and the community.

8. The right of employees and employers alike to organize for collective bargaining and social action; protection of both in the exercise of this right; the obligation of both to work for the public good; encouragement of cooperatives and other organizations among farmers and other groups.

9. Abolition of child labor; adequate provision for the protection, education, spiritual nurture and wholesome recreation of every child.

10. Protection of the family by the single standard of purity; educational preparation for marriage, home-making and parenthood.

11. Economic justice for the farmer in legislation, financing, transportation and the price of farm products as compared with the cost of machinery and other commodities which he must buy.

12. Extension of the primary cultural opportunities and social services now enjoyed by urban populations to the farm family.

13. Protection of the individual and society from the social, economic and moral waste of any traffic in intoxicants and habit-forming drugs.

14. Application of the Christian principle of redemption to the treatment of offenders; reform of penal and correctional methods and institutions, and of criminal court procedure.

15. Justice, opportunity and equal rights for all; mutual goodwill and cooperation among racial, economic and religious groups.

16. Repudiation of war, drastic reduction of armaments, participation in international agencies for the peaceable settlement of all controversies; the building of a cooperative world order.

17. Recognition and maintenance of the rights and responsibilities of free speech, free assembly, and a free press; the encouragement of free communication of mind with mind as essential to the discovery of truth.

Source: "Social Ideals of the Churches" (published by the Federal Council of Churches), pp. 18, 19. This statement published in 1932 succeeds the 1908 "Social Creed of Methodism."

3. ı *A THEOLOGY FOR THE SOCIAL GOSPEL* (1917)

Walter Rauschenbusch

In the following brief propositions I should like to offer a few suggestions, on behalf of the social gospel, for the theological formulations of the doctrine of the Kingdom. Something like this is needed to give us "a theology for the social gospel."

1. The Kingdom of God is divine in its origin, progress and consummation. It was initiated by Jesus Christ, in whom the prophetic spirit came to its

consummation, it is sustained by the Holy Spirit, and it will be brought to its fulfilment by the power of God in his own time. The passive and active resistance of the Kingdom of Evil at every stage of its advance is so great, and the human resources of the Kingdom of God so slender, that no explanation can satisfy a religious mind which does not see the power of God in its movements. The Kingdom of God, therefore, is miraculous all the way, and is the continuous revelation of the power, the righteousness, and the love of God. . . .

2. The Kingdom of God contains the teleology of the Christian religion. It translates theology from the static to the dynamic. It sees, not doctrines or rites to be conserved and perpetuated, but resistance to be overcome and great ends to be achieved. Since the Kingdom of God is the supreme purpose of God, we shall understand the Kingdom so far as we understand God, and we shall understand God so far as we understand his Kingdom. As long as organized sin is in the world, the Kingdom of God is characterized by conflict with evil. But if there were no evil, or after evil has been overcome, the Kingdom of God will still be the end to which God is lifting the race. It is realized not only by redemption, but also by the education of mankind and the revelation of his life within it.

3. Since God is in it, the Kingdom of God is always both present and future. Like God it is in all tenses, eternal in the midst of time. It is the energy of God realizing itself in human life. Its future lies among the mysteries of God. It invites and justifies prophecy, but all prophecy is fallible; it is valuable in so far as it grows out of action for the Kingdom and impels action. No theories about the future of the Kingdom of God are likely to be valuable or true which paralyze or postpone redemptive action on our part. To those who postpone, it is a theory and not a reality. It is for us to see the Kingdom of God as always coming, always pressing in on the present, always big with possibility, and always inviting immediate action. We walk by faith. Every human life is so placed that it can share with God in the creation of the Kingdom, or can resist and retard its progress. The Kingdom is for each of us the supreme task and the supreme gift of God. By accepting it as a task, we experience it as a gift. By labouring for it we enter into the joy and peace of the Kingdom as our divine fatherland and habitation.

4. Even before Christ, men of God saw the Kingdom of God as the great end to which all divine leadings were pointing. Every idealistic interpretation of the world, religious or philosophical, needs some such conception. Within the Christian religion the idea of the Kingdom gets its distinctive interpretation from Christ. (a) Jesus emancipated the idea of the Kingdom from previous nationalistic limitations and from the debasement of lower religious tendencies, and made it world-wide and spiritual. (b) He made the purpose of salvation essential in it. (c) He imposed his own mind, his personality, his love and holy will on the idea of the Kingdom. (d) He not only foretold it but initiated it by his life and work. . . .

5. The Kingdom of God is humanity organized according to the will of God. Interpreting it through the consciousness of Jesus we may affirm these

convictions about the ethical relations within the Kingdom: (a) Since Christ revealed the divine worth of life and personality, and since his salvation seeks the restoration and fulfilment of even the least, it follows that the Kingdom of God, at every stage of human development, tends toward a social order which will best guarantee to all personalities their freest and highest development. This involves the redemption of social life from the cramping influence of religious bigotry, from the repression of self-assertion in the relation of upper and lower classes, and from all forms of slavery in which human beings are treated as mere means to serve the ends of others. (b) Since love is the supreme law of Christ, the Kingdom of God implies a progressive reign of love in human affairs. We can see its advance wherever the free will of love supersedes the use of force and legal coercion as a regulative of the social order. This involves the redemption of society from political autocracies and economic oligarchies; the substitution of redemptive for vindictive penology; the abolition of constraint through hunger as part of the industrial system; and the abolition of war as the supreme expression of hate and the completest cessation of freedom. (c) The highest expression of love is the free surrender of what is truly our own, lives, property, and rights. A much lower but perhaps more decisive expression of love is the surrender of any opportunity to exploit men. No social group or organization can claim to be clearly within the Kingdom of God which drains others for its own ease, and resists the effort to abate this fundamental evil. This involves the redemption of society from private property in the natural resources of the earth, and from any condition in industry which makes monopoly profits possible. (d) The reign of love tends toward the progressive unity of mankind, but with the maintenance of individual liberty and the opportunity of nations to work out their own national peculiarities and ideals.

6. Since the Kingdom is the supreme end of God, it must be the purpose for which the Church exists. The measure in which it fulfils this purpose is also the measure of its spiritual authority and honour. The institutions of the Church, its activities, its worship, and its theology must in the long run be tested by its effectiveness in creating the Kingdom of God. . . .

7. Since the Kingdom is the supreme end, all problems of personal salvation must be reconsidered from the point of view of the Kingdom. It is not sufficient to set the two aims of Christianity side by side. There must be a synthesis, and theology must explain how the two react on each other. The entire redemptive work of Christ must also be reconsidered under this orientation. Early Greek theology saw salvation chiefly as the redemption from ignorance by the revelation of God and from earthliness by the impartation of immortality. It interpreted the work of Christ accordingly, and laid stress on his incarnation and resurrection. Western theology saw salvation mainly as forgiveness of guilt and freedom from punishment. It interpreted the work of Christ accordingly, and laid stress on the death and atonement. If the Kingdom of God was the guiding idea and chief end of Jesus—as we now know it was—we may be sure that every step in His life, including His death, was related to that aim and its realization, and when the idea of the Kingdom of God takes its due place in theology, the work of Christ will have to be interpreted afresh.

8. The Kingdom of God is not confined within the limits of the Church and its activities. It embraces the whole of human life. It is the Christian transfiguration of the social order. The Church is one social institution alongside of the family, the industrial organization of society, and the State. The Kingdom of God is in all these, and realizes itself through them all. During the Middle Ages all society was ruled and guided by the Church. Few of us would want modern life to return to such a condition. Functions which the Church used to perform, have now far outgrown its capacities. The Church is indispensable to the religious education of humanity and to the conservation of religion, but the greatest future awaits religion in the public life of humanity.

Source: Walter Rauschenbusch, *A Theology for the Social Gospel* (New York: Macmillan, 1917), pp. 131-45.

4. | "THE (ROMAN CATHOLIC) BISHOPS' PROGRAM OF SOCIAL RECONSTRUCTION" (1919)

Social Reconstruction

"Reconstruction" has of late been so tiresomely reiterated, not to say violently abused, that it has become to many of us a word of aversion. Politicians, social students, labor leaders, businessmen, charity workers, clergymen, and various other social groups have contributed to their quota of spoken words and printed pages to the discussion of the subject; yet the majority of us still find ourselves rather bewildered and helpless. We are unable to say what parts of our social system imperatively need reconstruction; how much of that which is imperatively necessary is likely to be seriously undertaken; or what specific methods and measures are best suited to realize that amount of reconstruction which is at once imperatively necessary and immediately feasible. . . .

Present Wage Rates Should be Sustained

Even if the great majority of workers were now in receipt of more than living wages, there are no good reasons why rates of pay should be lowered. After all, a living wage is not necessarily the full measure of justice. All the Catholic authorities on the subject explicitly declare that this is only the minimum of justice. In a country as rich as ours, there are very few cases in which it is possible to prove that the worker would be getting more than that to which he has a right if he were paid something in excess of this ethical minimum. Why, then, should we assume that this is the normal share of almost the whole laboring population? Since our industrial resources and instrumentalities are sufficient to provide more than a living wage for a very large population of the workers, why should we acquiesce in a theory which denies them this measure of the comforts of life? Such a policy is not only of very questionable morality, but is unsound economically. The large demand for goods which is created and maintained by high rates of wages and high purchasing power by the masses is the surest guarantee of a continuous and general operation of industrial establishments. It is the most effective instrument of prosperity for labor and capital alike. The principal beneficiaries of a general reduction of wages would be the less efficient among the capitalists, and the more comfortable sections of the consumers. The wage-earners would lose more in remuneration than they would gain from whatever fall in prices occurred as a direct result of the fall in wages. On grounds both of justice and sound economics, we should give our hearty support to all legitimate efforts made by labor to resist general wage reductions.

Housing for Working Classes

Housing projects for war workers which have been completed, or almost completed by the government of the United States, have cost some forty million dollars, and are found in eleven cities. While the federal government cannot continue this work in time of peace, the example and precedent that it has set, and the experience and knowledge that it has developed, should not be forthwith neglected and lost. The great cities in which congestion and other forms of bad housing are disgracefully apparent ought to take up and continue the work, at least to such an extent as will remove the worst features of a social condition that is a menace at once to industrial efficiency, civic health, good morals, and religion.

Reduction of the Cost of Living

During the war the cost of living has risen at least 75 percent above the level of 1913. Some check has been placed upon the upward trend by government fixing of prices in the case of bread and coal and a few other commodities. Even if we believe it desirable, we cannot ask that the government continue this action after the articles of peace have been signed; for neither public opinion nor Congress is ready for such a revolutionary policy. If the extortionate practices of monopoly were prevented by adequate laws and adequate law enforcement, prices would automatically be kept at as low a level as that to which they might be brought by direct government determination. Just what laws, in addition to those already on the statute books, are necessary to abolish monopolistic extortion is a question of detail that need not be considered here. In passing, it may be noted that government competition with monopolies that cannot be effectively restrained by the ordinary antitrust laws deserves more serious consideration than it has yet received.

More important and more effective than any government regulation of prices would be the establishment of co-operative stores. . . .

The Legal Minimum Wage

Turning now from those agencies and laws that have been put in operation during the war to the general subject of labor legislation and problems, we are glad to note that there is no longer any serious objection urged by impartial persons against the legal minimum wage. The several states should enact laws providing for the establishment of wage rates that will be at least sufficient for the decent maintenance of a family, in the case of all male adults, and adequate to the decent individual support of female workers. In the beginning the minimum wages for male workers should suffice only for the present needs of the family, but they should be gradually raised until they are adequate to meet future needs as well. That is, they should be ultimately high enough to make possible that amount of saving which is necessary to protect the worker and his family against sickness, accidents, invalidity, and old age.

Social Insurance

Until this level of legal minimum wages is reached the worker stands in need of the device of insurance. The State should make comprehensive provision for insurance against illness, invalidity, unemployment, and old age. So far as possible the insurance fund should be raised by a levy on industry, as is now done in the case of accident compensation. The industry in which a man is employed should provide with all that is necessary to meet all the needs of his entire life. Therefore, any contribution to the insurance fund from the general revenues of the State should be only slight and temporary. . . .

Labor Participation in Industrial Management

The right of labor to organize and to deal with employers through representatives has been asserted above in connection with the discussion of the War Labor Board. It is to be hoped that this right will never again be called in question by any considerable number of employers. In addition to this, labor ought gradually to receive greater representation in what the English group of Quaker employers have called the "industrial" part of business management— "The control of processes and machinery; nature of product; engagement and dismissal of employees; hours of work, rates of pay, bonuses, etc.; welfare work; shop discipline; relations with trade unions." The establishment of shop committees, working wherever possible with the trade union, is the method suggested by this group of employers for giving the employees the proper share of industrial management. There can be no doubt that a frank adoption of these means and ends by employers would not only promote the welfare of the workers, but vastly improve the relations between them and their employers, and increase the efficiency and productiveness of each establishment.

There is no need here to emphasize the importance of safety and sanitation in work places, as this is pretty generally recognized by legislation. What is required is an extension and strengthening of many of the existing statutes, and a better administration and enforcement of such laws everywhere.

Vocational Training

The need of industrial, or as it has come to be more generally called, vocational training, is now universally acknowledged. In the interest of the nation, as well as in that of the workers themselves, this training should be made substantially universal. While we cannot now discuss the subject in any detail, we do wish to set down two general observations. First, the vocational training should be offered in such forms and conditions as not to deprive the children of the working classes of at least the elements of a cultural education. A healthy democracy cannot tolerate a purely industrial or trade education for any class of its citizens. We do not want to have the children of the wage earners put into a special class in which they are marked as outside the sphere of opportunities for culture. The second observation is that the system of vocational training should not operate so as to weaken in any degree our parochial schools or any other class of private schools. Indeed, the opportunities of the system should be extended to all qualified private schools on exactly the same basis as to public schools. We want neither class divisions in education nor a State monopoly of education.

Child Labor

The question of education naturally suggests the subject of child labor. Public opinion in the majority of the states of our country has set its face inflexibly against the continuous employment of children in industry before the age of sixteen years. Within a reasonably short time all of our states, except some of the stagnant ones, will have laws providing for this reasonable standard. The education of public opinion must continue, but inasmuch as the process is slow, the abolition of child labor in certain sections seems unlikely to be brought about by the legislatures of those states, and since the Keating-Owen act has been declared unconstitutional, there seems to be no device by which this reproach to our country can be removed except that of taxing child labor out of existence. This method is embodied in an amendment to the Federal Revenue Bill which would impose a tax of 10 per cent on all goods made by children. . . .

Ultimate and Fundamental Reforms

Despite the practical and immediate character of the present statement, we cannot entirely neglect the question of ultimate aims and a systematic program; for other groups are busy issuing such systematic pronouncements, and we all need something of the kind as a philosophical foundation and as a satisfaction to our natural desire for comprehensive statements.

It seems clear that the present industrial system is destined to last for a long time in its main outlines. That is to say, private ownership of capital is not likely to be supplanted by a collectivist organization of industry at a date sufficiently near to justify any present action based on the hypothesis of its arrival. This forecast we recognize as not only extremely probable, but as highly desirable; for, other objections apart, Socialism would mean bureaucracy, political tyranny, the helplessness of the individual as a factor in the ordering of his own life, and in general social inefficiency and decadence.

Main Defects of Present System

Nevertheless, the present system stands in grievous need of considerable modifications and improvement. Its main defects are three: Enormous inefficiency and waste in the production and distribution of commodities; insufficient incomes for the great majority of wage earners, and unnecessarily large incomes for a small minority of privileged capitalists. . . .

A New Spirit a Vital Need

"Society," said Pope Leo XIII, "can be healed in no other way than by a return to Christian life and Christian institutions." The truth of these words is more widely perceived today than when they were written, more than twenty-seven years ago. Changes in our economic and political systems will have only partial and feeble efficiency if they be not reinforced by the Christian view of work and wealth. Neither the moderate reforms advocated in this paper nor any other program of betterment or reconstruction will prove reasonably effective without a reform in the spirit of both labor and capital. The laborer must come to realize that he owes his employer and society an honest day's work in return for a fair wage, and that conditions cannot be substantially improved until he roots out the desire to get a maximum of return for a minimum of service. The capitalist must likewise get a new viewpoint. He needs to learn the long-forgotten truth that wealth is stewardship, that profit-making is not the basic justification of business enterprise, and that there are such things as fair profits, fair interest, and fair prices. Above and before all, he must cultivate and strengthen within his mind the truth which many of his class have begun to grasp for the first time during the present war; namely, that the laborer is a human being, not merely an instrument of production; and that the laborer's right to a decent livelihood is the first moral charge upon industry. The employer has a right to get a reasonable living out of his business, but he has no right to interest on his investment until his employees have obtained at least living wages. This is the human and Christian, in contrast to the purely commercial and pagan, ethics of industry.

Source: *Our Bishops Speak . . . 1919-1951* (Milwaukee, 1952), pp. 243-44, 248, 251-57, 259-60.

5. I *THE CHURCH AGAINST THE WORLD* (1935)

H. Richard Niebuhr

The church is in bondage to capitalism. Capitalism in its contemporary form is more than a system of ownership and distribution of economic goods. It is a faith and a way of life. It is faith in wealth as the source of all life's blessings and as the savior of man from his deepest misery. It is the doctrine that man's most important activity is the production of economic goods and that all other things are dependent upon this. On the basis of this initial idolatry it develops a morality in which economic worth becomes the standard by which to measure all other values and the economic virtues take precedence over courage, temperance, wisdom and justice, over charity, humility and fidelity. Hence nature, love, life, truth, beauty and justice are exploited or made the servants of the high economic good. Everything, including the lives of workers, is made a utility, is desecrated and ultimately destroyed. Capitalism develops a discipline of its own but in the long run makes for the overthrow of all discipline since the service of its god demands the encouragement of unlimited desire for that which promises—but must fail—to satisfy the lust of the flesh and the pride of life.

The capitalist faith is not a disembodied spirit. It expresses itself in laws and social habits and transforms the whole of civilization. It fashions society into an economic organization in which production for profit becomes the central enterprise, in which the economic relations of men are regarded as their fundamental relations, in which economic privileges are most highly prized, and in which the resultant classes of men are set to struggle with one another for the economic goods. Education and government are brought under the sway of the faith. The family itself is modified by it. The structure of cities and their very architecture is influenced by the religion. So intimate is the relation between the civilization and the faith, that it is difficult to participate in the former without consenting to the latter and becoming entangled in its destructive morality. It was possible for Paul's converts to eat meat which had been offered to idols without compromising with paganism. But the products which come from the altars of this modern idolatry—the dividends, the privileges, the status, the struggle—are of such a sort that it is difficult to partake of them without becoming involved in the whole system of misplaced faith and perverted morality.

No antithesis could be greater than that which obtains between the gospel and capitalist faith. The church has known from the beginning that the love of money is the root of evil, that it is impossible to serve God and Mammon, that they that have riches shall hardly enter into life, that life does not consist in the abundance of things possessed, that the earth is the Lord's and that love, not self-interest, is the first law of life. Yet the church has become entangled with capitalist civilization to such an extent that it has compromised with capitalist faith and morality and become a servant of the world. So intimate have the bonds between capitalism and Protestantism become that the genealogists have suspected kinship. Some have ascribed the parentage of capitalism to Protestantism while others have seen in the latter the child of the former. But whatever may have been the relation between the modest system of private ownership which a Calvin or a Wesley allowed and the gospel they proclaimed, that which obtains between the high capitalism of the latter period and the church must fall under the rule of the seventh and not of the fifth command-ment, as a Hosea or a Jeremiah would have been quick to point out. The entan-glement with capitalism appears in the great economic interest of the church, in its debt structure, in its dependence through endowments upon the continued dividends of capitalism, and especially in its dependence upon the continued gifts of the privileged classes in the economic society. This entanglement has become the greater the more the church has attempted to keep pace with the development of capitalistic civilization, not without compromising with capital-ist ideas of success and efficiency. At the same time evidence of religious syncre-tism, of the combination of Christianity with capitalist religion, has appeared. The "building of the kingdom of God" has been confused in many a churchly pronouncement with the increase of church possessions or with the economic advancement of mankind. The church has often behaved as though the saving of civilization and particularly of capitalist civilization were its mission. It has failed to apply to the morality of that civilization the rigid standards which it did not fail to use where less powerful realities were concerned. The develop-ment may have been inevitable, nevertheless it was a fall.

The bondage of the church to nationalism has been more apparent than its bondage to capitalism, partly because nationalism is so evidently a religion, partly because it issues in the dramatic sacrifices of war—sacrifices more obvious if not more actual than those which capitalism demands and offers to its god. National-ism is no more to be confused with the principle of nationality than capitalism is to be confused with the principle of private property. Just as we can accept, with-out complaint against the past, the fact that a private property system replaced feudalism, so we can accept, without blaming our ancestors for moral delinquency, the rise of national organization in place of universal empire. But as the private property system became the soil in which the lust for possessions and the worship of wealth grew up, so the possibility of national independence provided oppor-tunity for the growth of religious nationalism, the worship of the nation, and the lust for national power and glory. And as religious capitalism perverted the private property system, so religious nationalism corrupted the nationalities. Nationalism regards the nation as the supreme value, the source of all life's meaning, as an end-in-itself and a law to itself. It seeks to persuade individuals and organizations to make national might and glory their main aim in life. It even achieves a certain deliverance of men by freeing them from their bondage to self. In our modern polytheism it enters into close relationship with capitalism, though not without friction and occasional conflict, and sometimes it appears to offer an alternative faith to those who have become disillusioned with wealth-worship. Since the ade-quacy of its god is continually called into question by the existence of other na-tional deities, it requires the demonstration of the omnipotence of nation and breeds an unlimited lust for national power and expansion. But since the god is limited the result is conflict, war and destruction. Despite the fact that the nationalist faith becomes obviously dominant only in times of sudden or continued political crisis, it has had constant and growing influence in the West, affecting particularly government and education.

The antithesis between the faith of the church and the nationalist idolatry has always been self-evident. The prophetic revolution out of which Christianity eventually came was a revolution against nationalist religion. The messianic career of Jesus developed in defiance of the nationalisms of Judaism and of Rome. In one sense Christianity emerged out of a man's disillusionment with the doctrine that the road to life and joy and justice lies through the exercise of political force and the growth of national power. The story of its rise is the history of long struggle with self-righteous political power. Yet in the modern world Christianity has fallen into dependence upon the political agencies which have become the instruments of nationalism and has compromised with the religion they promote. The division of Christendom into national units would have been a less serious matter had it not resulted so frequently in a division into nationalistic units. The close relation of church and state in some instances, the participation of the church in the political life in other cases, has been accompanied by a syncretism of nationalism and Christianity. The confusion of democracy with the Christian ideal of life in America, of racialism and the gospel in Germany, of Western nationalism and church missions in the Orient, testify to the compromise which has taken place. The churches have encouraged the nations to regard themselves as messianic powers and have supplied them with religious excuses for their imperialist expansions and aggressions. And in every time of crisis it has been possible for nationalism to convert the major part of the church, which substituted the pagan Baal for the Great Jehovah, without being well aware of what it did, and promoted a holy crusade in negation of the cross. The captivity of the church to the world of nationalism does not assume so dramatic a form as a rule, yet the difficulty of Christianity in achieving an international organization testifies to the reality of its bondage.

Capitalism and nationalism are variant forms of a faith which is more widespread in modern civilization than either. It is difficult to label this religion. It may be called humanism, but there is a humanism that, far from glorifying man, reminds him of his limitations the while it loves him in his feebleness and aspiration. It has become fashionable to name it liberalism, but there is a liberalism which is interested in human freedom as something to be achieved rather than something to be assumed and praised. It may be called modernism, but surely one can live in the modern world, accepting its science and engaging in its work, without falling into idolatry of the modern. The rather too technical term "anthropocentrism" seems to be the best designation of the faith. It is marked on its negative side by the rejection not only of the symbols of the creation, the fall and the salvation of men, but also of the belief in human dependence and limitation, in human wickedness and frailty, in divine forgiveness through the suffering of the innocent. Positively it affirms the sufficiency of man. Human desire is the source of all values. The mind and the will of man are sufficient instruments of his salvation. Evil is nothing but lack of develop-ment. Revolutionary second-birth is unnecessary. Although some elements of the anthropocentric faith are always present in human society, and although it was represented at the beginning of the modern development, it is not the source but rather the product of modern civilization. Growing out of the success of science and technology in understanding and modifying some of the conditions of life, it has substituted veneration of science for scientific knowledge, and glorification of human activity for its exercise. Following upon the long educa-tion in which Protestant and Catholic evangelism had brought Western men to a deep sense of their duty, the anthropocentrism glorified the mortal sense of man as his natural possession and taught him that he needed no other law than the one within. Yet, as in the case of capitalism and nationalism, the faith which grew out of modern culture has modified that culture. During the last gener-ations the anthropocentric faith has entered deeply into the structure of society and has contributed not a little to the megapolitanism and megalomania of contemporary civilization.

The compromise of the church with anthropocentrism has come almost imperceptibly in the course of its collaboration in the work of culture. It was hastened by the tenacity of Christian traditionalism, which appeared to leave churchmen with no alternative than one between worship of the letter and worship of the men who wrote the letters. Nevertheless, the compromise is a perversion of the Christian position. The more obvious expressions of the compromise have been frequent but perhaps less dangerous than the prevailing one by means of which Christianity appeared to remain true to itself while accepting the anthropocentric position. That compromise was the substitution of religion for the God of faith. Man's aspiration after God, his prayer, his worship was exalted in this syncretism into a saving power, worthy of a place alongside science and art. Religion was endowed with all the attributes of God-head, the while its basis was found in human nature itself. The adaptation of Christianity to the anthropocentric faith appeared in other ways: in the atten-uation of the conviction of sin and of the necessity of rebirth, in the substitution of the human claim to immortality for the Christian hope and fear of an after-life, in the glorification of religious heroes, and in the efforts of religious men and societies to become saviors.

The captive church is the church which has become entangled with this system or these systems of worldliness. It is a church which seeks to prove its usefulness to civilization, in terms of civilization's own demands. It is a church which has lost the distinctive note and the earnestness of a Christian discipline of life and has become what every religious institution tends to become—the teacher of the prevailing code of morals and the pantheon of the social gods. It is a church, moreover, which has become entangled with the world in its desire for the increase of its power and prestige and which shares the worldly fear of insecurity.

How the church became entangled and a captive in this way may be understood. To blame the past for errors which have brought us to this pass is to indulge in the ancient fallacy of saying that the fathers have eaten sour grapes and the children's teeth are set on edge. The function of the present is neither praise nor blame of the past. It is rather the realization of the prevailing situation and preparation for the next task.

Source: From H. Richard Niebuhr, *The Church Against the World* (Chicago: Willett, Clark & Company 1935), pp. 1-13.

6. ǀ *THE POLITICAL BEHAVIOR OF AMERICAN JEWS* (1956)

Lawrence Fuchs

As Rabbi Philip Bernstein puts it in his popular book, *What the Jews Believe*, "The Jewish outlook is by its very nature optimistic, progressive, forward-looking. . . . It prods Jews constantly to strive for a better world, to be in the thick and at the front of movements for social reform. Even the very Jewish radical who may ignore his Jewishness is the product of its messianic fervor."[1] This outlook, a product of Jewish insecurity and the Jewish value system, constitutes a political style, an approach to the issues of social organization. Implicit in this style is the view that man and his environment are malleable, that he is much more the creator of history than its creature. Implicit, too, is the notion that man's environment and his polity are made for him. Implicit is a dynamic view of law, that it is changing and made for man. It is more than accident that three of the five great legal names which Americans associate with sociological jurisprudence are Jewish names: Brandeis, Cardozo, and Frankfurter. (The others are Stone and Holmes.) And especially implicit in such a style is the belief that what happens in this life on this earth is very important, what happens here and now matters very much.

Christian Emphases

Contrast this view with that which the Christian theologians Bernard I. Bell and Reinhold Niebuhr assert is the orthodox Christian position. Bell raises the question, "But is man capable of getting better and better by his own natural development or is he doomed to failure unless God intervenes? It makes a great deal of difference which of these alternatives is correct, a difference not only in theoretical doctrine but also in one's attitude toward living, one's source of hope and happiness, in social action, too."[2] Christianity has been split in its answer to his question. Judaism has not. Orthodox Christianity stresses the

---

1. Philip S. Bernstein, *What the Jews Believe* (New York: Farrar, Straus and Young, 1950), p. 419.
2. Bernard I. Bell, *Crowd Culture* (New York: Harper & Brothers, 1952), p. 111.

concept of redemption only through God's intervention. In recent years the Neo-Calvinists have lamented the failure of Christians to hold fast to this fundamental theological tenet. They have insisted that any departure from the Christian emphasis on complete dependence on God for the betterment of his condition has led to what Bell calls "the exaggerated optimism about man which . . . is the chief cause of our decay."[3] The failure of too many Christians to adopt what Niebuhr calls "Christian realism" in understanding man's sinfulness, his egocentricity, and utter helplessness without God has in his judgment led Americans too often into the fallacies of communism and utopian ideas for world government.[4]

But the fact is that American Jews, not Christians, have served these causes far out of proportion to their numbers. The Neo-Calvinists have exaggerated the political effects of liberal and heretical Christianity. After all, the vast majority of Christians still believe that man is stained with original sin and cannot be redeemed without God's grace. When the American sociologist, Lester Ward, stressed that man's power over nature was unlimited he was rejected, while the ideas of William Graham Summner dominated the thinking of the Supreme Court for more than forty years. Dependence on God for the improvement of man's condition has been coupled in the orthodox view with the idea that faith and repentance—not works—brings redemption. Of course, many Christians have stressed works too, and it is impossible to speak of a single Christian position on any of these issues—so various and individualistic is Christian theology. The Catholics have had a long tradition of working among the poor, and in recent decades there have been many labor priests and waterfront priests, backed by Papal encyclicals, active in movements for social and economic reform. In the United States they have been joined by the followers of the Social Gospel movement led by Washington Gladden and Walter Rauschenbush. From the Social Gospel and similar movements came a Protestant emphasis on secularizing religion, on work in settlement houses, creation centers, adult education, and political reform. Quaker concern has always manifested itself in humanitarian works. In the late nineteenth and early twentieth century, "liberalism" stressing the goodness of man, works, and social action was an important theological current running through all of the major Protestant denominations. It would certainly be a mistake to underestimate the role of liberal and secular Christianity in American life.

But it would also be a mistake to exaggerate it. While a number of Catholic leaders have been in the forefront of social action on behalf of the oppressed, Catholic law teaches resignation and moderation to the poor. Catholic Church leaders in the United States have been militantly anti-Socialist. More important than the Catholic political mood are the Protestant influences on American politics. The only major Protestant movement which has been optimistic about man and stressed his powers to improve life through social and political action has been the Social Gospel.

---

3. Ibid.

4. Reinhold Niebuhr, *Christian Realism and Political Problems* (New York: Charles Scribner's Sons, 1953). See Chapters I and II and p. 183.

From the Anabaptists to the Fundamentalists, the political implications of the important Protestant theological movements, with the exception of the liberal "heresy" of the nineteenth century, have been conservative. Calvinism, Lutherism, Puritanism, Evangelicalism, Fundamentalism, and contemporary neo-Calvinism—all have tended to oppose the notion of social betterment through the state. Indeed, the Anabaptists reluctantly admitted that the state was necessary at all, and refused to assume any responsibility for it. Lutherans and Calvinists stressed the sinfulness of man. Crucial to the early Anglican position was the concept of justification through faith. Puritanism, which influenced all of the major Protestant denominations to some extent, emphasized asceticism. Fundamentalism has usually meant extreme social conservatism and suspicion of scientific and secular influences. The Evangelical movement in the first half of the nineteenth century insisted on the sinfulness of man, salvation through faith, and the need for conversion.

It is true that many of the leading evangelists were busily engaged in the front lines of various reform movements during this period, but these movements were usually aimed at the suppression of personal vice and immorality. They had nothing to do with the role of the state in society. Almost every single one of the leading evangelists opposed Andrew Jackson while supporting Sabbatarianism, temperance, and anti-slavery. In their theological writings Lyman Beecher, Charles Finney, Calvin Colton, Albert Barnes, and other evangelists showed considerable innovation, but they were politically conservative to a man. They worried over the souls of the poor but opposed poor relief, limitations on child labor, and extensions of the suffrage.[5] In fact, the great theological radicals (in their day) who have had the largest influence on American Protestantism—Calvin, Luther, and Wesley—were, unlike the Hebrew prophets of ancient times, politically conservative.

Surely, the Quakers and the Unitarians have been influential in American life; but who would argue that Quakerism has played a larger role in shaping American politics than Puritanism, or that a handful of Unitarians have had the impact of a movement such as Fundamentalism, which dominates whole sections of the country! Quaker concern may make Herbert Hoover a great private humanitarian, but other influences determine his politics.

Still, it will be said that Christian liberalism must have had considerable impact if only to judge by the violent reactions of the Fundamentalists and Neo-Calvinists. It did have a large impact, but its influence was mainly theological and not political. The debate between liberals and fundamentalists was primarily over such matters as biblical criticism and the deity of Christ. Liberal theology reached its zenith during the early decades of the twenties, the very years when conservatism dominated American politics. Liberal theology at least implied that a truly Christian society could be achieved here on earth, but not necessarily through social action. For example, one way of exercising Christian responsibility was through individual "stewardship." This did not mean taking

5. For a complete discussion of the evangelical movement in the North see Charles C. Cole, Jr., *The Social Ideas of the Northern Evangelists, 1826-1860* (New York: Columbia University Press, 1954).

literally Jesus' extreme denunciation of wealth, but it did mean that the wealthy Christian should part with some of his money through philanthropy. But charity, like exploitation, was not the concern of the state, and the Christian theory of stewardship bears no resemblance to Zedakeh.

While liberal theology did not necessarily mean liberal politics, it sometimes did. Individual Quakers such as John Howard who struggled for prison reform and William Wilberforce who fought slavery were indeed motivated by religious force. Horace Buschnell and Washington Gladden stressed the social implications of Christianity. The Social Gospel was "a new application of the Christian ethic to the demands of a new historical situation" —the industrial age.[6] In fact, many theologians stressed the teachings on social justice of the Hebrew prophets Amos and Micah. But unlike Amos and Micah, the Christian liberals did not demand a recasting of society. Most of them only hoped to make life more bearable on earth, and for a great many the emphasis was still on the world to come. Even Wilberforce preached to the impoverished to accept their lot in life, and Rauschenbusch never supposed that the kingdom of God could be produced by man's efforts. The Social Gospel was a popular movement in the United States for fifty years from 1870 through 1920, but it appears to have affected American politics only slightly throughout its growth. It reached its height in 1908 when it was symbolized by the organization of the Federal Council of the Churches of Christ in America. Ironically, that was the year William Howard Taft, a Unitarian and the candidate of the conservatives, defeated fundamentalist theologian and "liberal" politician William Jennings Bryan for the Presidency.

The optimism of the liberal theology of the late nineteenth century has fallen into disrepute in the aftermath of the great depression, genocide, two degrading world wars and the terrors of world communism. The Neo-Calvinist writings of Reinhold Niebuhr, J. V. Langmean Casserly, and others have re-emphasized the traditional Christian view of sinful man and its insistence that faith is the key to salvation. There can be little doubt that the Christian emphasis on faith and repentance as contrasted with the Jewish stress on works has influenced American political behavior. As one Jewish writer recently pointed out, faith is essentially personal and works are inherently social.[7] Contrast the recent urging of the executive director of the Rabbinical Assembly of American Rabbis to raise questions and criticize social institutions with the oft-held Lutheran position that Christ's kingdom is not of this world, "and that therefore it is the preacher's duty to preach repentance and faith and not to concern himself with worldly affairs."[8] Because faith is personal and works are usually social, the Christian efforts at social and economic reform, great as they have been, have been dwarfed by the energies which Christians have spent on the

6. John Dillenberger and Claude Welch, *Protestant Christianity* (New York: Charles Scribner's Sons, 1954), p. 245.

7. Joseph R. Narot, "Judaism, Christianity, and Salvation," *The Reconstructionist*, Vol. XX (April 23, 1954), p. 16.

8. William Warren Sweet, *Religion in the Development of American Culture, 1765-1840* (New York: Charles Scribner's Sons, 1952), p. 38.

saving of souls. Enormous Christian effort goes into missionary work and pastoral counseling, while the Jews hardly pay any attention to these affairs at all. Catholics place strong emphasis on the confessional. And the church is prepared to make its peace with any social order, authoritarian as well as democratic, so as to concentrate on its main job of personal salvation.

Because of the orthodox stress on the sinfulness of man and the necessity of faith for redemption, many Christians view as the greatest of all impieties any effort by man to bring about what God has promised. Thus, Arnold Toynbee has criticized the restoration of the state of Israel as a prideful usurpation of Divine Will. For the same reason the English historian, like many Neo-Calvinists, has termed the communist movement a "Christian heresy" because it strives to produce the kingdom of God on earth without God, thus denying the capacity of the Almighty to do the task alone. But if the communist movement is in a sense a Christian heresy, it is also Jewish orthodoxy—not the totalitarian or revolutionary aspects of world communism, but the quest for social justice through social action.

Although there are many exceptions, Jews have tended to emphasize the interrelatedness of religion with social organization, while numberless Christians have believed that their temporal interests could be divorced from their religious convictions. By comparison with the Jews the Christians have been otherworldly. Contrast, for example, the notion held by many Christians that celibacy (as sharp a break from this world as one can make) is the highest form of life with the view which Rabbi Bernstein says Jews hold—that "The reward of the good life is the good life."[9] Undoubtedly, there are hundreds of thousands of Christians who agree with Bernstein and his coreligionists, but there are also hundreds of thousands who do not. In a recent book on Christianity and social problems, H. Ralph Higgens describes three typical Christian approaches to social questions, not one of which is held by any sizable number of Jews.[10] The first he calls the "hands off view." Injustice and suffering are to be endured since they are unavoidable "and are to be used by the Christian as spiritual muscle-builders." The second is the "first aid kit approach" used to salve the wounds of an unjust social order. The third holds that nothing much can be done until all men have been converted. Each of these views, as Higgins points out, is melancholy and based on a concept of selfish man. The fact that these are not the only Christian views is borne out by Higgens' own plea for Christian action on social problems, stressing the relevance of Christian morality to social life in the tradition of liberal theology.

The main point is that while there are many Christian approaches to social and political questions, the Jewish position has been relatively unified. While orthodox Christianity stresses man's sinfulness, repentance, and otherworldliness,

---

9. Bernstein, *op. cit.*, pp. 4,65. Writes Bernstein (p. 4), "Most Jews have assented to the judgment of an olden Rabbinic teacher who (said) . . . 'One hour of repentance and good deeds in this world is better than the whole life of the world to come.' "

10. H. Ralph Higgens, *Christianity and America's Social Problems* (New York: Comet Press, 1952), p. 8.

the Jews appear to have emphasized man's potentialities, works, and life here and now. Orthodox Christian theology has tended to color American politics with a conservative cast from which Jews have been largely exempt. On the other hand, Jewish cultural and theological values have promoted a liberal and radical political style.

It cannot be urged too often that there are many exceptions to the general tendencies described above. Thousands of Methodists, Episcopalians, Presbyterians, Baptists, and Catholics to say nothing of Unitarians and Quakers are, in Bernstein's words, "optimistic" in politics, "strive for a better world," and are "in the thick . . . of movements for social reform." But tendencies there are, and among Jews aggressive and optimistic reformism in politics is found much more often than among their Christian countrymen.

None of this is to say that Christian theology is responsible for making America conservative. In fact, just the opposite is true. The United States is a liberal-democratic state, and the Judeo-Christian emphasis on love, justice, and human dignity is in no small measure responsible for democracy itself. But there is a conservative position within the framework of American politics which can be categorized by such notions as the importance of order, the sanctity of private property, the futility of social change, and the Herbert Hoover type of rugged individualism. These elements of conservatism in American politics may be mainly secular in origin, but they meet with little resistance from the major strains of Christian theology and with a great deal of opposition from Jewish cultural and theological values.

Jewish Solidarity in Politics

Accepting the view that Jewish insecurity and the Jewish value system primarily account for the political liberalism of American Israelites in recent times, the query remains, "Why do Jews take their values and norms from the ethno-religious group they belong to in making political judgments? Why don't they relate their political behavior to the norms of other reference groups they belong to, their class groups or occupational groups?"

Like all of us, Jews relate to many reference groups.[11] Jewish doctors may adopt either Jewish norms or those of the AMA in judging proposals for socialized medicine; Jewish lawyers may adopt Jewish norms in judging the use of the Fifth Amendment by crypto-communists or they may use those of the American Bar Association; Jewish taxpayers may employ Jewish values as points of reference for judging tax legislation or they may follow the views of a taxpayer's association. The evidence presented in the preceding chapters shows that

---

11. I have accepted the definition of the Sherifs that reference groups are "simply those groups to which the individual relates himself as a part or to which he aspires to relate himself psychologically." *Op. cit.*, p. 161. For a discussion of reference group material see Theodore Newcombe, Eugene L. Hartley, and others in *Readings in Social Psychology* (revised edition: New York: Henry Holt & Co., 1952), Part IV, B.

an unusual number of Jews do derive their political attitudes and opinions from being Jewish. It is that which makes them political liberals and internationalists. Why is it that membership in the Jewish group, apparently without regard to the depth of one's involvement in that group, is so vital in determining the vote behavior of Jews?

There are basically two answers to this, and one of them has already been provided. The Jewish religion and culture are centered on the here and now as the Christian religions and cultures are not. And there is evidence that younger Jews believe that the Jewish religion should become less and less concerned with theology and ritual and more and more concerned with secular social and economic problems.[12] But the fact that Judaism is this worldly does not mean that Jews will apply Jewish norms to worldly affairs in competition with other norms.

The main answer lies in the unusual cohesiveness and solidarity of the Jewish group. Through centuries of dispersion, persecution, and even genocide the Jews have persisted as a people. The Jews have survived because of the extraordinary will to survive. They have resisted conversion, eschewed intermarriage, and scorned suicide. In the ghettos they developed a strong feeling of common responsibility. Perhaps more than anything else it was the ghetto experience which produced cohesiveness among the Jews. As Louis Wirth explained in his monumental study on Jewish ghetto life:

> What makes the Jewish community—composed as it is in our metropolitan centers of so many heterogeneous elements—a community is its ability to act corporately. It has a common set of attitudes and values based upon common traditions, similar experiences, and common problems. In spite of its geographical separateness it is welded into a community because of conflict and pressure from without and collective action within. The Jewish community is a cultural community. It is as near an approach to communal life as the modern city has to offer.[13]

Wirth wrote in 1928, when the American ghettos were beginning to disintegrate in 1928 and the flow of orthodox Jews into the ghettos had just about stopped. But the spectre of anti-Semitism came to replace these unifying factors and to prevent the divisive effects of assimilation. Anti-Semitism made considerable headway in the 1920's and 1930's. Exclusion from good housing and better residential areas was extended. The quota system at schools, in professions, and in clubs barred Jews from access to influence and prestige. Then the depression and the rise of Hitler exacerbated tensions between Jew and Gentile. Over 100 anti-Semitic organizations sprouted during the 1930's, and Gerald L. K. Smith, Father Coughlin, and Gerald Winrod applauded Hitler's

---

12. Meyer Greenberg, "The Jewish Student at Yale," in *Race Prejudice and Discrimination*, op. cit., p. 317. Nathan Goldberg, "Religious and Social Attitudes of Jewish Youth in the U.S.A.," *Jewish Review*, Vol. 1 (December 1943), pp. 139-41.

13. Louis Wirth, op. cit., p. 279.

attempts to destroy European Jewry. The solidarity of the Jews was reinforced by these events, and the tight cohesiveness of American Jewry was assured for at least a few decades. Jewish doctors, lawyers, laborers, peddlers—all were made conscious of their Jewishness whether they wanted it or not. Their insecurity as Jews served to emphasize Jewish values as points of reference for political action. After the war the growth of Zionism in the United States reinforced cohesiveness still further. The total membership in Jewish voluntary organizations grew from 807,000 in 1935 to 1,085,000 in 1941 and 1,436,000 in 1945, a much higher rate of increase than for all voluntary associations in the United States.[14] Membership in nonpolitical organizations such as the Workmen's Circle remained stable, but membership in Jewish political groups grew by leaps and bounds. Meanwhile, Jewish charities received a sudden burst of support which went far beyond the average national increase despite the fact that the ghettos in the big cities continued to disband and circulation figures for the Yiddish press went steadily down.

The events during this time not only promoted Jewish unity, but they made the Jews the most politicized group in the United States. During most of the nineteenth century American Jews were relatively indifferent to politics. Apathy resulted partly from a lack of issues which interested Jews, partly because Jews were so busy doing other things, and partly because of the reluctance of Sephardic and German Jews to enter politics as such. While Rabbinical sermons in the twentieth century were highly secular, mid-nineteenth century Rabbis generally objected to what they called "politics in the pulpit."[15] The Jewish pulpit was usually silent on such topics as free trade, labor unions, and governmental relief. But during this period, leading Rabbis spoke out boldly on almost every major political question. The anti-Semitism and Zionism during these decades promoted group consciousness, which, in turn, made Jewish values influential in shaping the political behavior of American Jews.

There are other contributing sources of Jewish liberalism, but they are probably not of major significance. Lewis Browne has forcefully stated the proposition that Jews are liberals and radicals in politics because they are an urban people.[16] American Jews are concentrated in the urban centers, but many of them were village and peasant folk in East Europe before they came to America. And the fact remains, within the cities other groups sharply divided in politics on economic class lines whereas the Jews were not.

14. Leo Bogart, *The Response of Jews in America to The European Jewish Catastrophe, 1941-1945,* Unpublished M. A. Thesis, University of Chicago, 1948, p. 46.

15. Robert I. Kahn, *Liberalism as Reflected in Jewish Preaching in the English Language in The Mid-Nineteenth Century,* Ph.D. Thesis, Hebrew Union College, 1949, p. 71.

16. Lewis Browne, *How Odd of God* (New York: Macmillan, 1934), Chapter VI, especially pp. 216-22.

A Personal Conclusion

Some readers may object that I have asserted the liberalism of the Jews and discussed the sources of Jewish liberalism in too sweeping a manner. Need it be said that there are thousands, perhaps hundreds of thousands of American Jews who are not liberals? Of course there are Jewish reactionaries, but these are the exceptions. Still, it ought to be remembered that this book is about Jews in a specific place and a specific time, and that even in a few short years these generalizations may fall. I should not like to be caught in the position of the great German sociologist, Werner Sombart, who wrote emphatically in 1913 that the intellectualism and lack of sensuousness in the painting of the Jews was proof of their asceticism—at the very time the Jewish Pissaro, Soutine, and Modigliani were putting brushes to canvas.

It may be that Jewish liberalism and internationalism are on the wane, and that the Jewish political style is less often found than it was fifteen years ago. The latter seems especially true. But in recent years, as during the first twenty years of the Republic, American Jewry has taken the liberal position in politics, and generalizations about the causes of Jewish liberalism ought not to be abandoned merely because they are large. Since they seem to be true, I would happily acquiesce in Albert Einstein's judgment that "Abandonment of generalization (in the field of politics) . . . means to relinquish understanding altogether."

Source: From Lawrence H. Fuchs, *The Political Behavior of American Jews* (Glencoe, Ill.: The Free Press, 1956), pp. 171-203.

5 | THEOLOGICAL TENSION AND CONTEMPORARY AMERICAN POLITICS

The humanistic way of thinking which had proclaimed itself our guide, did not admit the existence of intrinsic evil in man, nor did it see any task higher than the attainment of happiness on earth. It started Western civilization on the dangerous trend of worshipping man and his material needs. . . . As humanism in its development was becoming more and more materialistic, it also increasingly allowed its concepts to be used first by socialism and then by communism. So that Karl Marx was able to say, in 1844, that 'communism is naturalized humanism.'[1]

ALEKSANDR I. SOLZHENITSYN

Angry at change, rigid in the application of chauvinistic slogans, absolutistic in morality [the anti-humanists or the religious right], threaten through political pressure or public denunciation whoever dares to disagree with their authoritarian positions. Using television, direct mail and economic boycott [the anti-humanists or the religious right], would sweep before them anyone who holds a different opinion.[2]

A. BARTLETT GIAMATTI

Eruption of student violence on college campuses in the mid-1960s, civil rights demonstrations in the early and mid-1960s, outbursts of Black civil disobedience and riots in the late 1960s, marches against the Vietnam War, agitation for and opposition to ERA, abortion and school busing, organization of opposition to nuclear development in the early 1980s, and efforts to reverse the U.S. Supreme

Court's decisions on school prayer and Bible reading are among the many marks of social turmoil from 1960 through the early 1980s.

While these highly visible and very vocal efforts divided and polarized American society, a conservative resurgence theologically and politically was taking place that had its generally recognized political beginning with the 1964 presidential candidacy of Barry Goldwater and its greatest success with the election of Ronald Reagan in 1980. While abhorring the turbulent liberal and radical demonstrations, the conservative movement began to counterattack with its own demonstrations as well as more effective intellectual, legal, and political efforts to influence public opinion and public policy.

Does the conservative resurgence in the midst of strident social turmoil portend another major turning point in the direction of American public policy that will change the landscape of American politics and government for the next several decades? Our primary purpose here is not to argue affirmatively but to see if the theological foundations for such a change are apparent. Certainly as Paul Goodman points out, a religious foundation rests beneath the social, economic, and political turmoil.

> I have imagined [in 1962] that the world-wide student protest had to do with changing political and moral institutions, to which I was sympathetic, but I now say [1969] that we had to do with a religious crisis of the magnitude of the Reformation in the fifteen hundreds, when not only all institutions but all learning had been corrupted. . . .[3]

THE CONSERVATIVE COALITION

At the outset it appears that a marriage of conservative theology with conservative economic, political, and social ideology, not unlike the liberal theological and ideological marriage of the New Deal, may be in the process of consummation. Certainly President Reagan drew upon both to gain his election by naming persons from both to high policy positions in his administration and by espousing many policy positions pleasing to both. And as Jimmy Carter before him, he professed to be "born again" in an effort to appeal to the conservative theological constituency.

From the conservative ideological school of thought came ideas and persons from such institutions as the American Enterprise Institute, the Hoover Institution at Stanford University, and the Heritage Foundation. From conservative theological institutions came support associated even with very conservative or fundamental theological schools like Bob Jones University and Hyles-Anderson College in addition to those of conservative theological persuasion in other places.

Some elements in the conservative movement, both political and ideological, raised questions about the depth of President Reagan's commitment to conservative causes after he became president, because he refused to appoint sufficient numbers of conservatives to top positions; retained moderate advisors in high positions, such as James Baker; relied too much on Vice President George Bush; and rejected the conservative position on several key issues, such as cutting back more on the federal government. Despite these attacks, both political and theological conservatives generally recognized they were better off with President Reagan even though he moderated his conservatism somewhat. Strategically, of course, these attacks had the purpose of steering President Reagan back in the desired direction by threatening him with the loss of his political base.

Just as during the founding period when the then dissenting academies, such as Harvard, Yale, and Princeton, opened their doors as a theological grassroots response to the needs then, there now appears to be a grassroots response to establish academies that dissent from the established theological and ideological modes of thought in the public and private secular school domain.

During the past two decades there has been an enormous theological impact on education, largely ignored in the secular press, as Christian elementary and secondary schools and colleges and universities have been opened in large numbers. Some estimates have indicated that Christian elementary and secondary schools have been opened in recent years at the average rate of three per day. Although over 50 years old and not a recent entrant among Christian colleges and universities like Liberty Baptist College (Jerry Falwell) and Hyles-Anderson College (Jack Hyles), Bob Jones University has nearly 7,000 students from all 50 states and about 30 foreign countries and offers graduate programs through the Ph.D. in many areas to supply personnel for the burgeoning Christian school market. While some of the new Christian colleges have less than 1,000 students, several are now into the thousands in enrollment, and there appears to be no lack of students for any of them.

Similarly, the principal church growth is no longer with the established denominational churches, but with theologically conservative churches, such as independent fundamental Baptists, Assembly of God, and Church of God (Pentecostal). Of course, highly visible to the general public is the growth of so-called Christian radio and television, such as the Christian Broadcasting Network.

Although conservative theological fermentation has been taking place during the past two decades, the question remains: Why? The 1978 Harvard University commencement address by Aleksandr Solzhenitsyn suggests that it is a latent reaction to liberal theological successes in public policy.

> Destructive and irresponsible freedom has been granted boundless space. Society has turned out to have scarce defense against the abyss

of human decadence, for example against misuse of liberty for moral violence against young people, such as motion pictures full of pornography, crime and horror. This is all considered to be a part of freedom and to be counterbalanced, in theory, by the young people's right not to look and not to accept. Life organized legalistically has thus shown its inability to defend itself against the corrosion of evil. . . .

The tilt of freedom toward evil has come about gradually, but it evidently stems from a humanistic and benevolent concept according to which man—the master of the world—does not bear any evil within himself, and all the defects of life are caused by misguided social systems which must therefore be corrected. . . .

In early democracies, as in American democracy at the time of its birth, all individual human rights were granted on the ground that man is God's creature. That is, freedom was given to the individual conditionally, in the assumption of his constant religious responsibility. Such was the heritage of the preceding one thousand years. Two hundred or even fifty years ago, it would have seemed impossible, in America, that an individual be granted boundless freedom with no purpose, simply for the satisfaction of his whims. Subsequently, however, all such limitations were eroded everywhere in the West; a total emancipation occurred from the moral heritage of Christian centuries with their great reserves of mercy and sacrifice. . . .

We are now paying for the mistakes which had not been properly appraised at the beginning of the journey. . . . We have placed too much hope in political and social reforms, only to find out that we were being deprived of our most precious possession: our spiritual life.[4]

Nowhere is the latent reaction to liberal successes more evident than in the South which had overwhelmingly favored the Democratic Party. The South, held in the solid Democratic Party column by virtue of Civil War issues remained there in presidential elections until the liberal ideological and theological positions of the national Democratic Party began to conflict seriously with the South's indigenous ideological and theological conservatism. Although integration first sparked southern discontent in the 1948 Democratic National Convention, gradually other liberal platform ideas and candidates incurred the ire of the South, including positions on school busing, federal aid to education, strong support of labor unions, abortion, and the proposed Equal Rights Amendment.

The theological tension today is between conservative theology on the one hand and humanist and liberation theology together with the remnants of social gospel and neo-orthodox theology on the other. Also emerging as a part of the liberal theological force today is "prophetic politics" which combines a variety of social gospel, neo-orthodox and humanist tendencies to the extent that it generally fits the mold of liberal theological views of government, politics, and public policy. Indeed, content analysis of "prophetic politics" reveals that in many ways it is very much like religious humanism. (See the *Documents* sections of Chapters Four and Five.) "Prophetic politics," particularly apparent in the major protestant denominations and the Roman Catholic Church, also places substantial emphasis upon the ecumenical movement to unite structurally protestant and Roman Catholic churches.

While some question whether or not humanism is a religion, leading humanists do not. *The Humanist Manifesto I* (1933)[5] declares "to establish such a religion (of humanism) is a major necessity of the present," and to "break with the past" in order to establish a "vital, fearless, and frank religion capable of furnishing adequate goals and personal satisfactions," is the goal of humanism. *The Humanist Manifesto II* (1973) uses the words religion and religious some 19 times while stating that "Faith, commensurate with advancing knowledge, is also necessary," among nontheists whose center of thought or worship is "nature, not deity." Not only is there an influential journal entitled *The Religious Humanist*, but one of the most prominent humanists, Julian Huxley, referred to his beliefs as "the religion of evolutionary humanism" while still another, Michael Kolenda, entitled his book on humanistic religion, *Religion Without God*. Of course, the U.S. Supreme Court recognized humanism as a religion in *Torcasco* v. *Watkins* (1961), and *The Secular Humanist Declaration* (1980)[6] concludes that "Secular humanism places trust in human intelligence rather than in divine guidance."

The basic tenets of humanist theology are: disbelief in God, belief in evolution, rejection of absolute morals, belief in the innate goodness of men to govern the world equitably, and emphasis upon internationalism and world government. Liberation theology contributes an emphasis upon the human right to be free from imperialism and authoritarian government.

Opposition to religious or secular humanism has become one of the principal rallying cries of conservatives, especially theological conservatives. In effect it is a negative strength for conservatives in that it provides an identifiable enemy.

Writing in *The Humanist*, John Dunphy provides a dramatic illustration of the strident conflict between historic conservative Christianity and the liberal theology of contemporary humanism:

> I am convinced that the battle for humankind's future must be waged and won in the public school classroom by teachers who correctly perceive their role as the proselytizers of a new faith: a religion of humanity that recognizes and respects what theologians call divinity in every human being. These teachers must embody the same selfless dedication as the most rabid fundamentalist preachers, for they will be ministers of another sort, utilizing a classroom instead of a pulpit to convey humanist values in whatever subject they teach, regardless of the educational level—preschool day care center or large state university. The classroom must and will become an arena of conflict between the old and the new—the rotting corpse of Christianity, together with all its adjacent evils and misery, and the new faith of humanism.[7]

The emphasis on human rights in humanist and liberation theology has helped raise such public policy issues as the abortion rights of women, the Equal Rights Amendment, homosexual rights, the rights of children, and others. Additionally nuclear disarmament and the strengthened role of international institutions are also emphases of humanist and liberation theology that have aroused conservative theological opposition. Also pitched battles over President Carter's abrogation of the Taiwan Treaty and relinquishing of the Panama Canal engaged strident conservative and liberal theological opposition to one another.

Ironically, traditional supporters of Israel began to wonder whether they could trust conservative or liberal theological leaders more. As President Carter and other Democratic leaders began to modify their pro-Israeli stance, Jewish leaders began to recognize conservative Protestants with their historic Old Testament reverence for Israel as a consistent and rather solid bastion of support. Conservative and fundamental protestant leaders like Jerry Falwell seem to take the position that Israel can do no wrong in the Middle East conflict, and they have encouraged as well as sponsored scores of thousands of conservative and fundamental Protestants to travel to the Holy Land each year.

For the Democratic and Republican Parties, this theological tension is not without practical consequences. For example, on policy issues, what the Democratic Party began to do in the late 1960s and through the 1970s was to cut itself off from its grassroots base of support among poor and less educated white Protestants, conservative Roman Catholics, and conservative and orthodox Jews. Each of these groups felt the threat of theologically liberal public policies either being carried out or proposed by the Democratic Party. Both President Reagan and the Moral Majority capitalized on this alienation from the Democratic Party and the successes and goals of liberal theology in public policy. For example, the 1980 National Party platforms differed sharply on abortion, the Equal Rights Amendment, the existence of the Department of Education, school busing, and prayer in the public schools as well as on many other issues with Republicans taking positions designed to attract alienated Democrats.

It is interesting, though not necessarily meaningful in and of itself, that the last time the Democratic Party used the word *God* in its platform was in 1960 while the Republican Party has made consistent platform references to God from 1948-1980, an indication of the importance of theological conservatism in Republican Party policy making. In 1976, Republicans made three platform references to God and one to *The Creator* while Democrats made none.

The basis for latent conservative theological reaction may be seen in grassroots alienation from national leadership groups on major theological issues in nationwide data comparing general public opinion with the opinion of leaders in seven groups: business, military, news media, government, education, law and justice, and science. This study of American values was done for Connecticut Mutual Life Insurance Company by Research and Forecasts, Inc. Is abortion morally wrong? Sixty-five (65) percent of the general public says "yes," but only 31.7 percent of the leaders. Is homosexuality morally wrong? Seventy-one (71) percent of the general public says "yes," but only 38.6 percent of the leaders. Should women with children work? Only 44 percent of the general public says "yes," but 72 percent of the leaders respond affirmatively.[8] Table 5.1 provides a summary of the Connecticut Mutual Life Insurance Co. survey, including the opinions of religious leaders, on several moral, theological, and political issues. It would appear from those data that conservative theological and political interest groups like the Moral Majority are tapping a large reservoir of public support on these issues.

Another conservative strength is that state and local laws and ordinances have historically reflected conservative theological positions, especially on such issues as homosexuality, adultery, and incest. Using as an example the State of Virginia's laws which are very similar to those in other states on these subjects, the dominant conservative position is readily evident.

> *Cohabitation*: "It is unlawful for unmarried persons to lewdly and lasciviously associate and cohabit together." (18.2-345)
> *Premarital Sex*: "It is unlawful for any unmarried person to have sexual intercourse voluntarily with another unmarried person." (18.2-344)
> *Adultery*: "It is unlawful for any married person voluntarily to have sexual intercourse with any person not his or her spouse." (18.2-365)
> *Homosexuality*: "Marriage is forbidden between persons of the same sex." (20.45-2)

Emergence of the neo-conservative movement brought another significant asset to the conservative alliance during the late 1970s and early 1980s. Primarily populated by liberal Democrats of the New Deal order who chaffed at efforts to weaken the American military among leading Democrats like George Mc-Govern and at the inability of governmental programs to solve pressing social problems, neo-conservatives began to make common cause with conservative Republicans on issues of mutual interest. Some, like United Nations Ambassador Jeanne Kirkpatrick, actually accepted positions in the administration of President Reagan.

Still another asset of the conservative coalition was the apparent visible access it has achieved with the White House, including an admission by President Reagan that he confers regularly with television preacher Jerry Falwell. Perception of a large grassroots following has for many years often allowed conservative religious leaders greater access to the White House than liberal religious leaders.[9]

Beginning in the late 1960s, conservative theological reactions to liberal theological successes in religious denominations and churches occurred. Major theological battles ensued between the two factions in such large denominations as the Missouri Synod Lutheran and the Southern Baptist Convention.

TABLE 5.1 General Public and Leadership Groups: Expressions of Moral Disapproval (in percent)

	Abortion	Pornographic Movies	Premarital Sex	Homosexuality	Adultery	Living with Someone before Marriage	Sex before 16	Lesbianism
General public	65	68	40	71	85	47	71	70
Leadership groups								
Religion	74	87	77	73	96	72	79	74
Business	42	70	38	51	76	37	69	53
Military	40	54	28	58	80	36	59	60
News media	35	46	20	38	72	24	54	37
Government	29	47	23	36	70	23	55	35
Education	26	50	27	30	62	30	46	28
Law & justice	25	41	17	30	60	19	46	30
Science	25	45	20	27	65	19	41	26

Source: Adapted from data in the *Wall Street Journal*, May 15, 1981, p. 34, as reported in a national survey by the Connecticut Mutual Life Insurance Company.

Conservative forces won in the Lutheran battle, but given the less structured and less authoritarian nature of the Southern Baptist Convention, no apparent winner could be declared after a decade of skirmishing. Liberals still controlled the denominational machinery, including the six Southern Baptist seminaries, but conservatives were able to consistently elect presidents of the Convention.

Elsewhere revived interest in orthodox Judaism emerged and conservative Roman Catholics joined with conservative protestant and Jewish organizations and leaders to fight for conservative interests on such public policy issues as opposition to abortion and the Equal Rights Amendment.

In the short run, the conservative reaction to liberal theological successes and goals in public policy (1) has led to the creation of theologically conservative interest groups to challenge long-established liberal theological interest groups, such as the Moral Majority versus the National Council of Churches, (2) has prompted additional direct political action by ministers and laymen from theologically conservative churches and organizations to support or to oppose public policy initiatives, such as school prayer and rights of homosexuals, and to elect or to defeat candidates for office, such as the defeat of George Mc-Govern and other liberal senators in 1980 and the election of Ronald Reagan, and (3) has caused division within established denominations over important issues, such as the Roman Catholic Church, wherein liberal bishops have been advocating nuclear disarmament while conservative Roman Catholics have been taking their church's traditional posture of supporting a strong military.

THE LIBERAL ALLIANCE

The liberal alliance, extensively discussed in Chapter 4, is certainly not without its own considerable strengths in this full scale war, including dominance of the media, leadership in the educational arena, assets of tenure and precedents in the judiciary, the growing ecumenical movement, and the favorable historical trend of gradual liberal theological ascendance over conservative theology.

First, with respect to the media, *The Washington Journalism Review* reports in a survey of master's degree students at the Columbia School of Journalism conducted by Linda Lichter, S. Robert Lichter, and Stanley Rothman that

- 80 percent say they seldom or never attend church while only 8 percent say they attend church regularly;
- 85 percent subscribe to liberal political ideology while only 11 percent are conservative ideologically;
- 90 percent preferred McGovern to Nixon in 1972, and only 4 percent voted for President Reagan in 1980;

- almost 40 percent favor public ownership of corporations;
- about 75 percent believe that the private enterprise system is unfair;
- over 70 percent believe that American society produces alienation;
- 93 percent favor giving homosexuals the right to teach in public schools; and
- 75 percent believe the United States exploits Third World countries.[10]

Still in another article by Lichter, Lichter, and Rothman, their overwhelming conclusion is that the principal leaders in determining what is portrayed on television are substantially liberal in their political and theological positions. They found that

- 75 percent classify themselves as political liberals;
- 44 percent say they have no religion;
- only 7 percent attend church regularly;
- a majority take liberal political and theological stands on specific economic, political and social issues; and
- an average of only 19.25 percent voted for Republican presidential candidates from 1968 through 1980 although Republican candidates won three of the four elections.[11]

Second, in colleges, universities, and seminaries, the liberal theological and ideological point of view prevails, especially among faculty teaching courses that address public policy issues, like political science, history, psychology, and sociology. As shown in Tables 5.2 through 5.7, theology faculty are decidedly liberal, particularly in the prestigious protestant denominations, as are liberal arts and social sciences faculty generally in higher education. Practically this has great impact in that the conservative point of view is less prevalent in the training of a substantial portion of the nation's clergy who preach from week to week in their churches and college professors who teach in college and university classrooms.

The federal judiciary, dominated by liberal Democratic judges nominated by President Carter in the largest single enlargement of the judiciary in history and working within the confines of liberal precedents handed down by the U.S. Supreme Court under the leadership of former Chief Justice Earl Warren, has seen some piecemeal conservative changes under the more conservative Chief Justice Warren Burger, but the basic outline of Warren Court decisions remains with the Burger Court usually either modifying or in some instances confirming them when they are challenged. Structural and positional dominance in the judiciary has made it difficult for conservatives to change interpretations of the fundamental law on such issues as school prayer and Bible reading, abortion, school busing, and other issues.

Within America's churches, the mainline denominations, such as Methodist, Episcopal, Presbyterian, American Baptist, and Lutheran, have been moving

TABLE 5.2   Ideological Inclinations of College Faculty, by Selected Disciplines, 1969 (in percent)

	Liberal	*Conservative*
All faculty	45	26
Social work	80	7
Sociology	79	6
Political science	69	10
Philosophy	70	10
Economics	63	14
History	66	13
Religion	56	20
Physics	52	23
Biochemistry	50	21
Music	37	31
Math	40	29
Civil engineering	23	47

Source: Adapted from 1969 Survey of the American Professoriate, Carnegie Commission on Higher Education. The difference between the percentages shown and 100 percent for each discipline is the group professing to be moderate ideologically.

TABLE 5.3   Comparative Ideological Inclinations: Theology Faculty, General Public, and College Graduates (in percent)

	Liberal	Conservative
Theology faculty	50	27
Theology faculty by denomination		
Episcopalian	78	11
Methodist	69	14
Presbyterian	63	19
Roman Catholic	60	10
American Baptist	54	16
Church of Christ	53	29
Lutheran	52	20
Southern Baptist	32	35
Other Baptist	17	65
Pentecostal	7	75
General public	21	47
College graduates	29	44

Source: Adapted from survey made by the Roper organization, October 24-31, 1981. The difference between the percentages shown and 100 percent for each group is portion professing to be moderate ideologically.

TABLE 5.4   Presidential Voting Patterns: Theology Faculty and General Public, 1972-80 (in percent)

	Democratic	Republican	Other
1972			
Theology faculty	61	37	2
General public	37	61	2
1976			
Theology faculty	69	29	1
General public	50	48	2
1980			
Theology faculty	55	32	14
General public	41	51	8

Source: Adapted from Richard Scammon and Alice V. McGillivary, eds., *America Votes* (Washington, D.C.: Congressional Quarterly Press, 1981).

TABLE 5.5 Contrasting Views on Welfare and Defense Spending: Theology Faculty and General Public (in percent)

	Welfare		Defense	
	Too Much	*Too Little*	*Too Much*	*Too Little*
All theology faculty	29	43	75	7
Theology faculty by denomination				
Episcopal	20	55	92	3
Roman Catholic	29	52	89	1
Methodist	17	63	88	1
Presbyterian	19	43	81	6
American Baptist	17	47	81	5
Lutheran	13	53	79	4
Church of Christ	32	43	78	5
Southern Baptist	42	30	67	13
Other Baptist	45	22	44	20
Pentecostal	75	9	31	16
General public	55	21	29	31
College educated	56	17	36	25
Roman Catholic public	58	19	31	28

Source: Adapted from survey conducted by the Roper Organization, October 24-31, 1981, as reported in *Roper Reports* 81-10. The difference between the percentages shown for each group and 100 percent are those who think spending is about right.

TABLE 5.6   Economic Inclinations of Theology Faculty (in percent)

	U.S. Should Have More Socialism	Could Adhere to Marxism
All theology faculty	37	36
Theology faculty by denomination		
Presbyterian	45	49
Methodist	49	49
Roman Catholic	45	31
Lutheran	41	53
Episcopal	49	68
Church of Christ	36	47
American Baptist	41	44
Other Baptist	9	9
Pentecostal	7	9

Source: Adapted from survey conducted by the Roper organization, October 24-31, 1981.

TABLE 5.7 Views on International Issues Among Theology Faculty

| | The United States | | Use of Nuclear Weapons |
	Is a Force for Good	Mistreats the Third World	Is Always Wrong
Episcopal	27	81	60
Presbyterian	40	82	60
Roman Catholic	59	85	60
Methodist	50	77	49
Church of Christ	53	76	48
Lutheran	53	81	46
American Baptist	56	69	39
Southern Baptist	69	60	29
Other Baptist	79	33	17
Pentecostal	83	35	7
All Theology Faculty	57	70	46

Source: Adapted from survey conducted by the Roper organization, October 24-31, 1981.

closer to merger and, indeed, are cooperating more with the Roman Catholic church. Ironically, former conservative darling Billy Graham has moved to build support among each of the mainline churches, including the solicitation of their active support for his crusades, consultation with the Vatican prior to his 1982 Russian trip and advocacy of liberal positions on such issues as nuclear development. As Billy Graham has become more liberal in his political and theological positions, Jerry Falwell and others have moved to fill his previous position among conservatives.

A simple analysis of history reveals the clear conclusion that gradually liberal theology has been triumphing over conservative theology. Thus, we see still another liberal strength in that the weight of history is on the side of the liberal alliance.

Strength of the liberal alliance is also shown in Figure 5.1 where the generally larger and more prestigious protestant denominations are clearly classified in the liberal theological and political quadrant. Those in the conservative theological and political quadrant are generally smaller and less prestigious. Three of the nation's largest church bodies, Southern Baptist, Roman Catholic, and Mormon, present special problems in categorizing, however.

First, while the six Southern Baptist seminaries and some 50 colleges and universities are generally more liberal in their theological and political orientations than rank-and-file Southern Baptists, a conservative is generally chosen to be president of the Southern Baptist Convention. Interestingly the Convention's Christian Life Commission and its associate state commissions that address social and political issues are generally liberal in their positions. We could probably safely conclude that the Southern Baptist Convention on the whole still remains in the conservative theological and political quadrant, but that it is substantially more liberal than 20 to 30 years ago.

Second, Roman Catholics present a problem like Southern Baptists, namely a political division between liberal Roman Catholic professors on the one hand and rank-and-file Roman Catholics on the other. The present Pope's efforts to insist upon that church's historically accepted theological and political positions for Roman Catholic professors illustrates the conflict between conservatism and liberalism. Of course, only in 1980 did Roman Catholics vote in a majority for a conservative candidate for president of the United States. Historically, rank-and-file Roman Catholics had identified more with the liberal economic policies of the New Deal and the Democratic Party. Threats, however, to Roman Catholic positions on issues like abortion have moved more Roman Catholics into the conservative camp. Additionally, however, Roman Catholic doctrine presents a special problem in that salvation, they believe, is not determined by "grace through faith in the Lord Jesus Christ" (Ephesians 2:8,9 and Titus 3:5) as Protestants believe, but also that other considerations are crucial like good works and one's relationship to the Roman Catholic church.

FIGURE 5.1   Political and Theological Relationships among Churches
and Denominations

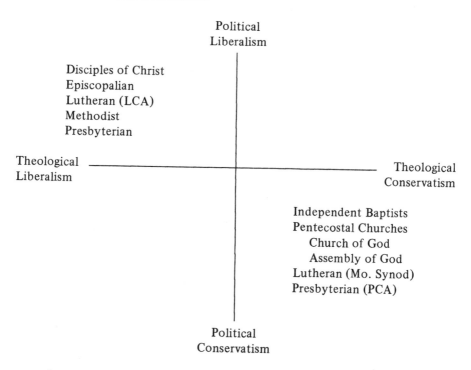

Source: Developed by author from analysis of survey research and other
data.

Third, Mormons present special problems similar to the Roman Catholic
church in that salvation is not premised upon "grace through faith in the Lord
Jesus Christ" alone, but upon good works and baptism. Also Mormons draw
upon the Book of Mormon in addition to the Holy Bible for their rules of faith
and practice just as Roman Catholics utilize church tradition besides the Holy
Bible. Protestants have traditionally relied only upon the Bible as the final rule
for faith and practice. Therefore, by historically accepted protestant standards,
Roman Catholics and Mormons would be liberal theologically. Politically,
however, rank-and-file Mormons are traditionally conservative while among
rank-and-file Roman Catholics, conservatism has been increasing as religious and
social issues become more important in political debate and voting. To help
solidify conservative and Republican voting strength among Roman Catholics,
President Reagan named an American Ambassador to the Vatican in 1984.

PEACEFUL COEXISTENCE?

As society, or at least those studying theological skirmishes, awaits the outcome of battle, they may well see more visible signs of warfare as events like book burnings in the name of theology, such as one at the First Unitarian Church of Baltimore, take place. Nat Hentoff's account in *The Progressive* aptly describes book burnings as yet another volley in a war that is now full scale.

> It happened one splendid Sunday morning in a church. Not Jerry Falwell's Baptist sanctuary in Lynchburg, Virginia, but rather the First Unitarian Church in Baltimore. On October 4, 1981, midway through the 11 A.M. service, pernicious ideas were burned at the altar. As reported by Frank P. L. Somerville, religion editor of the Baltimore *Sun*, centuries of Jewish, Christian, Islamic, and Hindu writings were 'expurgated' —because of sections defined as 'sexist'. . . . The congregation was much exalted: 'As the last flame died in the pot, and the organ pealed, there was applause,' Somerville wrote. . . . What an inspiring homily for the children attending services at a liberated church: They now know that the way to handle ideas they don't like is to set them on fire. . . . The stirring ceremony in Baltimore is just one more illustration that the spirit of the First Amendment is not being savaged only by malign forces of the Right, whether private or governmental. Campaigns to purge school libraries, for example, have been conducted by feminists as well as by Phyllis Schlafly. Yet, most liberal watchdogs of our freedom remain fixed on the Right as *the* enemy of free expression.[12]

While the forces of secular and religious humanism, including the "prophetic politics" position, among such churches and groups as the Roman Catholic church, major protestant denominations, and the Jewish faith, have much in common on issues like the use of nuclear weapons, they are not totally cohesive on other issues like abortion and governmental support for parochial schools. Where they agree, however, they are generally in opposition to the conservative theological voice. These tensions are revealed in the documents and readings that follow: (1) *Humanist Manifesto I* (1933), (2) *Black Theology and Black Power* (1969) by James H. Cone, (3) *Humanist Manifesto II* (1973), (4) "A Secular Humanist Declaration" (1980), (5) *Listen, America* (1980) by Jerry Falwell, (6) *A Christian Manifesto* (1981) by Francis Schaeffer, (7) "Toward a More Prophetic Politics" (1983) by Neal Riemer, and (8) "Resolutions of the World Congress of Fundamentalists" (1980, 1983).

During the founding era in American history, theology provided glue to hold society together, but now it appears to be tearing society apart, raising the very real question of whether America can survive as a free democratic society without a generally accepted moral and spiritual foundation of common values. Those from the conservative theological viewpoint would generally side with Theodore H. White, who said: "Although Christianity has never been the guarantee of a democratic state anywhere in the world, no democracy has ever thrived successfully for any period of time outside of Christian influence."[13] The humanist position, on the other hand, would generally conclude that for American democracy to survive, the vestiges of conservative Christian superiority in American society would need to be leveled. Can the one wipe out the other? Can they live in peaceful coexistence? It would appear that neither can eliminate the other just yet and that peaceful coexistence is impossible.

NOTES

1. Aleksandr I. Solzhenitsyn, *A World Split Apart* (New York: Harper & Row, 1978), pp. 49, 53.

2. The New York *Times*, September 1, 1981, p. 1.

3. In William G. McLoughlin, *Revivals, Awakenings and Reform* (Chicago: University of Chicago Press, 1978), p. 207.

4. Solzhenitsyn, pp. 21, 23, 49, 51, 57.

5. Analysis of and quotes from Humanist Manifestos One and Two come from Paul Kurtz, ed., *Humanist Manifestos One & Two* (Buffalo, N.Y.: Prometheus, 1973).

6. *Free Inquiry* (Winter, 1980): 3-6.

7. James Dunphy, "A Religion for a New Age," *The Humanist* 43 (January/February 1983): 26.

8. *Wall Street Journal*, May 15, 1981, p. 34.

9. Merlin Gustafson, Religious Interest Groups and the American Presidency, paper delivered at the 1982 American Political Science Association Convention, Denver, Colorado.

10. Linda Lichter, et al., "The Once and Future Journalists," *Washington Journalism Review*, December 1982, pp. 26, 27.

11. Linda Lichter, et al., "Hollywood and America: The Odd Couple," *Public Opinion*, December/January, 1983, pp. 54-59.

12. In *Today*, February 11, 1983, p. 6.

13. In Charles L. Wallis, ed., *Our American Heritage* (New York: Harper & Row, 1970), p. 53.

CONTEMPORARY AMERICAN POLITICS: SELECTED POLITICAL AND THEOLOGICAL DOCUMENTS

1. *Humanist Manifesto I* (1933)
2. *Black Theology and Black Power* (1969) by James H. Cone
3. *Humanist Manifesto II* (1973)
4. "A Secular Humanist Declaration" (1980)
5. *Listen, America* (1980) by Jerry Falwell
6. *A Christian Manifesto* (1981) by Francis Schaeffer
7. "Toward a More Prophetic Politics" (1983) by Neal Riemer
8. "From Civil Religion to Prophetic Church: American Bishops and the Bomb" (1983) by Mary Hanna
9. "Resolutions of the World Congress of Fundamentalists" (1980, 1983)

1. | *HUMANIST MANIFESTO I* (1933)

The time has come for widespread recognition of the radical changes in religious beliefs throughout the modern world. The time is past for mere revision of traditional attitudes. Science and economic change have disrupted the old beliefs. Religions the world over are under the necessity of coming to terms with new conditions created by a vastly increased knowledge and experience. In every field of human activity, the vital movement is now in the direction of a candid and explicit humanism. In order that religious humanism may be better understood we, the undersigned, desire to make certain affirmations which we believe the facts of our contemporary life demonstrate.

There is great danger of a final, and we believe fatal, identification of the word religion with doctrines and methods which have lost their significance and which are powerless to solve the problem of human living in the Twentieth Century. Religions have always been means for realizing the highest values of life. Their end has been accomplished through the interpretation of the total environing situation (theology or world view), the sense of values resulting therefrom (goal or ideal), and the technique (cult) established for realizing the satisfactory life. A change in any of these factors results in alteration of the outward forms of religion. This fact explains the changefulness of religions through the centuries. But through all changes religion itself remains constant in its quest for abiding values, an inseparable feature of human life.

Today man's larger understanding of the universe, his scientific achievements, and his deeper appreciation of brotherhood, have created a situation which requires a new statement of the means and purposes of religion. Such a vital, fearless, and frank religion capable of furnishing adequate social goals and personal satisfactions may appear to many people as a complete break with the past. While this age does owe a vast debt to traditional religions, it is none the less obvious that any religion that can hope to be a synthesizing and dynamic force for today must be shaped for the needs of this age. To establish such a religion is a major necessity of the present. It is a responsibility which rests upon this generation. We therefore affirm the following:

First: Religious humanists regard the universe as self-existing and not created.

Second: Humanism believes that man is a part of nature and that he has emerged as the result of a continuous process.

Third: Holding an organic view of life, humanists find that the traditional dualism of mind and body must be rejected.

Fourth: Humanism recognizes that man's religious culture and civilization, as clearly depicted by anthropology and history, are the product of a gradual development due to his interaction with his natural environment and with his social heritage. The individual born into a particular culture is largely molded to that culture.

Fifth: Humanism asserts that the nature of the universe depicted by modern science makes unacceptable any supernatural or cosmic guarantees of human values. Obviously humanism does not deny the possibility of realities as yet undiscovered, but it does insist that the way to determine the existence and value of any and all realities is by means of intelligent inquiry and by the assessment of their relation to human needs. Religion must formulate its hopes and plans in the light of the scientific spirit and method.

Sixth: We are convinced that the time has passed for theism, deism, modernism, and the several varieties of "new thought."

Seventh: Religion consists of those actions, purposes, and experiences which are humanly significant. Nothing human is alien to the religious. It includes labor, art, science, philosophy, love, friendship, recreation—all that is in its degree expressive of intelligently satisfying human living. The distinction between the sacred and the secular can no longer be maintained.

Eighth: Religious humanism considers the complete realization of human personality to be the end of man's life and seeks its development and fulfillment in the here and now. This is the explanation of the humanist's social passion.

Ninth: In place of the old attitudes involved in worship and prayer the humanist finds his religious emotions expressed in a heightened sense of personal life and in a cooperative effort to promote social well-being.

Tenth: It follows that there will be no uniquely religious emotions and attitudes of the kind hitherto associated with belief in the supernatural.

Eleventh: Man will learn to face the crises of life in terms of his knowledge of their naturalness and probability. Reasonable and manly attitudes will be fostered by education and supported by custom. We assume that humanism will take the path of social and mental hygiene and discourage sentimental and unreal hopes and wishful thinking.

Twelfth: Believing that religion must work increasingly for joy in living, religious humanists aim to foster the creative in man and to encourage achievements that add to the satisfactions of life.

Thirteenth: Religious humanism maintains that all associations and institutions exist for the fulfillment of human life. The intelligent evaluation, transformation, control, and direction of such associations and institutions with a view to the enhancement of human life is the purpose and program of humanism. Certainly religious institutions, their ritualistic forms, ecclesiastical methods, and communal activities must be reconstituted as rapidly as experience allows, in order to function effectively in the moden world.

Fourteenth: The humanists are firmly convinced that existing acquisitive and profit-motivated society has shown itself to be inadequate and that a radical change in methods, controls, and motives must be instituted. A socialized and cooperative economic order must be established to the end that the equitable distribution of the means of life be possible. The goal of humanism is a free and universal society in which people voluntarily and intelligently cooperate for the common good. Humanists demand a shared life in a shared world.

Fifteenth and last: We assert that humanism will (a) affirm life rather than deny it; (b) seek to elicit the possibilities of life, not flee from it, and (c) endeavor to establish the conditions of a satisfactory life for all, not merely for the few. By this positive morale and intention humanism will be guided and from this perspective and alignment the techniques and efforts of humanism will flow.

So stand the theses of religious humanism. Though we consider the religious forms and ideas of our fathers no longer adequate, the quest for the good life is still the central task for mankind. Man is at last becoming aware that he alone is responsible for the realization of the world of his dreams, that he has within himself the power for its achievement. He must set intelligence and will to the task.

Source: *Humanist Manifesto* (Buffalo, N.Y.: Prometheus, 1973), pp. 7-10.

2. | *BLACK THEOLOGY AND BLACK POWER* (1969)

James H. Cone

The question of authority has been and still is in some circles a much-debated religious question. Protestant Christianity was born because Martin Luther denied the absolute authority of the Pope in religious matters.

Ultimate and absolute authority in matters of faith can and must reside only in the Word of God, who was made flesh, died and rose again for our salvation, and abides for ever in His Church. In Him and through Him God has spoken to men; here only have we the unmistakable voice of God, unimpeded in its utterance by the weakness of sinful nature and the fallibility of sinful human thought.

For Luther, Christ alone is supreme authority and the Scripture is second only to Christ.

Within Protestantism, liberalism, fundamentalism, and neo-orthodoxy have exerted much time and energy discussing the question. Fundamentalists (sometimes referred to as conservatives) emphasize the verbal inspiration of Scripture and locate final authority in the infallibility of the text itself. The Scripture is God's Word in that "by a special, supernatural, extraordinary influence of the Holy Ghost, the sacred writers have been guided in their writing in such a way, as while their humanity was not superseded it was yet so dominated that their words became at the same time the words of God, and thus, in every case and all alike, infallible." Liberals would be much freer in their treatment of the Bible. Certainly they would not agree that the Scripture is infallible or is the supreme authority on matters of faith. They would be more inclined to emphasize the place of reason in matters of faith and life. The neo-orthodox theologians would emphasize the authority of God's disclosure of himself in Jesus Christ. They seem to represent the Reformation theology of the sixteenth century as expressed in Luther and Calvin.

In more recent times, the question of religious authority is not discussed in the way it used to be. In the past (especially among the fundamentalists, liberals, and neo-orthodox theologians), it was essentially a private debate among religious scholars abstracted from real life in the world. Politically, in America at least, it did not matter whose side one supported. None of the positions threatened the basic structure of the nation. Now, however, religious thinkers have begun to relate theological talk to worldly talk, and some have even begun to question the way men live in the society. This is clearly seen in writings of William Sloane Coffin, Jr., the Yale University chaplain; he not only wrote about it but acted in such a manner that he was tried, convicted, and sentenced for his "illegal" draft counseling. In a less dramatic fashion, the rise of the death-of-God theology means that religious authority not only involves one's participation in a churchly community but equally in the secular community.

It is within this larger context of "the world" that we are to understand Black Theology and religious authority. The discussion of authority must depart from the abstract debate among fundamentalist, liberalist, and neo-orthodox thinkers. Though there are expressions of these three major streams of Protestant thought within the black churches, Black Theology sees a prior authority that unites all black people and transcends these theological differences. It is this common experience among black people in America that Black Theology elevates as the supreme test of truth. To put it simply, Black Theology knows no authority more binding than the experience of oppression itself. This alone must be the ultimate authority in religious matters.

Concretely, this means that Black Theology is not prepared to accept any doctrine of God, man, Christ, or Scripture which contradicts the black demand for freedom now. It believes that any religious idea which exalts black dignity and creates a restless drive for freedom must be affirmed. All ideas which are opposed to the struggle for black self-determination or are irrelevant to it must be rejected as the work of the Antichrist.

Again, this does not mean that Black Theology makes the experience of Christ secondary to the experience of black oppression. Rather, it means that black people have come to know Christ precisely through oppression, because he has made himself synonymous with black oppression. Therefore, to deny the reality of black oppression and to affirm some other "reality" is to deny Christ. Through Christ, black people have come to know not only who he is but also who they are, and what they must do about that which would make them nothings. When the question is asked, "On what authority, in the last resort, do we base our claim that this or that doctrine is part of the Gospel and therefore true?" Black Theology must say: "If the doctrine is compatible with or enhances the drive for black freedom, then it is the gospel of Jesus Christ. If the doctrine is against or indifferent to the essence of blackness as expressed in Black Power, then it is the work of the Antichrist." It is as simple as that.

Black Theology is not prepared to discuss the doctrine of God, man, Christ, Church, Holy Spirit—the whole spectrum of Christian theology—without making each doctrine an analysis of the emancipation of black people. It believes that, in this time, moment, and situation, all Christian doctrines must be interpreted in such a manner that they unreservedly say something to black people who are living under unbearable oppression.

The most corrupting influence among the black churches was their adoption of the "white lie" that Christianity is primarily concerned with an otherworldly reality. White missionaries persuaded most black religious people that life on earth was insignificant because obedient servants of God could expect a "reward" in heaven after death.

Source: James H. Cone, *Black Theology and Black Power* (New York: Seabury, 1969), pp. 116-52.

3. I *HUMANIST MANIFESTO II* (1973)

Preface: It is forty years since Humanist Manifesto I (1933) appeared. Events since then make that earlier statement seem far too optimistic. Nazism has shown the depths of brutality of which humanity is capable. Other totalitarian regimes have suppressed human rights without ending poverty. Science has sometimes brought evil as well as good. Recent decades have shown that inhuman wars can be made in the name of peace. The beginnings of police states, even in democratic societies, widespread government espionage, and other abuses of power by military, political, and industrial elites, and the continuance of unyielding racism, all present a different and difficult social outlook. In various societies, the demands of women and minority groups for equal rights effectively challenge our generation.

As we approach the twenty-first century, however, an affirmative and hopeful vision is needed. Faith, commensurate with advancing knowledge, is also necessary. In the choice between despair and hope, humanists respond in this Humanist Manifesto II with a positive declaration for times of uncertainty.

As in 1933, humanists still believe that traditional theism, especially faith in the prayer-hearing God, assumed to love and care for persons, to hear and understand their prayers, and to be able to do something about them, is an unproved and outmoded faith. Salvationism, based on mere affirmation, still appears as harmful, diverting people with false hopes of heaven hereafter. Reasonable minds look to other means for survival.

Those who sign Humanist Manifesto II disclaim that they are setting forth a binding credo; their individual views would be stated in widely varying ways. This statement is, however, reaching for vision in a time that needs direction. It is social analysis in an effort at consensus. New statements should be developed to supersede this, but for today it is our conviction that humanism offers an alternative that can serve present-day needs and guide humankind toward the future.

Text of the Manifesto

The next century can be and should be the humanistic century. Dramatic scientific, technological, and ever-accelerating social and political changes crowd our awareness. We have virtually conquered the planet, explored the moon, overcome the natural limits of travel and communication; we stand at the dawn of a new age, ready to move farther into space and perhaps inhabit other planets. Using technology wisely, we can control our environment, conquer poverty, markedly reduce disease, extend our life-span, significantly modify our behavior, alter the course of human evolution and cultural development, unlock vast new powers, and provide humankind with unparalleled opportunity for achieving an abundant and meaningful life.

The future is, however, filled with dangers. In learning to apply the scientific method to nature and human life, we have opened the door to ecological damage, overpopulation, dehumanizing institutions, totalitarian repression, and nuclear and biochemical disaster. Faced with apocalyptic prophesies and doomsday scenarios, many flee in despair from reason and embrace irrational cults and theologies of withdrawal and retreat.

Traditional moral codes and newer irrational cults both fail to meet the pressing needs of today and tomorrow. False "theologies of hope" and messianic ideologies, substituting new dogmas for old, cannot cope with existing world realities. They separate rather than unite peoples.

Humanity, to survive, requires bold and daring measures. We need to extend the uses of scientific method, not renounce them, to fuse reason with compassion in order to build constructive social and moral values. Confronted by many possible futures, we must decide which to pursue. The ultimate goal should be the fulfillment of the potential for growth in each human personality —not for the favored few, but for all of humankind. Only a shared world and global measures will suffice.

A humanist outlook will tap the creativity of each human being and provide the vision and courage for us to work together. This outlook emphasizes the role human beings can play in their own spheres of action. The decades ahead call for dedicated, clear-minded men and women able to marshal the will, intelligence, and cooperative skills for shaping a desirable future. Humanism can provide the purpose and inspiration that so many seek; it can give personal meaning and significance to human life.

Many kinds of humanism exist in the contemporary world. The varieties and emphases of naturalistic humanism include "scientific," "ethical," "democratic," "religious," and "Marxist," humanism. Free thought, atheism, agnosticism, skepticism, deism, rationalism, ethical culture, and liberal religion all claim to be heir to the humanist tradition. Humanism traces its roots from ancient China, classical Greece and Rome, through the Renaissance and the Enlightenment, to the scientific revolution of the modern world. But views that merely reject theism are not equivalent to humanism. They lack commitment to the positive belief in the possibilities of human progress and to the values central to it. Many within religious groups, believing in the future of humanism, now claim humanist credentials. Humanism is an ethical process through which we all can move, above and beyond the divisive particulars, heroic personalities, dogmatic creeds, and ritual customs of past religions or their mere negation.

We affirm a set of common principles that can serve as a basis for united action—positive principles relevant to the present human condition. They are a design for a secular society on a planetary scale.

For these reasons, we submit this new Humanist Manifesto for the future of humankind; for us, it is a vision of hope, a direction for satisfying survival.

Religion

First: In the best sense, religion may inspire dedication to the highest ethical ideals. The cultivation of moral devotion and creative imagination is an expression of genuine "spiritual" experience and aspiration.

We believe, however, that traditional dogmatic or authoritarian religions that place revelation, God, ritual, or creed above human needs and experience do a disservice to the human species. Any account of nature should pass the tests of scientific evidence; in our judgment, the dogmas and myths of traditional religions do not do so. Even at this late date in human history, certain elementary facts based upon the critical use of scientific reason have to be restated. We find insufficient evidence for belief in the existence of a supernatural; it is either meaningless or irrelevant to the question of the survival and fulfillment of the human race. As nontheists, we begin with humans not God, nature not deity. Nature may indeed be broader and deeper than we now know; any new discoveries, however, will but enlarge our knowledge of the natural.

Some humanists believe we should reinterpret traditional religions and reinvest them with meanings appropriate to the current situation. Such redefinitions, however, often perpetuate old dependencies and escapisms; they easily become obscurantist, impeding the free use of the intellect. We need, instead, radically new human purposes and goals.

We appreciate the need to preserve the best ethical teachings in the religious traditions of humankind, many of which we share in common. But we reject those features of traditional religious morality that deny humans a full appreciation of their own potentialities and responsibilities. Traditional religions often offer solace to humans, but, as often, they inhibit humans from helping themselves or experiencing their full potentialities. Such institutions, creeds, and rituals often impede the will to serve others. Too often traditional faiths encourage dependence rather than independence, obedience rather than affirmation, fear rather than courage. More recently they have generated concerned social action, with many signs of relevance appearing in the wake of the "God is Dead" theologies. But we can discover no divine purpose or providence for the human species. While there is much that we do not know, humans are responsible for what we are or will become. No deity will save us; we must save ourselves.

Second: Promises of immortal salvation or fear of eternal damnation are both illusory and harmful. They distract humans from present concerns, from self-actualization, and from rectifying social injustices. Modern science discredits such historic concepts as the "ghost in the machine" and the "separable soul." Rather, science affirms that the human species is an emergence from natural evolutionary forces. As far as we know, the total personality is a function of the biological organism transacting in a social and cultural context. There is no credible evidence that life survives the death of the body. We continue to exist in our progeny and in the way that our lives have influenced others in our culture.

Traditional religions are surely not the only obstacles to human progress. Other ideologies also impede human advance. Some forms of political doctrine, for instance, function religiously, reflecting the worst features of orthodoxy and authoritarianism, especially when they sacrifice individuals on the altar of Utopian promises. Purely economic and political viewpoints, whether capitalist or communist, often function as religious and ideological dogma. Although humans undoubtedly need economic and political goals, they also need creative values by which to live.

Ethics

Third: We affirm that moral values derive their source from human experience. Ethics is autonomous and situational, needing no theological or ideological sanction. Ethics stems from human need and interest. To deny this distorts the whole basis of life. Human life has meaning because we create and develop our futures. Happiness and the creative realization of human needs and desires, individually and in shared enjoyment, are continuous themes of humanism. We strive for the good life, here and now. The goal is to pursue life's enrichment despite debasing forces of vulgarization, commercialization, bureaucratization, and dehumanization.

Fourth: Reason and intelligence are the most effective instruments that humankind possesses. There is no substitute: neither faith nor passion suffices in itself. The controlled use of scientific methods, which have transformed the natural and social sciences since the Renaissance, must be extended further in the solution of human problems. But reason must be tempered by humility, since no group has a monopoly of wisdom or virtue. Nor is there any guarantee that all problems can be solved or all questions answered. Yet critical intelligence, infused by a sense of human caring, is the best method that humanity has for resolving problems. Reason should be balanced with compassion and empathy and the whole person fulfilled. Thus, we are not advocating the use of scientific intelligence independent of or in opposition to emotion, for we believe in the cultivation of feeling and love. As science pushes back the boundary of the known, man's sense of wonder is continually renewed, and art, poetry, and music find their places, along with religion and ethics.

The Individual

Fifth: the preciousness and dignity of the individual person is a central humanist value. Individuals should be encouraged to realize their own creative talents and desires. We reject all religious, ideological, or moral codes that denigrate the individual, suppress freedom, dull intellect, dehumanize personality. We believe in maximum individual autonomy consonant with social responsibility. Although science can account for the causes of behavior, the possibilities of individual freedom of choice exist in human life and should be increased.

Sixth: In the area of sexuality, we believe that intolerant attitudes, often cultivated by orthodox religions and puritanical cultures, unduly repress sexual conduct. The right to birth control, abortion, and divorce should be recognized. While we do not approve of exploitive, denigrating forms of sexual expression, neither do we wish to prohibit, by law or social sanction, sexual behavior between consenting adults. The many varieties of sexual exploration should not in themselves be considered "evil." Without countenancing mindless permissiveness or unbridled promiscuity, a civilized society should be a tolerant one. Short of harming others or compelling them to do likewise, individuals should be permitted to express their sexual proclivities and pursue their life-styles as they desire. We wish to cultivate the development of a responsible attitude toward sexuality, in which humans are not exploited as sexual objects, and in which intimacy, sensitivity, respect, and honesty in interpersonal relations are encouraged. Moral education for children and adults is an important way of developing awareness and sexual maturity.

Democratic Society

Seventh: To enhance freedom and dignity the individual must experience a full range of civil liberties in all societies. This includes freedom of speech and the press, political democracy, the legal right of opposition to governmental policies, fair judicial process, religious liberty, freedom of association, and artistic, scientific, and cultural freedom. It also includes a recognition of an individual's right to die with dignity, euthanasia, and the right to suicide. We oppose the increasing invasion of privacy, by whatever means, in both totalitarian and democratic societies. We would safeguard, extend, and implement the principles of human freedom evolved from the Magna Carta to the Bill of Rights, the Rights of Man, and the Universal Declaration of Human Rights.

Eighth: We are committed to an open and democratic society. We must extend participatory democracy in its true sense to the economy, the school, the family, the workplace, and voluntary associations. Decision-making must be decentralized to include widespread involvement of people at all levels—social, political, and economic. All persons should have a voice in developing the values and goals that determine their lives. Institutions should be responsive to expressed desires and needs. The conditions of work, education, devotion, and play should be humanized. Alienating forces should be modified or eradicated and bureaucratic structures should be held to a minimum. People are more important than decalogues, rules, proscriptions, or regulations.

Ninth: The separation of church and state and the separation of ideology and state are imperatives. The state should encourage maximum freedom for different moral, political, religious, and social values in society. It should not favor any particular religious bodies through the use of public monies, nor espouse a single ideology and function thereby as an instrument of propaganda or oppression, particularly against dissenters.

Tenth: Humane societies should evaluate economic systems not by rhetoric or ideology, but by whether or not they increase economic well-being for all individuals and groups, minimize poverty and hardship, increase the sum of human satisfaction, and enhance the quality of life. Hence the door is open to alternative economic systems. We need to democratize the economy and judge it by its responsiveness to human needs, testing results in terms of the common good.

Eleventh: The principle of moral equality must be furthered through elimination of all discrimination based upon race, religion, sex, age, or national origin. This means equality of opportunity and recognition of talent and merit. Individuals should be encouraged to contribute to their own betterment. If unable, then society should provide means to satisfy their basic economic, health, and cultural needs, including, wherever resources make possible, a minimum guaranteed annual income. We are concerned for the welfare of the aged, the infirm, the disadvantaged, and also for the outcasts—the mentally retarded, abandoned or abused children, the handicapped, prisoners, and addicts —for all who are neglected or ignored by society. Practicing humanists should make it their vocation to humanize personal relations.

We believe in the right to universal education. Everyone has a right to the cultural opportunity to fulfill his or her unique capacities and talents. The schools should foster satisfying and productive living. They should be open at all levels to any and all; the achievement of excellence should be encouraged. Innovative and experimental forms of education are to be welcomed. The energy and idealism of the young deserve to be appreciated and channeled to constructive purposes.

We deplore racial, religious, ethnic, or class antagonisms. Although we believe in cultural diversity and encourage racial and ethnic pride, we reject separations which promote alienation and set people and groups against each other, we envision an integrated community where people have a maximum opportunity for free and voluntary association.

We are critical of sexism or sexual chauvinism—male or female. We believe in equal rights for both women and men to fulfill their unique careers and potentialities as they see fit, free of invidious discrimination.

World Community

Twelfth: We deplore the division of humankind on nationalistic grounds. We have reached a turning point in human history where the best option is to transcend the limits of national sovereignty and to move toward the building of a world community in which all sectors of the human family can participate. Thus we look to the development of a system of world law and a world order based upon transnational federal government. This would appreciate cultural pluralism and diversity. It would not exclude pride in national origins and accomplishments nor the handling of regional problems on a regional basis. Human progress, however, can no longer be achieved by focusing on one section of the world. Western or Eastern, developed or underdeveloped. For the first time in human history, no part of humankind can be isolated from any other. Each person's future is in some way linked to all. We thus reaffirm a commitment to the building of world community at the same time recognizing that this commits us to some hard choices.

Thirteenth: This world community must renounce the resort to violence and force as a method of solving international disputes. We believe in the peaceful adjudication of differences by international courts and by the development of the arts of negotiation and compromise. War is obsolete. So is the use of nuclear, biological, and chemical weapons. It is a planetary imperative to reduce the level of military expenditures and turn these savings to peaceful and people-oriented uses.

Fourteenth: The world community must engage in cooperative planning concerning the use of rapidly depleting resources. The planet earth must be considered a single ecosystem. Ecological damage, resource depletion, and excessive population growth must be checked by international concord. The cultivation and conservation of nature is a moral value; we should perceive ourselves as integral to the sources of our being in nature. We must free our world from needless pollution and waste, responsibility guarding and creating wealth, both natural and human. Exploitation of natural resources, uncurbed by social conscience, must end.

Fifteenth: The problems of economic growth and development can no longer be resolved by one nation alone; they are worldwide in scope. It is the moral obligation of the developed nations to provide—through an international authority that safeguards human rights—massive technical, agricultural, medical, and economic assistance, including birth control techniques, to the developing portions of the globe. World poverty must cease. Hence extreme disproportions in wealth, income, and economic growth should be reduced on a worldwide basis.

Sixteenth: Technology is a vital key to human progress and development. We deplore any neo-romantic efforts to condemn indiscriminately all technology and science or to counsel retreat from its further extension and use for the good of humankind. We would resist any moves to censor basic scientific research on moral, political, or social grounds. Technology must, however, be carefully judged by the consequences of its use; harmful and destructive changes should be avoided. We are particularly disturbed when technology and bureaucracy control, manipulate, or modify human beings without their consent. Technological feasibility does not imply social or cultural desirability.

Seventeenth: We must expand communication and transportation across frontiers. Travel restrictions must cease. The world must be open to diverse political, ideological, and moral viewpoints and evolve a worldwide system of television and radio for information and education. We thus call for full international cooperation in culture, science, the arts, and technology across ideological borders. We must learn to live openly together or we shall perish together.

Humanity as a Whole

In closing: The world cannot wait for a reconciliation of competing political or economic systems to solve its problems. These are the times for men and women of good will to further the building of a peaceful and prosperous world. We urge that parochial loyalties and inflexible moral and religious ideologies be transcended. We urge recognition of the common humanity of all people. We further urge the use of reason and compassion to produce the kind of world we want—a world in which peace, prosperity, freedom, and happiness are widely shared. Let us not abandon that vision in despair or cowardice.

We are responsible for what we are or will be. Let us work together for a humane world by means commensurate with humane ends. Destructive ideological differences among communism, capitalism, socialism, conservatism, liberalism, and radicalism should be overcome. Let us call for an end to terror and hatred. We will survive and prosper only in a world of shared humane values. We can initiate new directions for humankind; ancient rivalries can be superseded by broad-based cooperative efforts. The commitment to tolerance, understanding, and peaceful negotiation does not necessitate acquiescence to the status quo nor the damming up of dynamic and revolutionary forces. The true revolution is occurring and can continue in countless non-violent adjustments. But this entails the willingness to step forward onto new and expanding plateaus. At the present juncture of history, commitment to all humankind is the highest commitment of which we are capable; it transcends the narrow allegiances of church, state, party, class, or race in moving toward a wider vision of human potentiality. What more daring a goal for humankind than for each person to become, in ideal as well as practice, a citizen of a world community. It is a classical vision; we can now give it new vitality. Humanism thus interpreted is a moral force that has time on its side. We believe that humankind has the potential intelligence, good will, and cooperative skill to implement this commitment in the decades ahead.

Source: Humanist Manifesto, pp. 13-23.

4. I "A SECULAR HUMANIST DECLARATION" (1980)

Secular humanism is a vital force in the contemporary world. It is now under unwarranted and intemperate attack from various quarters. This declaration defends only that form of secular humanism which is explicitly committed to democracy. It is opposed to all varieties of belief that seek supernatural sanction for their values or espouse rule by dictatorship.

Democratic secular humanism has been a powerful force in world culture. Its ideals can be traced to the philosophers, scientists, and poets of classical Greece and Rome, to ancient Chinese Confucian society, to the Carvaka movement of India, and to other distinguished intellectual and moral traditions. Secularism and humanism were eclipsed in Europe during the Dark Ages, when religious piety eroded humankind's confidence in its own powers to solve human problems. They reappeared in force during the Renaissance with the reassertion of secular and humanist values in literature and the arts, again in the sixteenth and seventeenth centuries with the development of modern science and a naturalistic view of the universe, and their influence can be found in the eighteenth century in the Age of Reason and the Enlightenment. Democratic secular humanism has creatively flowered in modern times with the growth of freedom and democracy.

Countless millions of thoughtful persons have espoused secular humanist ideals, have lived significant lives, and have contributed to the building of a more humane and democratic world. The modern secular humanist outlook has led to the application of science and technology to the improvement of the human condition. This has had a positive effect on reducing poverty, suffering, and disease in various parts of the world, in extending longevity, on improving transportation and communication, and in making the good life possible for more and more people. It has led to the emancipation of hundreds of millions of people from the exercise of blind faith and fears of superstition and has contributed to their education and the enrichment of their lives. Secular humanism has provided an impetus for humans to solve their problems with intelligence and perseverance, to conquer geographic and social frontiers, and to extend the range of human exploration and adventure.

Regrettably, we are today faced with a variety of antisecularist trends: the reappearance of dogmatic authoritarian religions; fundamentalist, literalist, and doctrinaire Christianity; a rapidly growing and uncompromising Moslem clericalism in the Middle East and Asia; the reassertion of orthodox authority by the Roman Catholic papal hierarchy; nationalistic religious Judaism; and the reversion to obscurantist religions in Asia. New cults of unreason as well as bizarre paranormal and occult beliefs, such as belief in astrology, reincarnation, and the mysterious power of alleged psychics, are growing in many Western societies. These disturbing developments follow in the wake of the emergence in the earlier part of the twentieth century of intolerant messianic and totalitarian quasi-religious movements, such as fascism and communism. These religious activists not only are responsible for much of the terror and violence in the world today but stand in the way of solutions to the world's most serious problems.

Paradoxically, some of the critics of secular humanism maintain that it is a dangerous philosophy. Some assert that it is "morally corrupting" because it is committed to individual freedom, others that it condones "injustice" because it defends democratic due process. We who support democratic secular humanism deny such charges, which are based upon misunderstanding and misinterpretation, and we seek to outline a set of principles that most of us share. Secular humanism is not a dogma or a creed. There are wide differences of opinion among secular humanists on many issues. Nevertheless, there is a loose consensus with respect to several propositions. We are apprehensive that modern civilization is threatened by forces antithetical to reason, democracy, and freedom. Many religious believers will no doubt share with us a belief in many secular humanist and democratic values, and we welcome their joining with us in the defense of these ideals.

1. *Free Inquiry*. The first principle of democratic secular humanism is its commitment to free inquiry. We oppose any tyranny over the mind of man, any efforts by ecclesiastical, political, ideological, or social institutions to shackle free thought. In the past, such tyrannies have been directed by churches and states attempting to enforce the edicts of religious bigots. In the long struggle in the history of ideas, established institutions, both public and private, have attempted to censor inquiry, to impose orthodoxy on beliefs and values, and to excommunicate heretics and extirpate unbelievers. Today, the struggle for free inquiry has assumed new forms. Sectarian ideologies have become the

new theologies that use political parties and governments in their mission to crush dissident opinion.

Free inquiry entails recognition of civil liberties as integral to its pursuit, that is, a free press, freedom of communication, the right to organize opposition parties and to join voluntary associations, and freedom to cultivate and publish the fruits of scientific, philosophical, artistic, literary, moral and religious freedom. Free inquiry requires that we tolerate diversity of opinion and that we respect the right of individuals to express their beliefs, however unpopular they may be, without social or legal prohibition or fear of sanctions. Though we may tolerate contrasting points of view, this does not mean that they are immune to critical scrutiny. The guiding premise of those who believe in free inquiry is that truth is more likely to be discovered if the opportunity exists for the free exchange of opposing opinions; the process of interchange is frequently as important as the result. This applies not only to science and to everyday life, but to politics, economics, morality, and religion.

2. *Separation of Church and State.* Because of their commitment to freedom, secular humanists believe in the principle of the separation of church and state. The lessons of history are clear: wherever one religion or ideology is established and given a dominant position in the state, minority opinions are in jeopardy. A pluralistic, open democratic society allows all points of view to be heard. Any effort to impose an exclusive conception of Truth, Piety, Virtue, or Justice upon the whole of society is a violation of free inquiry. Clerical authorities should not be permitted to legislate their own parochial views—whether moral, philosophical, political, education, or social—for the rest of society.

Nor should tax revenues be exacted for the benefit or support of sectarian religious institutions. Individuals and voluntary associations should be free to accept or not to accept any belief and to support these convictions with whatever resources they may have, without being compelled by taxation to contribute to those religious faiths with which they do not agree. Similarly, church properties should share in the burden of public revenues and should not be exempt from taxation. Compulsory religious oaths and prayers in public institutions (political or educational) are also a violation of the separation principle.

Today, nontheistic as well as theistic religions compete for attention. Regrettably, in communist countries, the power of state is being used to impose an ideological doctrine on the society, without tolerating the expression of dissenting or heretical views. Here we see a modern secular version of the violation of the separation principle.

3. *The Ideal of Freedom.* There are many forms of totalitarianism in the modern world—secular and nonsecular—all of which we vigorously oppose. As democratic secularists, we consistently defend the ideal of freedom, not only freedom of conscience and belief from those ecclesiastical, political, and economic interests that seek to repress them, but genuine political liberty, democratic decision-making based upon majority rule, and respect for minority rights and the rule of law. We stand not only for freedom from religious control but for freedom from jingoistic government control as well. We are for the defense of basic human rights, including the right to protect life, liberty, and the pursuit of

happiness. In our view, a free society should also encourage some measure of economic freedom, subject only to such restrictions as are necessary in the public interest. This means that individuals and groups should be able to compete in the marketplace, organize free trade unions, and carry on their occupations and careers without undue interference by centralized political control. The right to private property is a human right without which other rights are nugatory. Where it is necessary to limit any of these rights in a democracy, the limitation should be justified in terms of its consequences in strengthening the entire structure of human rights.

4. *Ethics Based on Critical Intelligence*. The moral views of secular humanism have been subjected to criticism by religious fundamentalist theists. The secular humanist recognizes the central role of morality in human life. Indeed, ethics was developed as a branch of human knowledge long before religionists proclaimed their moral systems based upon divine authority. The field of ethics has had a distinguished list of thinkers contributing to its development: from Socrates, Democritus, Aristotle, Epicurus, and Epictetus, to Spinoza, Erasmus, Hume, Voltaire, Kant, Bentham, Mill, G. E. Moore, Bertrand Russell, John Dewey, and others. There is an influential philosophical tradition that maintains that ethics is an autonomous field of inquiry, that ethical judgments can be formulated independently of revealed religion, and that human beings can cultivate practical reason and wisdom and, by its application, achieve lives of virtue and excellence. Moreover, philosophers have emphasized the need to cultivate an appreciation for the requirements of social justice and for an individual's obligations and responsibilities toward others. Thus secularists deny that morality needs to be deduced from religious belief or that those who do not espouse a religious doctrine are immoral.

For secular humanists, ethical conduct is, or should be judged by critical reason, and their goal is to develop autonomous and responsible individuals, capable of making their own choices in life based upon an understanding of human behavior. Morality that is not God-based need not be antisocial, subjective, or promiscuous, nor need it lead to the breakdown of moral standards. Although we believe in tolerating diverse lifestyles and social manners, we do not think they are immune to criticism. Nor do we believe that any one church should impose its views of moral virtue and sin, sexual conduct, marriage, divorce, birth control, or abortion, or legislate them for the rest of society.

As secular humanists we believe in the central importance of the value of human happiness here and now. We are opposed to absolutist morality, yet we maintain that objective standards emerge, and ethical values and principles may be discovered, in the course of ethical deliberation.

Secular humanist ethics maintains that it is possible for human beings to lead meaningful and wholesome lives for themselves and in service to their fellow human beings without the need of religious commandments or the benefit of clergy. There have been any number of distinguished secularists and humanists who have demonstrated moral principles in their personal lives and works: Protagoras, Lucretius, Epicurus, Spinoza, Hume, Thomas Paine, Diderot, Mark Twain, George Eliot, John Stuart Mill, Ernest Renan, Charles Darwin,

Thomas Edison, Clarence Darrow, Robert Ingersoll, Gilbert Murray, Albert Schweitzer, Albert Einstein, Max Born, Margaret Sanger, and Bertrand Russell, among others.

5. *Moral Education*. We believe that moral development should be cultivated in children and young adults. We do not believe that any particular sect can claim important values as their exclusive property; hence it is the duty of public education to deal with these values. Accordingly, we support moral education in the schools that is designed to develop an appreciation for moral virtues, intelligence, and the building of character. We wish to encourage wherever possible the growth of moral awareness and the capacity for free choice and an understanding of the consequences thereof. We do not think it is moral to baptize infants, to confirm adolescents, or to impose a religious creed on young people before they are able to consent. Although children should learn about the history of religious moral practices, these young minds should not be indoctrinated in a faith before they are mature enough to evaluate the merits for themselves. It should be noted that secular humanism is not so much a specific morality as it is a method for the explanation and discovery of rational moral principles.

6. *Religious Skepticism*. As secular humanists, we are generally skeptical about supernatural claims. We recognize the importance of religious experience: that experience that redirects and gives meaning to the lives of human beings. We deny, however, that such experiences have anything to do with the supernatural. We are doubtful of traditional views of God and divinity. Symbolic and mythological interpretations of religion often serve as rationalizations for a sophisticated minority, leaving the bulk of mankind to flounder in theological confusion. We consider the universe to be a dynamic scene of natural forces that are most effectively understood by scientific inquiry. We are always open to the discovery of new possibilities and phenomena in nature. However, we find that traditional views of the existence of God either are meaningless, have not yet been demonstrated to be true, or are tyrannically exploitative. Secular humanists may be agnostics, atheists, rationalists, or skeptics, but they find insufficient evidence for the claim that some divine purpose exists for the universe. They reject the idea that God has intervened miraculously in history or revealed himself to a chosen few, or that he can save or redeem sinners. They believe that men and women are free and are responsible for their own destinies and that they cannot look toward some transcendent Being for salvation. We reject the divinity of Jesus, the divine mission of Moses, Mohammed, and other latter-day prophets and saints of the various sects and denominations. We do not accept as true the literal interpretation of the Old and New Testaments, the Koran, or other allegedly sacred religious documents, however important they may be as literature. Religions are pervasive sociological phenomena, and religious myths have long persisted in human history. In spite of the fact that human beings have found religions to be uplifting and a source of solace, we do not find their theological claims to be true. Religions have made negative as well as positive contributions toward the development of human civilization. Although they have helped to build hospitals and schools

and, at their best, have encouraged the spirit of love and charity, many have also caused human suffering by being intolerant of those who did not accept their dogmas or creeds. Some religions have been fanatical and repressive, narrowing human hopes, limiting aspirations, and precipitating religious wars and violence. While religions have no doubt offered comfort to the bereaved and dying by holding forth the promise of an immortal life, they have also aroused morbid fear and dread. We have found no convincing evidence that there is a separable "soul" or that it exists before birth or survives death. We must therefore conclude that the ethical life can be lived without the illusions of immortality or reincarnation. Human beings can develop the self-confidence necessary to ameliorate the human condition and to lead meaningful, productive lives.

7. *Reason*. We view with concern the current attack by non-secularists on reason and science. We are committed to the use of the rational methods of inquiry, logic, and evidence in developing knowledge and testing claims to truth. Since human beings are prone to err, we are open to the modification of all principles, including those governing inquiry, believing that they may be in need of constant correction. Although not so naïve as to believe that reason and science can easily solve all human problems, we nonetheless contend that they can make a major contribution to human knowledge and can be of benefit to humankind. We know of no better substitute for the cultivation of human intelligence.

8. *Science and Technology*. We believe the scientific method, though imperfect, is still the most reliable way of understanding the world. Hence, we look to the natural, biological, social, and behavioral sciences for knowledge of the universe and man's place within it. Modern astronomy and physics have opened up exciting new dimensions of the universe: they have enabled humankind to explore the universe by means of space travel. Biology and the social and behavioral sciences have expanded our understanding of human behavior. We are thus opposed in principle to any efforts to censor or limit scientific research without an overriding reason to do so.

While we are aware of, and oppose, the abuses of misapplied technology and its possible harmful consequences for the natural ecology of the human environment, we urge resistance to unthinking efforts to limit technological or scientific advances. We appreciate the great benefits that science and technology (especially basic and applied research) can bring to humankind, but we also recognize the need to balance scientific and technological advances with cultural explorations in art, music, and literature.

9. *Evolution*. Today the theory of evolution is again under heavy attack by religious fundamentalists. Although the theory of evolution cannot be said to have reached its final formulation, or to be an infallible principle of science, it is nonetheless supported impressively by the findings of many sciences. There may be some significant differences among scientists concerning the mechanics of evolution; yet the evolution of the species is supported so strongly by the weight of evidence that it is difficult to reject it. Accordingly, we deplore the efforts by fundamentalists (especially in the United States) to invade the science classrooms, requiring that creationist theory be taught to students and requiring

that it be included in biology textbooks. This is a serious threat both to academic freedom and to the integrity of the educational process. We believe that creationists surely should have the freedom to express their viewpoint in society. Moreover, we do not deny the value of examining theories of creation in educational courses on religion and the history of ideas; but it is a sham to mask an article of religious faith as a scientific truth and to inflict that doctrine on the scientific curriculum. If successful, creationists may seriously undermine the credibility of science itself.

10. *Education*. In our view, education should be the essential method of building humane, free, and democratic societies. The aims of education are many: the transmission of knowledge; training for occupations, careers, and democratic citizenship; and the encouragement of moral growth. Among its vital purposes should also be an attempt to develop the capacity for critical intelligence in both the individual and the community. Unfortunately, the schools are today being increasingly replaced by the mass media as the primary institutions of public information and education. Although the electronic media provide unparalleled opportunities for extending cultural enrichment and enjoyment, and powerful learning opportunities, there has been a serious misdirection of their purposes. In totalitarian societies, the media serve as the vehicle of propaganda and indoctrination. In democratic societies television, radio, films, and mass publishing too often cater to the lowest common denominator and have become banal wastelands. There is a pressing need to elevate standards of taste and appreciation. Of special concern to secularists is the fact that the media (particularly in the United States) are inordinately dominated by a pro-religious bias. The views of preachers, faith healers, and religious hucksters go largely unchallenged and the secular outlook is not given an opportunity for a fair hearing. We believe that television directors and producers have an obligation to redress the balance and revise their programming.

Indeed, there is a broader task that all those who believe in democratic secular humanist values will recognize, namely, the need to embark upon a long-term program of public education and enlightenment concerning the relevance of the secular outlook to the human condition.

Conclusion

Democratic secular humanism is too important for human civilization to abandon. Reasonable persons will surely recognize its profound contributions to human welfare. We are nevertheless surrounded by doomsday prophets of disaster, always wishing to turn the clock back—they are anti-science, anti-freedom, antihuman. In contrast, the secular humanistic outlook is basically melioristic, looking forward with hope rather than backward with despair. We are committed to extending the ideals of reason, freedom, individual and collective opportunity, and democracy throughout the world community. The problems that humankind will face in the future, as in the past, will no doubt be complex and difficult. However, if it is to prevail, it can only do so by enlisting resourcefulness and courage. Secular humanism places trust in human intelligence rather than in divine guidance. Skeptical of theories of redemption, damnation, and reincarnation, secular humanists attempt to approach the human situation in realistic terms: human beings are responsible for their own destinies.

We believe that it is possible to bring about a more humane world, one based upon the methods of reason and the principles of tolerance, compromise, and the negotiations of difference. We recognize the need for intellectual modesty and the willingness to revise beliefs in the light of criticism. Thus consensus is sometimes attainable. While emotions are important, we need not resort to the panaceas of salvation, to escape through illusion, or to some desperate leap toward passion and violence. We deplore the growth of intolerant sectarian creeds that foster hatred. In a world engulfed by obscurantism and irrationalism it is vital that the ideals of the secular city not be lost.

Source: *Free Inquiry*, Winter, 1980, pp. 3-6.

5. | *LISTEN, AMERICA* (1980)

Jerry Falwell

It is time that we come together and rise up against the tide of permissiveness and moral decay that is crushing in on our society from every side. America is at a crossroads as a nation; she is facing a fateful "Decade of Destiny" —the 1980s. I am speaking about survival and am calling upon those Americans who believe in decency and integrity to stand for what is good and what is right. It is time to face the truth that America is in trouble.

I have read the recent best sellers on the stands of America's bookstores. I have read the books of men of courage who are not afraid to stand and tell the American public the dangers they see. Nobel Laureate economist Milton Friedman, who has written the best seller *Free to Choose*, speaks of the suicidal course along which our beloved nation is proceeding. In his best seller *A Time for Truth*, William E. Simon, Secretary of the Treasury from 1974 to 1977, a period of the worst inflation and recession to rock our country in forty years, speaks of leaving Washington "a very frightened man." He states in his book that he declared time and time again to hundreds of subcommittees on Capitol Hill that "all the rhetoric about deficits and balanced budgets obscures the real danger that confronts us: the gradual disintegration of our free society." William Simon says, "Our country today sits at the very crossroads between freedom and totalitarian rule. If a majority of Americans do not soon understand this reality and help to turn the tide toward freedom, they ultimately will have no choice but to understand it at a time when it will be too late to do anything about it."

General Lewis W. Walt, who was assistant commandant of the Marine Corps from 1968 to 1971 and who served in combat during World War II, the

Korean War, and in Vietnam, winning two Navy Crosses, two Distinguished Service Medals, the Silver Star Medal, two Purple Hearts, and numerous other decorations, pleads with the American people in the Preface to his book *The Eleventh Hour*, "to fight a battle now to prevent a war tomorrow. Unless you respond—both veteran and youth—the sacrifices of the past and the promises of the future will vanish down the drain of history." In his best seller *Restoring the American Dream*, Robert J. Ringer says to Americans, "For you and me, the picture is pretty clear; we either restore the American dream right here and now or we most certainly will never live to experience it again." I could list many other excellent books that warn of our collapse.

At one time these men would have been called alarmists, but the truth is that many American people are coming to the realization that something must be done. They are ready to listen. Americans are looking at the 1980s with uncertainty.

I respect the writers of the books I have mentioned. They are intelligent men who are knowledgeable and who have concrete answers to the problems they pose in their area of expertise. But I do not believe that America will be turned around solely by working in the areas of politics, economics, and defense, as important as these may be. These are crucial issues that face us in the 1980s, but America can only be turned around as her people make godly, moral choices. When history records these ten years, I think it will be fair to project that this will have probably been, since the days of the American Revolution, the most important decade this nation has known. This is a grave statement because I believe that the outcome of how we stand as a free people at the end of this decade will depend upon the moral decisions we as a people make in the very near future.

Before we discuss America's moral dilemma let me summarize our military, economic, and political malaise. Even in these areas, a return to our founding principles is our sure and only hope.

The United States is for the first time, in my lifetime, and probably in the lifetime of my parents and grandparents, no longer the military might of the world.

I have read about the War Between the States; indeed that was a perilous time. No one questioned the fact, however, that our nation would survive that time. The First World War, that war that was to end all wars, was a very difficult time. Thousands perished, but no one ever doubted the survival of our republic. I was born in 1933 and do not recall the Great Depression. But I know that the Great Depression was a horrible time for many families and for our nation as a whole; but again, our existence was not at stake. I remember the Second World War. I remember well listening to the radio the day the Japanese bombed Pearl Harbor. The worst war in history occurred during a 4-year period that none of us can forget. There were 50 million deaths in that war. Hitler was certainly a formidable opponent, but yet, as an elementary school student eight years of age when we entered the war, I cannot remember anything but an optimistic outlook on the part of America's citizens. My schoolteachers, the news commentators, and everyone who spoke of the war spoke with a note tempered with encouragement and hope, even though everything was dark in those first months of the war. We believed that we were fully capable of rising to the occasion, and we did. I could go on and on. There was Korea, then Vietnam, but again the existence of our republic was never in question. The survival of this nation has been secure from long before I was born.

This is not true today. Recently I watched a film entitled The SALT Syndrome. This film was produced by the American Security Council and is a numerical and dramatic comparison of the military strength, both conventional and nuclear, of the United States and the Soviet Union. Much could be said about this film, but the bottom line reveals that in offensive nuclear weaponry, the United States is behind the Soviet Union two to one. That separation is widening daily as the United States spends less proportionately than the Soviet Union and as the Soviet Union continues to accelerate its expenditures. The United States is behind forty-seven to one in defensive weaponry. That breach is also widening due to a policy adopted in the United States in the 1960s. It is called Mutual Assured Destruction. The American people and the Soviet population have been placed in positions of hostages of one another, both reasonably concluding that the other would not attack.

Our legislators and governmental officials have not taken into consideration that the Soviets think nothing of lying and cheating. It is a fact that of the past twenty-seven treaties America has made with the Soviet Union, twenty-seven of them have been broken by the Soviet Union. Top governmental officials in our nation once said that if we would treat the Russians humanely, if we would show our sincerity by unilaterally disarming, by pulling back, by making concessions, that the Soviets would reciprocate because they too are decent people. Two nights after the Afghanistan invasion, the report came from Washington, D. C., that it was finally concluded that the intentions of the Soviets "are not good."

It is sad that it has taken a crisis like the invasion of Afghanistan to make our leaders realize the terrible threats of communism. The Soviet Union has watched the United States respond, not from what was once a point of strength, but from what is now a point of weakness. I believe that the Soviets had no doubt of what the reaction of the United States would be before they moved into Afghanistan.

It is only common sense that disarmament is suicide. The leaders of our country are responsible for taking care of the families of this nation. For the first time in two hundred years, we face a decade when it is doubtful if Americans will survive as a free people.

We as Americans can, as the old cliché goes, "put our heads in the sand." We can laugh and assume that things will always be as they are, when we really know that this is not being realistic. The fact is that we have a "will crisis" in this country today. We are not committed to victory. We are not committed to greatness. We have lost the will to stay strong and therefore have not won any wars we have fought since 1945.

The Soviets have always had only one goal, and that is to destroy capitalistic society. They are a nation committed to communism and to destroying the American way of life. Because of the overwhelming conventional and nuclear strength of the Soviet Union, it is now possible that the Soviet Government could demand our capitulation. Our willingness to pay the price of a nuclear conflict could well force our leadership into lowering our flag and surrendering the American people to the will of the Communist Party in Moscow. There has never been a time in our history when such a condition existed.

In the September 2, 1979, issue of the Detroit News we find this quote released by UPI: "Former U. S. Secretary of State Henry Kissinger assailed Western military policies Saturday and warned the time is fast approaching when the Soviet Union will be able to determine the world's destiny.

"'If present trends continue, the 1980s will be a period of massive crisis for all of us,' Kissinger told a symposium on the future of NATO. 'The dominant fact of the current military situation is that the NATO countries are falling behind in every significant military category. Never in history has it happened that a nation achieved superiority in all significant weapons categories without seeking to translate this at some point into some foreign-policy benefit.'

"He added: 'The Soviets have been building forces for traditional military missions capable of destroying the forces of the U. S., so that in the 1980s we will be in a position where many of our strategic forces and all land-based forces will be vulnerable.'"

I believe that John Gorton summed it up well when he said at the time he was Prime Minister of Australia: "I wonder if anybody has thought what the situation of comparatively small nations would be if there were not in existence a United States of America with a heritage and a willingness to see that small nations who might otherwise not be able to protect themselves, are given some shield. Imagine what the situation would be if there were not a great and giant country prepared to make such sacrifices!"

America is in desperate trouble economically. A strong national defense requires the monies to maintain that defense. Common sense tells us that you cannot spend more than you are taking in for a long period of time without eventual bankruptcy. When government begins to print more and more money without backing, it soon becomes worthless, and financial collapse then becomes inevitable. Economists are quick to point out that freedom is directly related to our free-enterprise system and that our Congress is responsible for the economic and energy crises that America is now experiencing.

Economist Milton Friedman points out that currently more than 40 percent of our income is disposed of on our behalf by government at the federal, state, and local levels. He points out in his book *Free to Choose* that as late as 1938 federal government spending amounted to only 3 percent of the national income.

Today government has become all-powerful as we have exchanged freedom for security. For all too many years, Americans have been educated to dependence rather than to liberty. A whole generation of Americans has grown up brainwashed by television and textbooks to believe that it is the responsibility of government to take resources from some and bestow them upon others. This idea certainly was alien to the Founding Fathers of our country.

Welfarism has grown because Americans have forgotten how to tithe and give offerings. Until the early days of this century, it was widely recognized that churches and other private institutions carried the primary responsibility, not merely for education, but also for health care and charity. The way to defeat welfarism in America is for those who wish to see God's law restored to our country to tithe fully to organizations that will remove from government those tasks that are more properly addressed by religious and private organizations.

Our nation's growing welfare system alone threatens our country with bankruptcy. It is time that we realized the working population of America cannot indefinitely carry on the burden of the governmental spending.

Currently, our government is running annual deficits of more than fifty billion dollars. Our government's accumulated long-term debt is more than five trillion dollars. The inflation rate in the United States is nearly 19 percent. Our government is now printing money at a rate that is more than twice as fast as our economy is growing. Our currency does not have substantial gold backing, and consequently has shockingly little value.

Milton Friedman points out, "The economic controls that have proliferated in the United States in recent decades have not only restricted our freedom to use our economic resources, they have also affected our freedom of speech, of press, and of religion."

The free enterprise system is clearly outlined in the Book of Proverbs in the Bible. Jesus Christ made it clear that the work ethic was a part of His plan for man. Ownership of property is biblical. Competition in business is biblical. Ambitious and successful business management is clearly outlined as a part of God's plan for His people. Our Founding Fathers warned against centralized government power, concluding that the concentration of government corrupts and sooner or later leads to abuse and tyranny. Robert Ringer sums up the economic situation in America, "If the devastating cycle of politically expedient promises/government-function, spending/direct taxation and inflation is not halted and drastically reduced, attempts to use free enterprise as a scapegoat will accelerate. And as taxation and regulation of business increase, motivation to produce will die, leading inevitably to a nationalization of industry. This is the step which will take America from the decaying stage to the death stage. It happened in Greece; it happened in Rome; it happened in every civilization that tried to provide the free lunch for its citizens and then blamed businessmen for its financial collapse."

The third crisis facing our nation today is a vacuum of leadership. One of the greatest needs in our nation today is for effective leadership. A special section of an August 6, 1979, *Time* magazine issues "A Cry for Leadership" and quotes Ortega y Gasset: "Before long there will be heard throughout the planet a formidable cry, rising like the howling of innumerable dogs to the stars, asking for someone or something to take command. . ." In this special section, historian Eugene Genovese is quoted as saying, "It would be very difficult to point out a set of values about which you could say that most Americans could agree. I think our society has become largely purposeless." The special section continues, "The task of the nation's leaders in the eighties will be to rediscover new themes of purpose in American life." *Time* quotes former U. S. Commissioner of Education Ernest Boyer as saying, "Conditions are building that will revitalize leadership. People are not willing to live endlessly with ambiguity. There is something within us that is violated by feeling that we are adrift."

The all-too-prevalent feelings of many Americans about leadership in America today is summed up by Douglas Fraser, UAW president. When asked by *Time* correspondents, "What living American leaders have been most effective in changing things for the better?" Mr. Fraser made this comment: "I can't think of any leaders. Isn't this sad? That's what's wrong with this country! That's exactly what's wrong." An April 16, 1979, *U. S. News & World Report* states the findings of its sixth nationwide leadership survey, "Who Runs America," and reports that more than ever top Americans are doubting the quality of the nation's direction and that influential citizens are hungry for decisive White House leadership. Florida Attorney General Jim Smith says in this article, "Americans are crying out for persons in responsible elected positions to provide leadership. Unfortunately, most elected public officials spend too much time analyzing the political angles rather than making the tough decisions. The American people will accept some hardships." This survey indicates that sixteen of the twenty most influential citizens in the United States have positions in government. Although finding fault with leadership in the White House and on Capitol Hill, America's policymakers have little disagreement on who runs the United States: the federal government and its officials.

The sad fact today is that many of our top governmental officials care more about getting a vote than doing and standing for what is right and good for America. Edmund Burke once said, "Men are qualified for civil liberties in exact proportion to their disposition to put moral chains upon their own appetites."

In the thirteenth chapter of the Book of Romans in the Bible we find these verses: "Let every soul be subject unto the higher powers. For there is no power but of God: The powers that be are ordained of God. For rulers are not a terror to good works, but to the evil. Wilt thou then not be afraid of the power? Do that which is good, and thou shalt have praise of the same: For he is the minister of God to thee for good. But if thou do that which is evil, be afraid; for he beareth not the sword in vain: For he is the minister of God, a revenger to execute wrath upon him that doeth evil. Wherefore ye must needs be subject, not only for wrath, but also for conscience sake. For this cause pay ye tribute also: For they are God's ministers, attending continually upon this very thing."

Obvious facts can be concluded from these verses. The authority, "the higher powers" —the President, the Congress, the judiciary—are ordained of God. This does not imply that all persons in places of authority are godly people. It does, however, mean that they are in their position, whether they are aware of the fact or not, by divine ordination. The Bible states that rulers are not a terror to good works, but to evil works. Law-abiding citizens need not be afraid of leaders. The leader is the minister of God to the people for good. Because they are to respect and obey the leaders in authority, Americans have a grave responsibility to vote in those leaders who will rule America justly, under divine guidance. Good citizens are concerned, informed, active, and law-abiding. The only grounds for citizens refusing to obey the law would be when human law violates divine law.

Why do we have so few good leaders? Why is it that political and judicial decisions are made that horrify America? You will find that when society begins to fall apart spiritually, what we find missing is the mighty man, that man who is willing, with courage and confidence, to stand up for that which is right. We are hard-pressed to find today that man in a governmental position, that man of war, that judge, that prophet, that preacher who is willing to call sin by its right name. Vanishing from the scene is the prudent, the wise person, the ancient, the old, the honorable people, the grandparents who will stand up for righteousness year after year, generation after generation, and be an example to us. For the first time in history, we have few elderly honorable people on the national scene. We have few we can look to and say, "Here is an example of godliness in leadership." Instead we find confusion and selfishness, which is destroying the very basis of our society.

We must review our government and see where our leadership has taken us today and where our future leaders must take us tomorrow if we are to remain a free America. It is a sad fact today that Americans have made a god of government. They are looking to government rather than to God, who ordained government. The United States is a republic where laws rule. Although the people of the United States have a vote, America is not a democracy in the sense that the majority rules. Her citizens elect representatives who represent them and govern them by laws. I believe that God promoted America to a greatness no other nation has ever enjoyed because her heritage is one of a republic governed by laws predicated on the Bible.

America is facing a vacuum of leadership not only in regard to her elected officials, but also among her citizens who are not standing for what is right and decent. We need in America today powerful, dynamic, and godly leadership. Male leadership in our families is affecting male leadership in our churches, and it is affecting male leadership in our society. As we look across our nation today we find a tremendous vacuum of godly men who are willing to be the kind of spiritual leaders who are necessary not only to change a nation, but also to change the churches within our nation and the basic units of our entire society, our families.

If a man is not a student of the Word of God and does not know what the Bible says, I question his ability to be an effective leader. Whatever he leads, whether it be his family, his church, or his nation, will not be properly led without this priority. God alone has the wisdom to tell men and women where this world is going, where it needs to go, and how it can be redirected. Only by godly leadership can America be put back on a divine course. God will give national healing if men and women will pray and meet God's conditions, but we must have leadership in America to deliver God's message.

We must reverse the trend America finds herself in today. Young people between the ages of twenty-five and forty have been born and reared in a different world than Americans of years past. The television set has been their primary baby-sitter. From the television set they have learned situation ethics and immorality—they have learned a loss of respect for human life. They have learned to disrespect the family as God has established it. They have been educated in a public school system that is permeated with secular humanism. They have been taught that the Bible is just another book of literature. They have been taught that there are no absolutes in our world today. They have been introduced to the drug culture. They have been reared by the family and by the public school in a society that is greatly void of discipline and character-building. These same young people have been reared under the influence of a government that has taught them socialism and welfarism. They have been taught to believe that the world owes them a living whether they work or not.

I believe that America was built on integrity, on faith in God, and on hard work. I do not believe that anyone has ever been successful in life without being willing to add that last ingredient—diligence or hard work. We now have second- and third-generation welfare recipients. Welfare is not always wrong. There are those who do need welfare, but we have reared a generation that understands neither the dignity nor the importance of work.

Every American who looks at the facts must share a deep concern and burden for our country. We are not unduly concerned when we say that there are some very dark clouds on America's horizon. I am not a pessimist, but it is indeed a time for truth. If Americans will face the truth, our nation can be turned around and can be saved from the evils and the destruction that have fallen upon every other nation that has turned its back on God.

There is no excuse for what is happening in our country. We must, from the highest office in the land right down to the shoeshine boy in the airport, have a return to biblical basics. If the Congress of our United States will take its stand on that which is right and wrong, and if our President, our judiciary system, and our state and local leaders will take their stand on holy living, we can turn this country around.

I personally feel that the home and the family are still held in reverence by the vast majority of the American public. I believe there is still a vast number of Americans who love their country, are patriotic, and are willing to sacrifice for her. I remember the time when it was positive to be patriotic, and as far as I am concerned, it still is. I remember as boy, when the flag was raised, everyone stood proudly and put his hand upon his heart and pledged allegiance with gratitude. I remember when the band struck up "The Stars and Stripes Forever," we stood and goose pimples would run all over me. I remember when I was in elementary school during World War II, when every report from the other shores meant something to us. We were not out demonstrating against our boys who were dying in Europe and Asia. We were praying for them and thanking God for them and buying war bonds to help pay for the materials and artillery they needed to fight and win and come back.

I believe that Americans want to see this country come back to basics, back to values, back to biblical morality, back to sensibility, and back to patriotism. Americans are looking for leadership and guidance. It is fair to ask the question, "If 84 percent of the American people still believe in morality, why is America having such internal problems?" We must look for the answer to the highest places in every level of government. We have a lack of leadership in

America. But Americans have been lax in voting in and out of office the right and the wrong people.

My responsibility as a preacher of the Gospel is one of influence, not of control, and that is the responsibility of each individual citizen. Through the ballot box Americans must provide for strong moral leadership at every level. If our country will get back on the track in sensibility and moral sanity, the crises that I have herein mentioned will work out in the course of time and with God's blessings.

It is now time to take a stand on certain moral issues, and we can only stand if we have leaders. We must stand against the Equal Rights Amendment, the feminist revolution, and the homosexual revolution. We must have a revival in this country. It can come if we will realize the danger and heed the admonition of God found in 2 Chronicles 7:14, "If my people, which are called by my name, shall humble themselves, and pray, and seek my face, and turn from their wicked ways; then will I hear from heaven, and will forgive their sin, and will heal their land."

As a preacher of the Gospel, I not only believe in prayer and preaching, I also believe in good citizenship. If a labor union in America has the right to organize and improve its working conditions, then I believe that the churches and the pastors, the priests, and the rabbis of America have a responsibility, not just the right, to see to it that the moral climate and conscience of Americans is such that this nation can be healed inwardly. If it is healed inwardly, then it will heal itself outwardly.

It is not easy to go against the tide and do what is right. This nation can be brought back to God, but there must first be an awareness of sin. The Bible declares, "Righteousness exalteth a nation: But sin is a reproach to any people." (Pr. 14:34) It is right living that has made America the greatest nation on earth, and with all of her shortcomings and failures, America is without question the greatest nation on the face of God's earth. We as Americans must recommit ourselves to keeping her that way. Our prayers must certainly be behind our President and our Congress. We are commissioned by Scripture (1. Tm. 2:1-3) to pray for those who are in authority, but we would also remind our leaders that the future of this great nation is in their hands. One day they will stand before God accountable with what they have done to ensure our future. God has charged us as Americans with great privileges, but to whom much is given "much is required." We are faced with great responsibilities. Today, more than at any time in history, America needs men and women of God who have an understanding of the times and are not afraid to stand up for what is right.

Americans have been silent much too long. We have stood by and watched as American power and influence have been systematically weakened in every sphere of the world.

We are not a perfect nation, but we are still a free nation because we have the blessing of God upon us. We must continue to follow in a path that will ensure that blessing. We must not forget the words of our national anthem, "Oh! thus be it ever when free men shall stand/Between their loved homes and the war's desolation!/Blest with victory and peace, may the heav'n rescued land/Praise the Power that hath made and preserved us a nation./Then conquer

we must, when our cause it is just,/And this be our motto: 'In God is our trust.'"
We must not forget that it is God Almighty who has made and preserved us a
nation.

Let us never forget that as our Constitution declares, we are endowed by
our Creator with certain inalienable rights. It is only as we abide by those laws
established by our Creator that He will continue to bless us with these rights.
We are endowed our rights to freedom and liberty and the pursuit of happiness
by the God who created man to be free and equal.

The hope of reversing the trends of decay in our republic now lies with the
Christian public in America. We cannot expect help from the liberals. They
certainly are not going to call our nation back to righteousness and neither are
the pornographers, the smut peddlers, and those who are corrupting our youth.
Moral Americans must be willing to put their reputations, their fortunes, and
their very lives on the line for this great nation of ours. Would that we had the
courage of our forefathers who knew the great responsibility that freedom
carries with it. Patrick Henry said, "It is natural to man to indulge in the illusions of hope. We are apt to shut our eyes against a painful truth. . . . Is this the
part of wise men, engaged in a great and arduous struggle for liberty? Are we
disposed to be a number of those who, having eyes, see not, and having ears,
hear not, the things which so nearly concern their temporal salvation? For
my part, whatever anguish of spirit it may cost, I am willing to know the whole
truth; to know the worst and to provide for it. . . . Is life so dear or peace so
sweet, as to be purchased at the price of chains or slavery? Forbid it, Almighty
God! I know not what course others may take, but as for me, give me liberty
or give me death!"

More than ever before in the history of humanity, we must have heroes,
those men and women who will stand for what is right and stand against what is
wrong, no matter what it costs. Today we need men and women of character
and integrity who will commit themselves to letting their posterity know the
freedom that our Founding Fathers established for this nation. Let us stand
by that statement in the Declaration of Independence that cost our forefathers
so much: ". . . with a firm Reliance on the Protection of divine Providence, we
mutually pledge to each other our lives, our Fortunes, and our sacred Honor."

Our Founding Fathers separated church and state in function, but never
intended to establish a government void of God. As is evidenced by our Constitution, good people in America must exert an influence and provide a conscience
and climate of morality in which it is difficult to go wrong, not difficult for
people to go right in America.

I am positive in my belief regarding the Constitution that God led in the
development of that document, and as a result, we here in America have enjoyed
204 years of unparalleled freedom. The most positive people in the world are
people who believe the Bible to be the Word of God. The Bible contains a positive message. It is a message written by 40 men over a period of approximately
1,500 years under divine inspiration. It is God's message of love, redemption,
and deliverance for a fallen race. What could be more positive than the message
of redemption in the Bible? But God will force Himself upon no man. Each
individual American must make His choice.

Peter Marshall knew that the choices of individuals determine the destiny of a nation. He immigrated to the United States as a young man and worked his way through seminary by digging ditches and doing newspaper work. His years in the ministry culminated with the pastorate of the historic New York Avenue Presbyterian Church in Washington, D. C. (Abraham Lincoln's church), located two blocks from the White House. Dr. Marshall became chaplain of the Senate in January 1947. He died suddenly in January 1949 while still holding office. He was a dynamic Christian and was called by many a reporter the "conscience of the Senate."

Peter Marshall summed it up well when in a sermon to the New York Presbyterian Church he challenged its members with these words: "Today, we are living in a time when enough individuals, choosing to go to hell, will pull the nation down to hell with them. The choices you make in moral and religious questions determine the way America will go. The choice before us is plain, Christ or chaos, conviction or compromise, discipline or disintegration. I am rather tired about hearing about our rights and privileges as American citizens. The time has come, it now is, when we ought to hear about the duties and responsibilities of our citizenship. America's future depends upon her accepting and demonstrating God's government. It is just as plain and clear as that."

Americans must no longer linger in ignorance and apathy. We cannot be silent about the sins that are destroying this nation. The choice is ours. We must turn America around or prepare for inevitable destruction. I am listening to the sounds that threaten to take away our liberties in America. And I have listened to God's admonitions and His direction—the only hopes of saving America. Are you listening too?

Source: Jerry Falwell, *Listen, America* (New York: Doubleday, 1980), pp. 7-23.

6. I *A CHRISTIAN MANIFESTO* (1981)

Francis Schaeffer

The Abolition of Truth and Morality

The basic problem of the Christians in this country in the last eighty years or so, in regard to society and in regard to government, is that they have seen things in bits and pieces instead of totals.

They have very gradually become disturbed over permissiveness, pornography, the public schools, the breakdown of the family, and finally abortion. But they have not seen this as a totality—each thing being a part, a symptom, of a much larger problem. They have failed to see that all of this has come about due to a shift in world view—that is, through a fundamental change in the overall way people think and view the world and life as a whole. This shift has been away from a world view that was at least vaguely Christian in people's memory (even if they were not individually Christian) toward something completely different—toward a world view based upon the idea that the final reality is impersonal matter or energy shaped into its present form by impersonal chance. They have not seen that this world view has taken the place of the one that had previously dominated Northern European culture, including the United States, which was at least Christian in memory, even if the individuals were not individually Christian.

These two world views stand as totals in complete antithesis to each other in content and also in their natural results—including sociological and governmental results, and specifically including law.

It is not that these two world views are different only in how they understand the nature of reality and existence. They also inevitably produce totally different results. The operative word here is inevitably. It is not just that they happen to bring forth different results, but it is absolutely inevitable that they will bring forth different results.

Why have the Christians been so slow to understand this? There are various reasons but the central one is a defective view of Christianity. This has its roots in the Pietist movement under the leadership of P. J. Spener in the seventeenth century. Pietism began as a healthy protest against formalism and a too abstract Christianity. But it had a deficient, "platonic" spirituality. It was platonic in the sense that Pietism made a sharp division between the "spiritual" and the "material" world—giving little, or no, importance to the "material" world. The totality of human existence was not afforded a proper place. In particular it neglected the intellectual dimension of Christianity.

Christianity and spirituality were shut up to a small, isolated part of life. The totality of reality was ignored by the pietistic thinking. Let me quickly say that in one sense Christians should be pietists in that Christianity is not just a set of doctrines, even the right doctrines. Every doctrine is in some way to have an effect upon our lives. But the poor side of Pietism and its resulting platonic outlook has really been a tragedy not only in many people's individual lives, but in our total culture.

True spirituality covers all of reality. There are things the Bible tells us as absolutes which are sinful—which do not conform to the character of God. But aside from these the Lordship of Christ covers all of life and all of life equally. It is not only that true spirituality covers all of life, but it covers all parts of the spectrum of life equally. In this sense there is nothing concerning reality that is not spiritual.

Related to this, it seems to me, is the fact that many Christians do not mean what I mean when I say Christianity is true, or Truth. They are Christians and they believe in, let us say, the truth of creation, the truth of the virgin birth, the truth of Christ's miracles, Christ's substitutionary death, and His coming again. But they stop there with these and other individual truths.

When I say Christianity is true I mean it is true to total reality—the total of what is, beginning with the central reality, the objective existence of the personal-infinite God. Christianity is not just a series of truths but Truth—Truth about all of reality. And the holding to that Truth intellectually—and then in some poor way living upon that Truth, the Truth of what is—brings forth not only certain personal results, but also governmental and legal results.

Now let's go over to the other side—to those who hold the materialistic final reality concept. They saw the complete and total difference between the two positions more quickly than Christians. There were the Huxleys, George Bernard Shaw (1856-1950), and many others who understood a long time ago that there are two total concepts of reality and that it was one total reality against the other and not just a set of isolated and separated differences. The *Humanist Manifesto I*, published in 1933, showed with crystal clarity their comprehension of the totality of what is involved. It was to our shame that Julian (1887-1975) and Aldous Huxley (1894-1963), and the others like them, understood much earlier than Christians that these two world views are two total concepts of reality standing in antithesis to each other. We should be utterly ashamed that this is the fact.

They understood not only that there were two totally different concepts but that they would bring forth two totally different conclusions, both for individuals and for society. What we must understand is that the two world views really do bring forth with inevitable certainty not only personal differences, but also total differences in regard to society, government, and law.

There is no way to mix these two total world views. They are separate entities that cannot be synthesized. Yet we must say that liberal theology, the very essence of it from its beginning, is an attempt to mix the two. Liberal theology tried to bring forth a mixture soon after the Enlightenment and has tried to synthesize these two views right up to our own day. But in each case when the chips are down these liberal theologians have always come down, as naturally as a ship coming into home port, on the side of the nonreligious humanist. They do this with certainty because what their liberal theology really is is humanism expressed in theological terms instead of philosophic or other terms.

An example of this coming down naturally on the side of the nonreligious humanists is the article by Charles Hartshorne in the January 21, 1981, issue of *The Christian Century*, pages 42-45. Its title is, "Concerning Abortion, an Attempt at a Rational View." He begins by equating the fact that the human fetus is alive with the fact that mosquitoes and bacteria are also alive. That is, he begins by assuming that human life is not unique. He then continues by saying that even after the baby is born it is not fully human until its social relations develop (though he says the infant does have some primitive social relations an unborn fetus does not have). His conclusion is, "Nevertheless, I have little sympathy with the idea that infanticide is just another form of murder. Persons who are already functionally persons in the full sense have more important rights even than infants." He then, logically, takes the next step: "Does this distinction apply to the killing of a hopelessly senile person or one in a permanent coma? For me it does." No atheistic humanist could say it with greater clarity. It is significant at this point to note that many of the denominations controlled by liberal theology have come out, publicly and strongly, in favor of abortion.

Dr. Martin E. Marty is one of the respected, theologically liberal spokesmen. He is an associate editor of *The Christian Century* and Fairfax M. Cone distinguished service professor at the University of Chicago divinity school. He is often quoted in the secular press as the spokesman for "mainstream" Christianity. In a *Christian Century* article in the January 7-14, 1981 issue (pages 13-17 with an addition on page 31), he has an article entitled: "Dear Republicans: A Letter on Humanisms." In it he brilliantly confuses the terms "being human," humanism, the humanities and being "in love with humanity." Why does he do this? As a historian he knows the distinctions of those words, but when one is done with these pages the poor reader who knows no better is left with the eradication of the total distinction between the Christian position and the humanist one. I admire the cleverness of the article, but I regret that in it Dr. Marty has come down on the nonreligious humanist side, by confusing the issues so totally.

It would be well at this point to stress that we should not confuse the very different things which Dr. Marty did confuse. Humanitarianism is being kind and helpful to people, treating people humanly. The humanities are the studies of literature, art, music, etc. —those things which are the products of human creativity. Humanism is the placing of Man at the center of all things and making him the measure of all things.

Thus, Christians should be the most humanitarian of all people. And Christians certainly should be interested in the humanities as the product of human creativity, made possible because people are uniquely made in the image of the great Creator. In this sense of being interested in the humanities it would be proper to speak of a Christian humanist. This is especially so in the past usage of that term. This would then mean that such a Christian is interested (as we all should be) in the product of people's creativity. In this sense, for example, Calvin could be called a Christian humanist because he knew the works of the Roman writer Seneca so very well. John Milton and many other Christian poets could also be so called because of their knowledge not only of their own day but also of antiquity.

But in contrast to being humanitarian and being interested in the humanities Christians should be inalterably opposed to the false and destructive humanism, which is false to the Bible and equally false to what Man is.

Along with this we must keep distinct the "humanist world view" of which we have been speaking and such a thing as the "Humanist Society," which produced the *Humanist Manifestos I* and *II* (1933 and 1973). The Humanist Society is made up of a relatively small group of people (some of whom, however, have been influential—John Dewey, Sir Julian Huxley, Jacques Monod, B. F. Skinner, etc.). By way of contrast, the humanist world view includes many thousands of adherents and today controls the consensus in society, much of the media, much of what is taught in our schools, and much of the arbitrary law being produced by the various departments of government.

The term humanism used in this wider, more prevalent way means Man beginning from himself, with no knowledge except what he himself can discover and no standards outside of himself. In this view Man is the measure of all things, as the Enlightenment expressed it.

Nowhere have the divergent results of the two total concepts of reality, the Judeo-Christian and the humanist world view, been more open to observation than in government and law.

We of Northern Europe (and we must remember that the United States, Canada, Australia, New Zealand and so on are extensions of Northern Europe) take our form-freedom balance in government for granted as though it were natural. There is form in acknowledging the obligations in society, and there is freedom in acknowledging the rights of the individual. We have form, we have freedom; there is freedom, there is form. There is a balance here which we have come to take as natural in the world. It is not natural in the world. We are utterly foolish if we look at the long span of history and read the daily newspapers giving today's history and do not understand that the form-freedom balance in government which we have had in Northern Europe since the Reformation and in the countries extended from it is unique in the world, past and present.

That is not to say that no one wrestled with these questions before the Reformation nor that no one produced anything worthwhile. One can think for example, of the Conciliar Movement in the late medieval church and the early medieval parliaments. Especially one must consider the ancient English Common Law and in relation to that Common Law (and all English Law) there is Henry De Bracton. I will mention more about him in a moment.

Those who hold the material-energy, chance concept of reality, whether they are Marxist or non-Marxist, not only do not know the truth of the final reality, God, they do not know who Man is. Their concept of Man is what Man is not, just as their concept of the final reality is what final reality is not. Since their concept of Man is mistaken, their concept of society and of law is mistaken, and they have no sufficient base for either society or law.

They have reduced Man to even less than his natural finiteness by seeing him only as a complex arrangement of molecules, made complex by blind chance. Instead of seeing him as something great who is significant even in his sinning, they see Man in his essence only as an intrinsically competitive animal, that has no other basic operating principle than natural selection brought about by the strongest, fittest, ending on top. And they see Man as acting in this way both individually and collectively as society.

Even on the basis of Man's finiteness having people swear in court in the name of humanity, as some have advocated, saying something like, "We pledge our honor before all mankind" would be insufficient enough. But reduced to the materialistic view of Man, it is even less. Although many nice words may be used, in reality law constituted on this basis can only mean brute force.

In this setting Jeremy Bentham's (1748-1842) *Utilitarianism* can be and must be all that law means. And this must inevitably lead to the conclusion of Oliver Wendell Holmes Jr. (1841-1935): "The life of the law has not been logic: it has been experience." That is, there is no basis for law except Man's limited, finite experience. And especially with the Darwinian, survival-of-the-fittest concept of Man (which Holmes held) that must, and will, lead to Holmes' final conclusion: law is "the majority vote of that nation that could lick all others."

The problem always was, and is, What is an adequate base for law? What is adequate so that the human aspiration for freedom can exist without anarchy, and yet provides a form that will not become arbitrary tyranny?

In contrast to the materialistic concept, Man in reality is made in the image of God and has real humanness. This humanness has produced varying degrees of success in government, bringing forth governments that were more than only the dominance of brute force.

And those in the stream of the Judeo-Christian world view have had something more. The influence of the Judeo-Christian world view can be perhaps most readily observed in Henry De Bracton's influence on British Law. An English judge living in the thirteenth century, he wrote *De Legibus et Consuetudinibus* (c. 1250).

Bracton, in the stream of the Judeo-Christian world view, said:

> And that he (the King) ought to be under the law appears clearly in the
> analogy of Jesus Christ, whose vice-regent on earth he is, for though
> many ways were open to Him for his ineffable redemption of the
> human race, the true mercy of God chose this most powerful way to
> destroy the devil's work, he would not use the power of force but the
> reason of justice.

In other words, God in his sheer power could have crushed Satan in his revolt by the use of that sufficient power. But because of God's character, justice came before the use of power alone. Therefore Christ died that justice, rooted in what God is, would be the solution. Bracton codified this: Christ's example, because of who He is, is our standard, our rule, our measure. Therefore power is not first, but justice is first in society and law. The prince may have the power to control and to rule, but he does not have the right to do so without justice. This was the basis of English Common Law. The Magna Carta (1215) was written within thirty-five years (or less) of Bracton's *De Legibus* and in the midst of the same universal thinking in England at that time.

The Reformation (300 years after Bracton) refined and clarified this further. It got rid of the encrustations that had been added to the Judeo-Christian world view and clarified the point of authority—with authority resting in the Scripture rather than church and Scripture, or state and Scripture. This not only had meaning in regard to doctrine but clarified the base for law.

That base was God's written Law, back through the New Testament to Moses' written Law; and the content and authority of that written Law is rooted back to Him who is the final reality. Thus, neither church nor state were equal to, let alone above, that Law. The base for law is not divided, and no one has the right to place anything, including king, state or church, above the content of God's Law.

What the Reformation did was to return most clearly and consistently to the origins, to the final reality, God; but equally to the reality of Man—not only Man's personal needs (such as salvation), but also Man's social needs.

What we have had for four hundred years, produced from this clarity, is unique in contrast to the situation that has existed in the world in forms of government. Some of you have been taught that the Greek city states had our concepts in government. It simply is not true. All one has to do is read Plato's *Republic* to have this come across with tremendous force.

When the men of our State Department, especially after World War II, went all over the world trying to implant our form-freedom balance in government downward on cultures whose philosophy and religion would never have produced it, it has, in almost every case, ended in some form of totalitarianism or authoritarianism.

The humanists push for "freedom," but have no Christian consensus to contain it, that "freedom" leads to chaos or to slavery under the state (or under an elite). Humanism, with its lack of any final base for values or law, always leads to chaos. It then naturally leads to some form of authoritarianism to control the chaos. Having produced the sickness, humanism gives more of the same kind of medicine for a cure. With its mistaken concept of final reality, it has no intrinsic reason to be interested in the individual, the human being. Its natural interest is the two collectives: the state and society.

Foundations for Faith and Freedom

The Founding Fathers of the United States (in varying degrees) understood very well the relationship between one's world view and government. John Witherspoon (1723-1794) has always been important to me personally, and he is even more so since I have read just recently a biography of him by David Walker Woods. John Witherspoon, a Presbyterian minister and president of what is now Princeton University, was the only pastor to sign the Declaration of Independence. He was a very important man during the founding of the country. He linked the Christian thinking represented by the College of New Jersey (now Princeton University) with the work he did both on the Declaration of Independence and on countless very important committees in the founding of the country. This linkage of Christian thinking and the concepts of government were not incidental but fundamental. John Witherspoon knew and stood consciously in the stream of Samuel Rutherford, a Scotsman who lived from 1600-1661 and who wrote *Lex Rex* in 1644. Lex rex means law is king—a phrase that was absolutely earthshaking. Prior to that it had been rex lex, the king is law. In *Lex Rex* he wrote that the law, and no one else, is king. Therefore, the heads of government are under the law, not a law unto themselves.

Jefferson, who was a deist, and others, knew they stood in the stream of John Locke (1632-1704), and while Locke had secularized *Lex Rex* he had drawn heavily from it. These men really knew what they were doing. We are not reading back into history what was not there. We cannot say too strongly that they really understood the basis of the government which they were founding. Think of this great flaming phrase: "certain inalienable rights." Who gives the rights? The state? Then they are not inalienable because the state can change them and take them away. Where do the rights come from? They understood that they were founding the country upon the concept that goes back into the Judeo-Christian thinking that there is Someone there who gave the inalienable rights. Another phrase also stood there: "In God we trust." With this there is no confusion of what they were talking about. They publicly recognized that law could be king because there was a Law Giver, a Person to give the inalienable rights.

Most people do not realize that there was a paid chaplain in Congress even before the Revolutionary War ended. Also we find that prior to the founding of the national congress all the early provincial congresses in all thirteen colonies always opened with prayer. And from the very beginning, prayer opened the national congress. These men truly understood what they were doing. They knew they were building on the Supreme Being who was the Creator, the final reality. And they knew that without that foundation everything in the Declaration of Independence and all that followed would be sheer unadulterated nonsense. These were brilliant men who understood exactly what was involved.

As soon as the war was over they called the first Thanksgiving Day. Do you realize that the first Thanksgiving Day in this country was called immediately by the Congress at the end of the war? Witherspoon's sermon on that day shows their perspective: "A republic once equally poised must either preserve its virtue or lose its liberty." Don't you wish that everybody in America would recite that, and truly understand it, every morning? "A republic once equally poised must either preserve its virtue or lose its liberty." Earlier in a speech Witherspoon had stressed: "He is the best friend of American liberty who is most sincere and active in promoting pure and undefiled religion." And for Witherspoon, and the cultural consensus of that day, that meant Christianity as it had come to them through the Reformation. This was the consensus which then gave religious freedom to all—including the "free thinkers" of that day and the humanists of our day.

This concept was the same as William Penn (1644-1718) had expressed earlier: "If we are not governed by God, then we will be ruled by tyrants." This consensus was as natural as breathing in the United States at that time. We must not forget that many of those who came to America from Europe came for religious purposes. As they arrived, most of them established their own individual civil governments based upon the Bible. It is, therefore, totally foreign to the basic nature of America at the time of the writing of the Constitution to argue a separation doctrine that implies a secular state.

When the First Amendment was passed it only had two purposes. The first purpose was that there would be no established, national church for the united thirteen states. To say it another way: There would be no "Church of the United States." James Madison (1751-1836) clearly articulated this concept of separation when explaining the First Amendment's protection of religious liberty. He said that the First Amendment to the Constitution was prompted because "the people feared one sect might obtain a preeminence, or two combine together, and establish a religion to which they would compel others to conform."

Nevertheless, a number of the individual states had state churches, and even that was not considered in conflict with the First Amendment. "At the outbreak of the American Revolution, nine of the thirteen colonies had conferred special benefits upon one church to the exclusion of others." "In all but one of the thirteen states, the states taxed the people to support the preaching of the gospel and to build churches." "It was not until 1798 that the Virginia legislature repealed all its laws supporting churches." "In Massachusetts the Massachusetts Constitution was not amended until 1853 to eliminate the tax-supported church provisions."

The second purpose of the First Amendment was the very opposite from what is being made of it today. It states expressly that government should not impede or interfere with the free practice of religion.

Those were the two purposes of the First Amendment as it was written.

As Justice Douglas wrote for the majority of the Supreme Court in the United States v. Ballard case in 1944:

> The First Amendment has a dual aspect. It not only "forestalls compulsion by law of the acceptance of any creed or the practice of any form of worship" but also "safeguards the free exercise of the chosen form of religion."

Today the separation of church and state in America is used to silence the church. When Christians speak out on issues, the hue and cry from the humanist state and media is that Christians, and all religions, are prohibited from speaking since there is a separation of church and state. The way the concept is used today is totally reversed from the original intent. It is not rooted in history. The modern concept of separation is an argument for a total separation of religion from the state. The consequence of the acceptance of this doctrine leads to the removal of religion as an influence in civil government. This fact is well illustrated by John W. Whitehead in his book *The Second American Revolution*. It is used today as a false political dictum in order to restrict the influence of Christian ideas. As Franky Schaeffer V says in the *Plan for Action*:

> It has been convenient and expedient for the secular humanist, the materialist, the so-called liberal, the feminist, the genetic engineer, the bureaucrat, the Supreme Court Justice, to use this arbitrary division between church and state as a ready excuse. It is used, as an easily identifiable rallying point, to subdue the opinions of that vast body of citizens who represent those with religious convictions.

To have suggested the state separated from religion and religious influence would have amazed the Founding Fathers. The French Revolution that took place shortly afterwards, with its continuing excesses and final failure leading quickly to Napoleon and an authoritative rule, only emphasized the difference between the base upon which the United States was founded and the base upon which the French Revolution was founded. History is clear and the men of that day understood it. Terry Eastland said in *Commentary* magazine:

> As a matter of historical fact, the Founding Fathers believed that the public interest was served by the promotion of religion. The Northwest Ordinance of 1787, which set aside federal property in the territory for schools and which was passed again by Congress in 1789, is instructive. 'Religion, morality, and knowledge being necessary to good

government and the happiness of mankind,' read the act, 'schools and the means of learning shall forever be encouraged.' . . .

In 1811 the New York state court upheld an indictment for blasphemous utterances against Christ, and in its ruling, given by Chief Justice Kent, the court said, "We are Christian people, and the morality of the country is deeply engrafted upon Christianity." Fifty years later this same court said that "Christianity may be conceded to be the established religion."

The Pennsylvania state court also affirmed the conviction of a man on charges of blasphemy, here against the Holy Scriptures. The Court said: "Christianity, general Christianity is, and always has been, a part of the common law of Pennsylvania . . . not Christianity founded on any particular religious tenets; nor Christianity with an established church and tithes and spiritual courts; but Christianity with liberty of conscience to all men." . . .

The establishment of Protestant Christianity was one not only of law but also, and far more importantly, of culture. Protestant Christianity supplied the nation with its "system of values" —to use the modern phrase—and would do so until the 1920's when the cake of Protestant custom seemed most noticeably to begin crumbling.

As we continue to examine the question of law in relation to the founding of the country, we next encounter Sir William Blackstone (1723-1780). William Blackstone was an English jurist who in the 1760's wrote a very famous work called *Commentaries on the Law of England*. By the time the Declaration of Independence was signed, there were probably more copies of his *Commentaries* in America than in Britain. His *Commentaries* shaped the perspective of American law at that time, and when you read them it is very clear exactly upon what that law was based.

To William Blackstone there were only two foundations for law, nature and revelation, and he stated clearly that he was speaking of the "holy Scripture." That was William Blackstone. And up to the recent past not to have been a master of William Blackstone's *Commentaries* would have meant that you would not have graduated from law school.

There were other well-known lawyers who spelled these things out with total clarity. Joseph Story in his 1829 inaugural address as Dane Professor of Law at Harvard University said, "There never has been a period in which Common Law did not recognize Christianity as laying at its foundation."

Concerning John Adams (1735-1826) Terry Eastland says:

> . . . most people agreed that our law was rooted, as John Adams had said, in a common moral and religious tradition, one that stretched back to the time Moses went up on Mount Sinai. Similarly almost everyone agreed that our liberties were God-given and should be exercised responsibly. There was a distinction between liberty and license.

What we find then as we look back is that the men who founded the United States of America really understood that upon which they were building their concepts of law and the concepts of government. And until the takeover of our government and law by this other entity, the materialistic, humanistic, chance world view, these things remained the base of government and law.

The Destruction of Faith and Freedom

And now it is all gone!

In most law schools today almost no one studies William Blackstone unless he or she is taking a course in the history of law. We live in a secularized society and in secularized, sociological law. By sociological law we mean law that has no fixed base but law in which a group of people decides what is sociologically good for society at the given moment; and what they arbitrarily decide becomes law. Oliver Wendell Holmes (1841-1935) made totally clear that this was his position. Frederick Moore Vinson (1890-1953), former Chief Justice of the United States Surpeme Court, said, "Nothing is more certain in modern society than the principle that there are no absolutes." Those who hold this position themselves call it sociological law.

As the new sociological law has moved away from the original base of the Creator giving the "inalienable rights," etc., it has been natural that this sociological law has then also moved away from the Constitution. William Bentley Ball, in his paper entitled "Religious Liberty: The Constitutional Frontier," says:

> I propose that secularism militates against religious liberty, and indeed against personal freedoms generally, for two reasons: first, the familiar fact that secularism does not recognize the existence of the "higher law"; second, because, that being so, secularism tends toward decisions based on the pragmatic public policy of the moment and inevitably tends to resist the submitting of those policies to the "higher" criteria of a constitution.

This moving away from the Constitution is not only by court rulings, for example the First Amendment rulings, which are the very reversal of the original purpose of the First Amendment, but in other ways as well. Quoting again from the same paper by William Bentley Ball:

> Our problem consists also, as perhaps this paper has well enough indicated, of more general constitutional concepts. Let me refer to but two: the unconstitutional delegation of legislative power and ultra vires. The first is where the legislature hands over its powers to agents through the conferral of regulatory power unaccompanied by strict standards. The second is where the agents make up powers on their own—assume powers not given them by the legislature. Under the first, the government of laws largely disappears and the government of men largely replaces it. Under the second, agents' personal "homemade" law replaces the law of the elected representatives of the people.

Naturally, this shift from the Judeo-Christian basis for law and the shift away from the restraints of the Constitution automatically militates against religious liberty. Mr. Ball closes his paper:

> Fundamentally, in relation to personal liberty, the Constitution was aimed at restraint of the State. Today, in case after case relating to religious liberty, we encounter the bizarre presumption that it is the

other way around; that the State is justified in whatever action, and that religion bears a great burden of proof to overcome that presumption.

It is our job, as Christian lawyers, to destroy the presumption at every turn.

As lawyers discuss the changes in law in the United States, often they speak of the influence of the laws passed in relationship to the Mormons and to the laws involved in the reentrance of the southern states into the national government after the Civil War. These indeed must be considered. But they were not the reason for the drastic change in law in our country. The reason was the takeover by the totally other world view which would never have given the form and freedom in government we have had in Northern Europe (including the United States). That is the central factor in the change.

It is parallel to the difference between modern science beginning with Copernicus and Galileo and the materialistic science which took over in the last century. Materialistic thought would never have produced modern science. Modern science was produced on the Christian base. That is, because an intelligent Creator had created the universe we can in some measure understand the universe and there is, therefore, a reason for observation and experimentation to be optimistically pursued.

Then there was a shift into materialistic science based on a philosophic change to the materialistic concept of final reality. This shift was based on no addition to the facts known. It was a choice, in faith, to see things that way. No clearer expression of this could be given than Carl Sagan's arrogant statement on public television—made without any scientific proof for the statement—to 140 million viewers: "The cosmos is all that is or ever was or ever will be." He opened the series Cosmos, with this essentially creedal declaration and went on to build every subsequent conclusion upon it.

There is exactly the same parallel in law. The materialistic-energy, chance concept of final reality never would have produced the form and freedom in government we have in this country and in other Reformation countries. But now it has arbitrarily and arrogantly supplanted the historic Judeo-Christian consensus that provided the base for form and freedom in government. The Judeo-Christian consensus gave greater freedoms than the world has ever known, but it also contained the freedoms so that they did not pound society to pieces. The materialistic concept of reality would not have produced the form-freedom balance, and now that it has taken over it cannot maintain the balance. It has destroyed it.

Will Durant and his wife Ariel together wrote *The Story of Civilization*. The Durants received the 1976 Humanist Pioneer Award. In The Humanist magazine of February 1977, Will Durant summed up the humanist problem with regard to personal ethics and social order: "Moreover, we shall find it no easy task to mold a natural ethic strong enough to maintain moral restraint and social order without the support of super-natural consolations, hopes, and fears."

Poor Will Durant! It is not just difficult, it is impossible. He should have remembered the quotation he and Ariel Durant gave from the agnostic Renan in their book *The Lessons of History*. According to the Durants, Renan said in 1866: "If Rationalism wishes to govern the world without regard to the religious needs of the soul, the experience of the French Revolution is there to teach us the consequences of such a blunder." And the Durants themselves say in the same context: "There is no significant example in history, before our time, of a society successfully maintaining moral life without the aid of religion."

Along with the decline of the Judeo-Christian consensus we have come to a new definition and connotation of "pluralism." Until recently it meant that the Christianity flowing from the Reformation is not now as dominant in the country and in society as it was in the early days of the nation. After about 1848 the great influx of immigrants to the United States meant a sharp increase in viewpoints not shaped by Reformation Christianity. This, of course, is the situation which exists today. Thus as we stand for religious freedom today, we need to realize that this must include a general religious freedom from the control of the state for all religion. It will not mean just freedom for those who are Christians. It is then up to Christians to show that Christianity is the Truth of total reality in the open marketplace of freedom.

This greater mixture in the United States, however, is now used as an excuse for the new meaning and connotation of pluralism. It now is used to mean that all types of situations are spread out before us, and that it really is up to each individual to grab one or the other on the way past, according to the whim of personal preference. What you take is only a matter of personal choice, with one choice as valid as another. Pluralism has come to mean that everything is acceptable. This new concept of pluralism suddenly is everywhere. There is no right or wrong; it is just a matter of your personal preference. On a recent *Sixty Minutes* program on television, for example, the questions of euthanasia of the old and the growing of marijuana as California's largest paying crop were presented this way. One choice is as valid as another. It is just a matter of personal preference. This new definition and connotation of pluralism is presented in many forms, not only in personal ethics, but in society's ethics and in the choices concerning law.

Now I have a question. In these shifts that have come in law, where were the Christian lawyers during the crucial shift from forty years ago to just a few years ago? These shifts have all come, or have mostly come, in the last eighty years, and the great, titanic shifts have come in the last forty years. Within our lifetime the great shifts in law have taken place. Now that this has happened we can say, surely the Christian lawyers should have seen the change taking place and stood on the wall and blown the trumpets loud and clear. A nonlawyer like myself has a right to feel somewhat let down because the Christian lawyers did not blow the trumpets clearly between, let us say, 1940 and 1970.

When I wrote *How Should We Then Live?* from 1974 to 1976 I worked out of a knowledge of secular philosophy. I moved from the results in secular philosophy, to the results in liberal theology, to the results in the arts, and then I turned to the courts, and especially the Supreme Court. I read Oliver Wendell Holmes and others, and I must say, I was totally appalled by what I read. It was an exact parallel to what I had already known so well from my years of study in philosophy, theology, and the other disciplines.

In the book and film series *How Should We Then Live?* I used the Supreme Court abortion case as the clearest illustration of arbitrary sociological law. But it was only the clearest illustration. The law is shot through with this kind of ruling. It is similar to choosing Fletcher's situational ethics and pointing to it as the clearest illustration of how our society now functions with no fixed ethics. This is only the clearest illustration, because in many ways our society functions on unfixed, situational ethics.

The abortion case in law is exactly the same. It is only the clearest case. Law in this country has become situational law, using the term Fletcher used for his ethics. That is, a small group of people decide arbitrarily what, from their viewpoint, is for the good of society at that precise moment and they make it law, binding the whole society by their personal arbitrary decisions.

But of course! What would we expect? These things are the natural, inevitable results of the material-energy, humanistic concept of the final basic reality. From the material-energy, chance concept of final reality, final reality is, and must be by its nature, silent as to values, principles, or any basis for law. There is no way to ascertain "the ought" from "the is." Not only should we have known what this would have produced, but on the basis of this viewpoint of reality, we should have recognized that there are no other conclusions that this view could produce. It is a natural result of really believing that the basic reality of all things is merely material-energy, shaped into its present form by impersonal chance.

No, we must say that the Christians in the legal profession did not ring the bell, and we are indeed very, very far down the road toward a totally humanistic culture. At this moment we are in a humanistic culture, but we are happily not in a totally humanistic culture. But what we must realize is that the drift has been all in this direction. If it is not turned around we will move very rapidly into a totally humanistic culture.

The law, and especially the courts, is the vehicle to force this total humanistic way of thinking upon the entire population. This is what has happened. The abortion law is a perfect example. The Supreme Court abortion ruling invalidated abortion laws in all fifty states, even though it seems clear that in 1973 the majority of Americans were against abortion. It did not matter. The Supreme Court arbitrarily ruled that abortion was legal, and overnight they overthrew the state laws and forced onto American thinking not only that abortion was legal, but that it was ethical. They, as an elite, thus forced their will on the majority, even though their ruling was arbitrary both legally and medically. Thus law and the courts became the vehicle for forcing a totally secular concept on the population.

But I would say for the comfort of the Christian lawyers, it was not only the lawyers that did not blow the trumpet. Certainly the Bible-believing theologians were not very good at blowing trumpets either. In 1893 Dr. Charles A. Briggs had been put out of the Presbyterian ministry for teaching liberal theology. I would repeat that liberal theology is only humanism in theological terms. Then after Dr. Briggs was put out of the Presbyterian ministry there largely followed a tremendously great silence. Until the twenties and the thirties, few, if any, among the Bible-believing theologians blew a loud horn. By that time it was too late as most of the old line denominations had come under the dominance of liberal theology at the two power centers of the bureaucracies and the seminaries. By then voices were raised. But with rare exceptions, by that time it was too late. From then on, the liberal theologians would increasingly side with the secular humanists in matters of life style and the rulings of socio-logical law.

And those Bible-believing theologians who did see the theological danger seemed totally blind to what was happening in law and in the total culture. Thus the theologians did no better in seeing the shift from one world view to a totally different world view. Nor did Christian educators do any better either. The failed responsibility covers a wide swath. Christian educators, Christian theo-logians, Christian lawyers—none of them blew loud trumpets until we were a long, long way down the road toward a humanistically based culture.

But, while this may spread the problem of responsibility around, that does not help us today—except to realize that if we are going to do better we must stop being experts in only seeing these things in bits and pieces. We have to understand that it is one total entity opposed to the other total entity. It con-cerns truth in regard to final and total reality—not just religious reality, but total reality. And our view of final reality—whether it is material-energy, shaped by impersonal chance, or the living God and Creator—will determine our position on every crucial issue we face today. It will determine our views on the value and dignity of people, the base for the kind of life the individual and society lives, the direction law will take, and whether there will be freedom or some form of authoritarian dominance.

Source: Francis A. Schaeffer, *A Christian Manifesto* (Westchester, Illinois, 1981), pp. 17-51.

7. I "TOWARD A MORE PROPHETIC POLITICS" (1983)

Neal Riemer

The future of the democratic revolution will not be secure unless we are willing to explore, in theory and practice, the probability of the possibility of a more Prophetic Politics. A powerful case can be made for moving beyond Machia-vellian Politics, the "Lion and Fox" Politics of the Nation-State. We need to protect the truly vital interests of human beings, and local political communities have an important role to play in such protection. But we can no longer convinc-ingly argue that nations protect those vital interests. Nation-state idolatry remains an obstacle to human life, human rights, human needs, around the globe. Utopian Politics, the Harmonious Politics of Earthly Salvation, is wrongly rooted in the premise of an eventual conflict-less society. We cannot abolish con-flict. We can articulate superior patterns of accommodation among contending interests. Constitutionalism is an evolving concept. But it is a mistake to assume that the constitutional pattern of Liberal Democratic Politics is the end of the constitutional line. Despite its weaknesses, it is very good; but it is not good enough. Democratic revisionist, pluralist, welfare-state attempts to make it more "realistic" and responsive should not blind us to the weaknesses of the "Conservative Politics of Pluralist Balance." This balance may suit the rich, the powerful, the white, the male; but poor people, weak people, people of color, and women cannot conclude that Liberal Democratic politics is operating adequately on their behalf. We have hardly begun to open up the whole problem of greater worker control over their primary life in Liberal Democratic ecological health and cultural quality of life in Liberal Democratic Politics.

As we consider the probability of the possibility of a more Prophetic Politics, it is important to keep in mind the distinction I have tried to establish between Prophetic and Utopian Politics. It is lamentable that the fear of messianic madness—whether in Left or Right totalitarianism—has led us to equate, and reject, both "utopian" and "prophetic." We have failed to see that the prophetic impulse does not lead to Lenin, Stalin, and the Gulag Archipelago, or to the Grand Inquisitor, Hitler, and Auschwitz. It is also sad that — rejecting Utopian Politics and disgusted with Machiavellian Politics — we have been tempted to conclude that our safest harbor in a world in which false prophets preach "miracle, mystery, and authority," or the end of alienation, is Liberal Democratic Politics. It is sad because that harbor is not the safest harbor. Indeed, if we are to safeguard the future of the democratic revolution, if we are to respond to the challenges of twenty-first-century politics, we are called to voyage, not to rest. Only if we see that we can distinguish between Prophetic and Utopian Politics can we move away from Machiavellian Politics without embracing Utopian Politics, and without concluding that Liberal Democratic Politics is the way to achieve the right balance in the politics of the twenty-first century. The recovery of the prophetic may be the precondition for a sound and creative, a superior democratic and constitutional, politics in the twenty-first century. The possibility is a live one. Our task is to demonstrate the probability of that possibility.

But what would a more prophetic politics look like in actual practice? Here we can only sketch a few examples in four crucial domains and emphasize our conviction that the probability of the possibility of such a politics rests upon a reasoned faith in the sense of cardinal commandments of our Judaic-Christian religious heritage, in the worth of soundly prescriptive democratic and constitutional principles, and in the ability of political actors to make enlightened self-interest the standard of statesmanship. Here, then, and briefly, we can—ever mindful of the risks inherent in enunciating any concrete program for the contemporary world—pull together our previous hints about a more prophetic program for practical politics.

The four domains in my sketch involve (1) peace, (2) human rights, (3) economic well-being, and (4) ecological health. In each of these areas we can move beyond the idolatry and narrowness of the often power-mad and deceitful nation-state without succumbing to falsely utopian notions about creating an angelic new person in a miraculously new earthly society where all conflict, tyranny, want, and imbalance have been entirely eliminated. But we can—and, indeed, must—succeed in reducing the dangers of nuclear war, in abolishing gross tyrannical acts, in more equitably distributing power and wealth, and in cleaning up our ecological home.

1. *Peace*: We can move to abolish nuclear war as a means for settling disputes between nations. Today such war serves no rational purpose. In such war there can be no winners, only losers. Enlightened self-interest dictates the abolition of nuclear war. The practical steps toward this end can prudently start with a mutual and verifiable freeze on the further development and deployment of nuclear weapons; can continue with staged reductions of all nuclear weapons until nuclear arsenals are reduced to zero; and can then progress to staged reductions of conventional armaments which today, in most countries, are far in excess of legitimate defense needs. Obviously, these efforts must be accompanied by political and economic measures to reduce tensions among the superpowers and to encourage constitutional accommodations that are mutually profitable.

2. *Human Rights*: Persistent and systematic violations of human rights—for example, political murder or torture—must not only be outlawed (as in the rhetoric of U.N. pronouncements) but be made subject to effective international sanctions, administered by an international civil rights commission. "Thou shalt not torture" must join the prophetic commandment, "Thou shalt not make nuclear war." The practice of a more prophetic politics calls for particular attention to the "least free." This means, for example, imaginative efforts to give to workers a greater voice in their primary life activity—their work—through their trade union, schemes for "co-determination," shared managerial responsibility, and joint ownership. Concern for the "least free" also calls—for example, in the United States—for continuing efforts to open doors for blacks and other ethnic groups that have been subject to persistent and systematic discrimination: through programs which strike a judicious balance between equality of opportunity and equality of results. Concern for the "least free" also means more result-oriented efforts to end male chauvinism and to recognize the unique contributions of women. It means more than honoring the liberal ideal of liberty and equality. It means recognizing household work and the bearing and rearing of children as "production." It means paying attention to nurturance, broadly conceived, as it extends beyond conception and family to care for the planet earth. Here nurturing peace and human rights joins with the nurturing of economic well-being and our ecological home.

3. *Economic Well-being*: Political actors in the global community need to establish minimum standards of economic well-being. We need a global "safety net." We cannot afford, for example, to tolerate people starving to death. Of course, we cannot—currently—miraculously lift the level of well-being of all peoples *overnight*—and assure them superior (or even decent) housing, medical care, education—but we certainly *can now* overcome famine; and we *can now* slowly raise the level of economic well-being toward a standard of decency. The battle to triumph over poverty will not be easy, but—in conjunction with disarmament efforts, major economic reforms, and population stabilization—a significant diminution of poverty is not only possible but highly probable.

4. *Ecological Health*: National, regional, and global steps *can* be taken to reduce the worst global pollution, stabilize population growth in excess of supporting resources, and prudently husband our life-sustaining resources. The prophetic affirmation of life not only demands an end to nuclear war (as an indispensable first step toward the end of all catastrophic war); it not only demands the protection of human rights against tyranny; it not only demands food for the hungry, it also demands prudent care of the planet earth. Widespread support for environmental protection bespeaks an enlightened self-interest in protecting the only globe we have to live and conduct our politics on.

This brief, and admittedly sketchy, picture of the practice of prophetic politics in four crucial domains may serve its purpose if it illustrates, however incompletely, the character of politics as a genuinely civilizing enterprise. Such a politics would be a superior democratic and constitutional enterprise. Such a politics is nourished by the prophetic vision, stimulated by prophetic criticism, enjoined to achieve creative constitutional breakthroughs in the prophetic tradition, and encouraged to anticipate and deal with future problems.

Source: Neal Riemer, "Toward a More Prophetic Politics," *Humanities in Society* 6 (Winter, 1983): 13-16.

8. | "FROM CIVIL RELIGION TO PROPHETIC CHURCH: AMERICAN BISHOPS AND THE BOMB" (1983)

Mary Hanna

In 1968 Professor Dorothy Dohen published a book called *Nationalism and American Catholicism*, the only serious study of the subject ever done. Dohen insisted that throughout its history the American Catholic Church had been acquiescent to the status quo.[1] Her book documented the Church's persistently conservative, nationalistic and patriotic attitudes. The study showed the bishops to have been the biggest hawks in our skies.

American bishops loyally supported every war in our history. During the Civil War, Archbishop John Hughes said, "There is but one rule for a Catholic wherever he is, and that is to fight on the side where he finds himself." John Cardinal Gibbons, during the Spanish-American War, told Catholics that they owed "absolute and unreserved obedience" to the nation's call. In the early 1960s Francis Cardinal Spellman paid a Christmas visit to American troops stationed in Vietnam. When a reporter asked his opinion of American involvement in the war, he answered by paraphrasing a quote from ninteenth-century

---

1. Dorothy Dohen, *Nationalism and American Catholicism* (New York: Oxford University Press, 1968), pp. 52-53.

naval hero Stephen Decatur: "My country, may it always be right. But right or wrong, my country."[2]

Given this history, it is no wonder that much of the media and Americans in general reacted with surprise when this past May the National Conference of Catholic Bishops issued a pastoral letter strongly denouncing nuclear warfare.[3] Newspapers termed the letter "a watershed" and "a landmark experience." *Newsweek* magazine called it "the most ambitious and daring political statement the bishops have ever made." Columnist Mary McGrory wrote, "There was, after all, a time when an American president could take for granted Catholic support for any foreign policy venture against godless Communism." In the last twenty years, however, the American Catholic Church has gone through a series of changes that have transformed its hierarchy, its organization and its attitudes toward politics. Those changes almost made predictable the Church's consideration and rejection of nuclear warfare. One can clearly trace the pattern of change that transformed the Catholic Church from a bulwark of civil religion in America to its adoption today of an independent, even radical role.

Historical factors conditioned the American Catholic Church's support for nationalism, patriotism and conservatism. During much of the last century the Church and its hierarchy were dominated by the Irish who came from the Mother Country with an ingrained habit of fusing religious and national feeling. Frequent, often violent anti-Catholic nativist attacks made Church leaders fearful of even the appearance of anti-Americanism, of anything less than total allegiance to the nation. The tremendous mixture of Catholic ethnic groups who came here—Irish, Poles, Germans, Italians—threatened the unity and stability of the Church. The bishops responded by stressing assimilation and conformity to American speech, values and traditions. In the twentieth century Church opposition to Communism made it more supportive than ever of American military and defense policies.

These attitudes began to change in the 1960s with the reforms mandated by the Ecumenical Council, Vatican II, and with the internal stresses generated in the American Church by the Vietnam War and later by the abortion issue. Finally, there is the fact that the bishops today are a new breed, different in education, experience and outlook from their predecessors.

When I was interviewing Church leaders in the 1970s for my book *Catholics and American Politics*, their strongest, most spontaneous reactions were to the Ecumenical Council.[4] Again and again, they talked of the revolutionary effect they felt it had had on the Church and on themselves. No Church Council had met for almost a century before Pope John XXIII called Vatican II in 1962. A Church Council is an assembly of all the world's bishops. When such a

---

2. Ibid., pp. 140, 146-47.

3. National Conference of Catholic Bishops, *The Challenge of Peace: God's Promise and Our Response* (Washington, D.C.: Origins, National Catholic Documentary Service, 19 May 1983).

4. Mary Hanna, *Catholics and American Politics* (Cambridge: Harvard University Press, 1979).

hierarchical assembly meets at the summons of the Pope, the decisions it makes and he approves become the "law," in effect, of the Church.

Vatican II proved one of the most active in history. It set out not just to reform liturgy and ritual but to move the Church in a new direction, into far more active participation in social and political affairs. The Council stressed that the Church as an institution and Catholics in general had a positive obligation to involve themselves in the problems of the world. "Vatican II gave us a kind of 'license' to act," the leaders of a national Catholic lay group told me.[5] An official with the United States Catholic Conference (USCC), the administrative arm of the National Bishops Conference, said, "The Council addressed itself to everyone, the whole Church. It said social justice involved the participation of all the faithful."[6]

The Council also issued a series of documents which denounced various political, social and economic ills—poverty, illiteracy, political repression, etc. —as morally wrong under Christian doctrine and urged Catholics to work to alleviate them. The importance of these documents in providing theological underpinning for Catholic action on political issues was alluded to again and again by the Church leaders I interviewed. A bishop called them "blueprints for action."

"Twenty or thirty years ago," he said, "the Catholic people had no concept of acting on issues like welfare rights, war action. It just wasn't the kind of thing they did. There wasn't a teaching foundation for it, either. Of course, there were some documents; the Eightieth Year Letter built on *Quadragessimo Anno*, for example. But these earlier documents were much more philosophical, theological letters. These were not designed for taking action for change, which rather was an outgrowth of Vatican II."[7]

More than any other part of the Catholic world, American Catholicism responded to the calls for reform and action. In the middle and the late 1960s, thousands of nuns, priests and lay people became involved with the civil rights, anti-poverty and anti-war movements. Public attention focused on the unusual and dramatic spectacle of nuns and priests demonstrating in the streets. Almost unnoticed but vitally important was the fact that the American Church began to move quickly to institutionalize change.

---

5. The quotations from Church leaders used in this paper all come from interviews conducted between 1973 and 1975 for my book, *Catholics and American Politics*. I interviewed bishops, officials with the National Bishops Conference and the United States Catholic Conference, editors of the major Catholic publications, leaders of the various national nuns' and priests' federations and major organizations of the laity. In the usual academic practice, interviewees were promised anonymity and so are referred to not by name but by interview number. The woman quoted in the text thus is Church leader no. 10.

6. Church leader interview no. 15.

7. Church leader interview no. 13. *Quadragessimo Anno* (Fortieth Year) was an encyclical issued by Pope Pius XI in 1931. It confirmed the Church's concern for such social issues as the rights of labor. The Eightieth Year Letter (*Octogesima Adveniens*) was a letter issued by Pope Paul VI in 1971 discussing the encyclical of Pius XI and other encyclicals in the light of Vatican II reforms.

The organizational changes the Church has undergone have not really been analyzed but the Church today is a very different body from what it was twenty years ago. During the postconciliar period, many new organizations were added, old organizations were transformed and a professional, lay expertise, hitherto almost non-existent in the American Church, became the rule. One of the new professionals, working for the USCC, spoke of the tie between the increase in new and renewed Church organizations and the development of Church political interest.

"Important is the creation of Church and Church-related organizations around these social justice issues," he insisted. "There is a whole series of new organizations now working to implement these issues. The Sisters Network is one example. Then Catholic Charities has expanded lately into whole new areas. There are the Jesuit Office for the Social Ministry, Catholics Concerned for the Urban Ministry, the National Council for American Nuns, the National Federation of Priests' Councils, the Conference of Major Superiors of Men."[8]

The United States Catholic Conference itself, a complex bureaucratic and administrative structure originally formed during World War I, underwent the creation of new departments or the addition of new divisions to older departments. All the changes were specifically designed to facilitate Church activity in the area of general social and political concerns. Among the new departments and division, organized in the later 1960s, were the Campaign for Human Development, an anti-poverty program that funds community action organizations without regard for race or creed; the International Affairs Department, concerned with the social and economic development of third world nations; and the Division of Peace and Justice, developed at the suggestion of Pope Paul VI to work for peace, economic developments and social justice.

With these new organizations came an influx of professionals, lawyers, social scientists, educators and communication specialists. A Church which had been led largely by clerics with seminary educations saw the emergence of a broad professional stratum, highly, usually secularly, trained and dedicated to the kinds of reform Vatican II had advocated. These new organizations and the new experts meant that permanent institutions developed which would provide the expertise and, often, the impetus to push the Church as a whole and the bishops toward action on social and political questions. "We have been differently trained and shaped by the Vatican Council," explained one of the new USCC professionals, "and we aren't satisfied to address ourselves to the same old

---

8. Church leader interview no. 20. Sisters Network is an organization designed to educate nuns, particularly, on political issues and to teach practical political strategies such as lobbying. The Jesuit Office for the Social Ministry is an organization devoted to educating the public and public officials on social justice issues. Catholics Concerned for the Urban Ministry is a group of lay and clerical Catholics, writers, teachers, social workers, and so on, who exchange ideas and programs to promote more effective Church work in urban ghetto areas. The National Council of American Nuns, the National Federation of Priests' Councils and the Conference of Major Superiors of Men are examples of the coalitions of religions referred to above.

questions."[9] The influence of these new organizations and professionals quickly became apparent as American Catholics and their Church became more and more involved with the Vietnam War.

The anti-war movement forced Catholic bishops for the first time in our history to seriously examine and judge an American war in terms of Catholic teachings regarding war. This experience was an important progenitor of the recent letter denouncing nuclear war.

World War I had produced only one American Catholic conscientious objector; World War II, about 200, nearly all of them followers of Dorothy Day's Catholic Worker movement. During the buildup of the Vietnam War, however, the first young man to publicly burn his draft card was David Miller, a young Catholic. Hundreds of young Catholics, like him, were stirred into questioning the war by the dramatic speeches and deeds of the priestly Berrigan brothers and other Catholic anti-war leaders and by the just-ended Ecumenical Council's resolutions on war.

These resolutions had questioned the morality of modern warfare, especially tactics such as terrorism, the bombing of cities, the indiscriminate killing of noncombatants, and the unprecedented dangers posed by biological and chemical weapons and nuclear bomb. By the late 1960s American Catholic attitudes had changed dramatically. The greatest percentage increase in conscientious objection occurred in this formerly more supportive religious group.[10]

This meant a problem for the Church and the bishops. Draft boards across the country were rejecting requests by young Catholic men for conscientious objector status, forcing them into exile or jail. There was no basis for granting conscientious objector status, the board ruled, since Catholicism in this country had not traditionally been associated with religious pacifist convictions. The United States Catholic Conference began a thorough study of the ancient, almost forgotten Catholic "just war" theory and how it might apply to the Vietnam conflict.

Of medieval origin, the "just war" theory holds that a Catholic must judge whether or not a war is "just" and his participation in it morally permissible according to several criteria. The war must be declared only as a last resort by a lawful authority, for a just cause, using just means, and with reasonable expectation of success. Most important, the military action cannot produce a greater evil than it seeks to correct. Hence the principle of "proportionality." This proportionality principle became a central issue in the bishops' assessment of the Vietnam War and now of nuclear warfare.

Pushed by the arguments of the "just war" theory, by the dramatic actions of anti-war priests like the Berrigan brothers, and by the plight of so many young Catholic men, the bishops began to reverse their traditional habit of support for America's wars. The reversal was a slow and painful one. In 1968 they issued a pastoral letter, asking an end to the draft and a modification of

---

9. Church leader interview no. 20.

10. James Finn, "American Catholics and Social Movements," in *Contemporary Catholicism in the United States*, ed. Philip Gleason (Notre Dame: University of Notre Dame Press, 1969), p. 144.

the Selective Service Act to permit conscientious objector status for Catholics. They also questioned the "inhuman dimensions of suffering" involved in the Vietnam conflict and whether that did not violate the "just war" principle of proportionality. They raised the question but didn't answer it. "They said they didn't know enough," one activist bishop reported in disgust, "that they had to trust our national leaders, even though they themselves had issued a document saying every citizen had an obligation to analyze government acts."[11]

The forces pushing the bishops to act intensified after their 1968 letter. More and more bishops individually began to take public stands opposing the war and to urge an official, collective statement. Finally, at their annual meeting in November 1971, the National Conference of Catholic Bishops issued a *Resolution on South East Asia*, declaring the war unjust and demanding its end.

"It seems clear to us," the bishops wrote, "that whatever good we hope to achieve through continued involvement in this war is now outweighed by the destruction of human life and of moral values which it inflicts. It is our firm conviction, therefore, that the speedy end of this war is a moral imperative of the highest priority."[12]

The Catholic hierarchy had reversed its traditional position in regard to perhaps the most crucial of all political questions: the issue of war and peace and support for the nation's war. There were hostile and baffled reactions among the Catholic people in many dioceses and ". . . when they went back home," said one bishop, "some of them told their people that they really didn't mean that."[13] This was the position of only a minority, however. The next year the National Bishops Conference denounced the war in even stronger terms and urged amnesty for war resisters and deserters.

Their letter on Vietnam was a decisive break with the past and put the bishops on a new path toward different and greater political activity. When I interviewed Church leaders in 1973, there was a feeling among many of them that the Vietnam letter spelled a kind of declaration of independence for the Church. Church leaders, they said, would now be much readier than they had been in the past to challenge political decisions they believed morally wrong. One USCC official said flatly, "The super-patriotic phase is over."[14] In an article, Jesuit priest and political scientist Edward Duff reported the same reaction and commented about the Catholic anti-war movement: "[They] have challenged in the public mind the automatic identification of American Catholicism with the status quo, its alliance with prevailing patriotic causes, its ambition to be accepted."[15]

The bishops' experience with the Vietnam War did more than end unquestioning acceptance of American policy. Their discussions of the "just war"

---

11. Church leader interview no. 13.
12. National Conference of Catholic Bishops, *Resolution of South East Asia* (Washington, D.C.: USCC Publications Office, November 1971).
13. Church leader interview no. 13.
14. Church leader interview no. 15.
15. Edward J. Duff, "The Burden of the Berrigans," in *The Berrigans*, ed. William V. Casey (New York: Praeger, 1971), p. 27.

theory were beginning to make some of them think about the morality of nuclear warfare. As early as 1973 several bishops told me that they thought the "just war" theory prohibited the use of nuclear weapons. "That's something we're going to have to deal with down the road," predicted one.[16]

The bishops' letter condemning nuclear war also contains a seven-paragraph section entitled "True Peace Calls for 'Reverence for Life,'" which is a denunciation of abortion. Some of the media suggested that it was an impromptu attempt to appease conservative Catholics. Columnists Rowland Evans and Robert Novack described the abortion section as "a late insertion," implying that it had been hastily added during the bishops' meeting. They termed the linking of abortion and war an "exotic new definition of pro-life."[17]

This section of the nuclear letter was no last-minute amendment. It appeared in the earlier drafts of the letter. There is also nothing new in the Church's connecting abortion and war. American bishops have been linking these two issues for at least ten years. The inclusion of a condemnation of abortion in their letter on nuclear war was a natural outcome of the way the bishops have come to think about right to life over the past decade. Their experience with the abortion issue was as important as the Vietnam War in bringing them to publicly condemn nuclear warfare.

The abortion issue was important for two reasons. Fighting abortion helped to make political activity a habit in the Church, rather than an innovation—as their action on Vietnam first seemed. Second, the more expansive definition of right to life, which the abortion issue quickly assumed, forced the bishops into continued consideration of all kinds of social justice issues, including war and peace.

I interviewed Church leaders shortly after the 1973 Supreme Court decision legalizing abortion. A number of leaders told me that that decision, *Roe* v. *Wade*, had been the final step in politicizing the Church hierarchy. The Supreme Court decision, one USCC official said, "was the real watershed. Among the bishops there had still been a residue reluctance to participate in politics but even the residue was washed away by the abortion issue."[18] Another Church leader said, "The abortion issue did more to radicalize the Church than anything else I can think of."[19]

Church reaction was so vehement because bishops and other Church leaders saw the abortion issue as a clash between conflicting value systems. In the Church's view the Supreme Court was telling Catholics that they must conform to what the Church saw as an increasingly materialistic, secular American value system. The editor of a major Catholic magazine insisted that ". . . abortion is a clash of value systems. We are being pushed to the wall and the fundamental problem of the American political system comes to the fore, its moral neutrality, the inability to define moral truth—see the Supreme Court

---

16. Church leader interview no. 14.
17. Rowland Evans and Robert Novak, "Bishops Aligned Closer to Mondale than Reagan." Syndicated column published in many newspapers, 5 May 1983.
18. Church leader interview no. 21.
19. Church leader interview no. 15.

decision."[20] One of the youngest, most liberal bishops in the Church said, "Sociologists would say that the traditional suspicion of Catholics had died. Of course, the Supreme Court decision finished that."[21]

Whether the bishops and other Church leaders were right or not in interpreting the Court's decision as anti-Catholic, this view of abortion as a value conflict was widespread among Catholics. It mobilized the Church politically as never before in its history. Organizations to fight abortion were developed around the country. Money was raised; polls were taken; demonstrations were held; bishops appeared personally before congressional committee hearings. The abortion issue helped the bishops become accustomed to speaking and acting on political issues. As in the case of the Vietnam War, the bishops again, on moral grounds, were publicly opposing official government policy.

Almost all lay and clerical Catholic leaders agreed with the Church's stance on abortion. Liberal Catholics, concerned about a number of social and economic issues, however, early pressed the bishops to embrace a wide definition of right to live. A nun, active in the anti-poverty program told me, in trying to explain the feelings of Catholic liberals, ". . . I have never seen so much power put behind an issue. The flood of literature that is coming out on the abortion issue! The groups that are being formed to fight! We haven't seen the bishops of the Church exercise this kind of power on other issues, on justice, for example, or poverty. Sometimes I almost forget that I myself am opposed to abortion because I spend so much time trying to bring the whole thing into some kind of balance."[22]

There already was theological justification for regarding the right to life as involving more than abortion. In 1965 the Ecumenical Council had issued a document asserting a broad definition. "This Council lays stress on reverence for man . . . taking into account first of all his life and the means necessary to living it with dignity." It declared that whatever is opposed to life itself, whatever violates the integrity of the human person or insults human dignity, are "infamies." The Council then listed these life-depriving and life-degrading infamies as not only, or even primarily, abortion but also murder, genocide, euthanasia, mental and physical coercion and suffering, subhuman living conditions, arbitrary imprisonment and harsh working conditions.[23]

The National Bishops Conference used the Council resolution as its basis for establishing a respect-for-life ideology encompassing a similarly wide range of conditions denying life or a decent life. In 1972 the bishops began sponsoring annual "Respect Life" programs to be held in parishes around the country. The 1972 program focused on abortion but also on war, violence, hunger and poverty. The 1973 program expanded respect for life to include the mentally retarded, the aging, youth, social justice at home and abroad, international

---

20. Church leader interview no. 17.
21. Church leader interview no. 13.
22. Church leader interview no. 6.
23. National Conference of Catholic Bishops/United States Catholic Conference, *Documentation on the Right to Life and Abortion* (Washington, D.C.: USCC Publications Office, 1974), pp. 71-72.

development and, again, peace and war. This broader conception of respect for life moved the bishops in 1974 to condemn capital punishment.

Year after year, the bishops were forced to consider warfare, especially nuclear warfare, not only in terms of the Church's "just war" theory but also in terms of its teachings on right to life. Their May 1983 letter described the nuclear race as ". . . a threat to human life and human civilization which is without precedence."[24]

"My predecessor now says that he was bishop in a golden age and that he got out just in time," a bishop told me during our interview. "There was an aura of dignity around bishops before. They worked with a few Chancery officials. They went to a few dinners. Now, you must get right out of the Chancery. You must do a lot of listening. There's coresponsibility now."[25]

He was right. Bishops now are a new breed in a new era. The Ecumenical Council, the Vietnam War and the abortion issue brought Catholic bishops to the point where they have defied the administration and issued a wide-ranging condemnation of nuclear war and the nuclear race. But the letter would probably never have happened if it were not for the fact that American Catholic bishops today are different in education, experience and outlook from the bishops of the earlier, immigrant Church.

Earlier, bishops were largely educated in seminaries, sometimes of poor quality given the Church's limited resources. Their exposure to American life was often limited. The usual career path for a bishop was a few years in parish work and then years spent slowly climbing through the ranks of the administrative apparatus of the Church. Their outlook on life was often narrow, formed by the working-class, ghettoized, immigrant roots from which, like most American Catholics, they sprang.

Many of today's bishops have been educated in secular as well as theological subjects, often at the great universities of this country and Europe. Since a mandatory retirement age for bishops was instituted by Pope Paul VI after the Vatican Council, bishops now tend to be younger as a group than their predecessors of twenty or thirty years ago. More than two-thirds of the men who voted for the anti-nuclear letter were named to their bishoprics after 1972. That means that most American bishops today were formed by the Vatican Council and by the tumultuous decade of the 1960s. They are not monastic men but men who have taken direct roles in many of the political events of the last two decades.

The men who were most active on the committee which drafted the nuclear war letter are good examples of these new bishops. Bishop Thomas Gumbleton was a superior scholar, singled out during his seminary years for advanced study in Rome. In the early 1970s he became an anti-war activist and was one of the men who uncovered the "tiger cages" in Vietnam, the underground bamboo cells where the South Vietnamese government was secretly holding political prisoners. Bishop John O'Connor holds both a doctor of philosophy degree in political science and rear admiral rank in the U.S. Navy.

---

24. National Conference of Catholic Bishops, *The Challenge of Peace*, 13.
25. Church leader interview no. 14.

He served for years as chaplain in both the Atlantic and Pacific fleets, was chief of chaplains for the Navy and wrote three books, *Principles and Problems of Naval Leadership*, *A Chaplain Looks at Vietnam* and *In Defense of Life* (which contained many ideas later incorporated into the bishops' nuclear war letter). Joseph Cardinal Bernardin has a master's degree in education. He is a former president of the National Conference of Catholic Bishops, involved in many social and political issues during his tenure. At President Gerald Ford's request, he helped plan the resettlement of Vietnamese refugees.

These men demonstrate how different today's Catholic hierarchy is, not just through their lives and educational and occupational experience, but also through the way in which they went about preparing the drafts of the bishops' letter on nuclear war. Here they showed their own experience in social and political affairs and the new professionalism of Church organizations and Church leaders.

First, these bishops hired a professional consultant, Dr. Bruce Martin Russett, professor of political science at Yale University and a noted expert on international relations and strategic policy. They set up a committee staff, including Reverend J. Bryan Hehir, head of the USCC Office of International Justice and Peace, a man who has been directing research on international questions for the bishops for more than ten years. They then held fourteen hearings. Over a period of a year the bishops listened to witnesses such as defense and national security officials Harold Brown, James Schlesinger, Helmut Sonnenfeld, Casper Weinberger and Lawrence Eagleberger; moral theologians like Gordon Zahn and George Weigel; and military men like retired General George Seignious and retired Admiral Noel Gaylor.[26] The bishops on the ad hoc committee responsible for the draft letter on nuclear warfare are men known for their spirituality and surely they prayed over the letter. They also went about preparing the drafts just as a congressional committee prepares legislation.

"The Church is like a barge," the editor of a Catholic magazine told me. "It seems to move so slowly but somehow it always gets there and always keeps moving. In the last ten years alone, this barge which seems to have moved so slowly has covered so much ground! It's unbelievable. The change has been immense."[27] I interviewed him in 1973. Much more change has occurred since then. The change which brought the Catholic Church from being a mainstay of civil religion to adopting a more "prophetic" stance was evolutionary and slow. It came about through a combination of a reforming Church Council, the politicizing effect of two traumatic issues (Vietnam and abortion) and the emergence of new and different leaders. Now, whether one agrees with the bishops or not, one can't deny that, like the prophets of old, they have challenged the thinking of our government and Americans in general. As Rabbi Marc Tannenbaum of the

---

26. National Conference of Catholic Bishops, *Third Draft of Pastoral Letter, The Challenge of Peace: God's Promise and Our Responses* (Washington, D.C.: Origins, National Catholic Documentary Service, 14 April 1983), pp. 726-27.

27. Church leader interview no. 5.

American Jewish Committee has said, "The letter is an historic contribution to advancing the supreme moral issue of this modern age—saving the human family from the terrors of potential nuclear holocaust."

Source: Mary Hanna, "From Civil Religion to Prophetic Church: American Bishops and the Bomb," *Humanities in Society* 6 (Winter 1983): 41-51.

9. | " RESOLUTIONS OF THE WORLD CONGRESS OF FUNDAMENTALISTS" (1980, 1983)

1. *Regarding Fundamentalism*
   A fundamentalist is a born-again believer in the Lord Jesus Christ who:
   1. Maintains an immovable allegiance to the inerrant, infallible, and verbally inspired Bible.
   2. Believes that whatever the Bible says, is so.
   3. Judges all things by the Bible and is judged only by the Bible.
   4. Affirms the foundational truths of the historic Christian Faith:
      a. The doctrine of the Trinity
      b. The incarnation, virgin birth, substitutionary atonement, bodily resurrection and glorious ascension, and Second Coming of the Lord Jesus Christ
      c. The new birth through regeneration of the Holy Spirit
      d. The resurrection of the ungodly to final judgment and eternal death
      e. The resurrection of saints to life eternal
      f. The fellowship of the saints, who are the body of Christ
   5. Practices fidelity to that Faith and endeavors to preach it to every creature.
   6. Exposes and separates from all ecclesiastical denial of that Faith, compromise with error, and apostasy from the Truth.
   7. Earnestly contends for the Faith once delivered. . . .

2. *Regarding Humanism*
   The World Congress of Fundamentalists believes that humanism as set forth in the Humanist Manifesto of 1933 and 1973 constitutes a new religion which promulgates the theory that traditional, dogmatic and authoritarian religions that place the revelation of God above needs and experiences do a disservice to the human species, and that humanism begins with humans, not God; which considers promises of eternal salvation or fear of eternal damnation both illusionary and harmful; which looks favorably upon abortion, divorce, and free sexual expression, including the rights of individuals to pursue their sexual proclivities (including homosexuality); which makes Death irrelevant and man central and autonomous. We believe humanism is a false religion; therefore,

we pledge ourselves to do everything possible to expose and oppose humanism in whatever form it takes. . . .

3. *Regarding the Scriptures*

The World Congress of Fundamentalists affirms its belief in the Bible, both Old and New Testaments (66 canonical books), as the verbally and plenarily inspired, inerrant, and infallible World of God in the autographs, and rejects the books known as the Apocrypha as the inspired Word of God. We condemn paraphrases such as "The Living Bible" and "Good News for Modern Man" and the products of unbelieving and liberal scholarship such as the Revised Standard Version and the New English Bible, and recognize the unique and special place of the Authorized (King James) Version in the English-speaking world, and we also reject the modern fad of exalting any version or translation to the position held uniquely by the original writings. . . .

4. *Regarding World Evangelism*

The World Congress of Fundamentalists takes seriously the command to evangelize the world and urges that we intensify our efforts to make possible the presentation of the Gospel message to all peoples in the fulfillment of the Great Commission, while at the same time avoiding compromise and inclusivism in our presentation of the good news of the Gospel of Christ. . . .

5. *Regarding Sexual Immorality*

The World Congress of Fundamentalists deplores and condemns all moral aberrations, including pornography, prostitution, sexual exploitation, homosexuality, and lesbianism as being under the curse and condemnation of Almighty God, and views all attempts to justify, condone, or legitimatize these as an affront to a holy God and a denial of the plain teaching of Scripture. Further, we go on record as declaring that abortion is murder. . . .

6. *Regarding the Lord's Day*

The Scriptures clearly teach that our Lord Jesus Christ arose from the dead on the first day of the week, that the Holy Spirit came on the Day of Pentecost the day after the Sabbath, and that the early Church worshiped on the first day of the week—the Lord's Day.

Therefore, the Congress calls upon its constituency to sanctify the Lord's Day, to resist every effort to secularize the same, and to be faithful in maintaining it as a holy day, and not as a holiday, by diligent attendance at the Lord's house and dedication to the Lord's service. . . .

7. *Resolution on Communism*

WHEREAS Marxian Socialism has proved to be the greatest failure of the 20th century, while professing to be the superior society destined by history to triumph, but which cannot feed itself, and is saved from collapse only by the indefensible support of the so-called "imperialistic" nations through their money, food grains, and willingness to allow open subversion, and

WHEREAS the three basic doctrines of communism (there is no God, man is an animal, and everything is economically determined) require the serious attention and condemnation of every right-thinking Christian leader the world over, and

WHEREAS basic human rights are practically non-existent in the Soviet Union, China, and their satellite allies, producing history's most monstrous system of slavery, and

WHEREAS we can almost hear in Manila the sound of the tramping of the marching millions living under communism trying by all means and at any cost to escape into Hong Kong, through the Berlin Wall and any other possible points of entry into the free world, and

WHEREAS the so-called "Liberation Theology" which has emerged in the Latin world and spread widely through liberal institutions is brazenly endeavoring to equate Marxism with radical Christian social action as the fulfillment of the Christian faith, and. . . .

WHEREAS Bible-believing Christians must view communism as total depravity, with no redeeming social values of commendable aspect, requiring Christian leaders to first understand it, and then to totally reject it, and

WHEREAS the Reagan political victory for the presidency of the United States, bringing the elimination of so many left-wing liberals in the U. S. Senate, and drastically altering the whole approach of the free world toward communism, provides an unparalleled opportunity to strike a telling blow against the forces of oppression and aggression,

BE IT RESOLVED

THAT we encourage the governments of the free world to develop and maintain strong defense forces against ambitious, expansionist communist programs, and take a firm anti-communist stand.

THAT preachers everywhere mount a determined offensive against the philosophy of dialectical materialism in the realm of theory as well as against all forms of communist terrorism as it works out in political reality.

THAT the myths of communism be exploded, their deceit unmasked, and their hypocrisy exposed, as they demand civil rights everywhere else while denying this to all peoples under their military and psychological control.

THAT the pro-communist and ecumenical forces of the World Council of Churches, the National Council of Churches, and other regional organizations of the apostasy be repudiated, such as their continued support of worldwide subversion of anti-communist governments in the Third World.

8. *Regarding the World Council of Churches*

We express serious alarm at the apostasy now accelerating within the WCC. In particular we repudiate the inclusion of religious leaders from Buddhism, Hinduism, Islam and Judaism on the platform of the recent assembly in Vancouver, British Columbia, the continuing propagation of Marxist and so-called "liberation" philosophy, the promotion of the doctrine that the Holy Spirit is female, the accelerating Rome-ward tendency, and the continued funding by the WCC of terrorist organizations on the continent of Africa.

Source: "Resolutions of the World Congress of Fundamentalists" (1980, 1983).

THE THEOLOGICAL DIMENSIONS OF PRESIDENTIAL LEADERSHIP

6

Americans treat America as a religion. Hatred for political opponents waxes theological. Like separate islands, the political religions of the land are connected through a single office. The president is the one pontiff bridging all.[1]

MICHAEL NOVAK

While the ideological dimensions of presidential leadership are generally obvious, the theological dimensions, though less obvious, are no less important, especially as they relate to the ideological. Ideologically it is naturally and properly assumed with clear historical support that a president's ideology affects how he performs in office. To wit, using some obvious examples, Lyndon Johnson from a liberal ideological background, contrasts sharply with Ronald Reagan from a conservative background with respect to a variety of aspects of presidential leadership, but especially public policy. The basic policy approach of a liberal president tends to increase while a conservative president tends to reduce, or at least desires to do so, the size and scope of the national government.

Reprinted with permission from *Presidential Studies Quarterly*, Center for the Study of the Presidency, New York.

IMPORTANCE OF PRESIDENTIAL THEOLOGY

The importance of a theological understanding of presidential leadership may be established in several ways. First, the presidency quite often is referred to in theological terms, such as "faith in the presidency," "trust in presidential leadership," "a sacred office," "confidence in presidential leadership," or "saving the presidency."

Second, leading presidential analysts, observers, and presidents themselves have used theological analogies, metaphors, and similes to describe the presidency. Theodore Roosevelt referred to the office as a "bully pulpit" while Franklin Roosevelt said it is "preeminently a place of moral leadership." Richard Nixon said:

> To a crisis of the *spirit*, we need an answer of the *spirit*. We can build a *great cathedral* of the *spirit*. We have endured a long night of the American *spirit*. But as our eyes catch the dimness of the first rays of dawn, let us not curse the remaining *dark*, let us gather the *light*. Our destiny offers not the *cup* of despair, but the *chalice* of opportunity.[2] (emphasis supplied)

New York *Times* journalist James Reston concluded that "the White House is the pulpit of the nation and the president is its chaplain."[3] Then perhaps presidential scholar Clinton Rossiter rose or stooped to the highest or lowest use of theological terminology, depending on one's perspective, when he said of Lincoln that he was "the martyred Christ of democracy's passion play."[4]

Campaigns for the presidency offer a third reason for understanding the theological dimensions of presidential leadership. The 1976 and 1980 presidential campaigns present excellent verbal as well as visual examples of theological symbol manipulation by presidential candidates. In 1976, candidate Jimmy Carter said he was "born again," a not-so-subtle code word from John 3 designed to woo the substantial segment of the American electorate that claims to be "born again." And the Sunday immediately prior to election day, President Ford, an Episcopalian, was prominently pictured shaking hands with the Southern Baptist Convention's best known conservative preacher, W. A. Criswell, while entering the front door of the First Baptist Church, Dallas, Texas. In 1980 candidate Ronald Reagan appeared before a theologically conservative meeting hosted by the Religious Roundtable in Texas where he proclaimed his faith in the Genesis account of creation and expressed support for prayer in the public schools.

Still a fourth reason for expanding our understanding concerns the use of theological rhetoric in support of public policy aims. Lincoln's Gettysburg Address, his Second Inaugural and his earlier "house divided" speech are replete with numerous theological themes. But perhaps more than any other president,

William McKinley's policy toward the Philippines reveals the significant relationship between theology and public policy.

> The truth is I didn't want the Philippines, and when they came
> to us a gift from the gods I did not know what to do with them ...
> I sought counsel ... I walked the floor of the White House night
> after night until midnight, and I am not ashamed to tell you gentle-
> men, that I went down on my knees and prayed to Almighty God
> for light and guidance more than one night. And late one night it
> came to me this way—I don't know how it was but it came ... there
> was nothing left for us to do but to take them all, and to educate
> the Filipinos, and uplift and civilize and Christianize them, and by
> God's grace do the very best we could by them as our fellowmen for
> whom Christ died.[5]

As he entered the presidential office during the Depression, Franklin
Roosevelt used biblical terminology when he declared that "the money changers
have fled from their high seats in the temple of civilization."[6] In defense of his
voting rights bill in 1965, President Johnson stated before Congress:

> ... should we double our wealth and conquer the stars and still be
> unequal to this issue, then we will have failed as a people and as a
> nation.
>
> For with a country as with a person, *'What is a man profited, if he
> shall gain the whole world, and lose his own soul?'*
>
> Above the pyramid on the great seal of the United States it says in
> Latin, 'God has favored our undertaking.'
>
> God will not favor everything we do. It is rather our duty to divine
> His will. I cannot help but believe that He truly understands and that
> He really favors the undertaking that we begin here tonight.[7] (emphasis
> supplied)

Fifth, a substantial body of scholarship, particularly among sociologists,
theologians, and historians, documents a civil religion replete with its own
terminology generally considered inoffensive to a broad theological spectrum.
As Conrad Cherry has pointed out:

> Throughout their history Americans have been possessed by an
> acute sense of divine election. They have fancied themselves a New
> Israel, a people chosen for the awesome responsibility of serving as a
> light to the nations, a city set upon a hill. This preponderating self-
> image, in its original form as well as in its myriad mutations, has served
> as both a stimulus of creative American energy and a source of Ameri-
> can self-righteousness. It has long been, in other words, the essence of
> America's motivating mythology.[8]

While William McKinley's Philippine statement may be considered outside the accepted boundary lines of the civil religion, both conservative and liberal presidents on the whole have drawn liberally from biblical and theological terminology to establish the credibility of their political aspirations and policy objectives. Many of the most famous of all political slogans have biblical and theological overtones, such as "the white man's burden" and "manifest destiny," that helped presidents and others inspire the populace.

Although probably no president excelled Lincoln in the use of the terminology of civil religion, Jefferson may have come close. For example, he proposed that the seal of the United States portray "the children of Israel in the wilderness led by a cloud by day and a pillar by night."[9] In his second inaugural, he declared: "I shall need . . . the favor of that Being in whose hands we are, who led our fathers, as Israel of old, from their native land and planted them in a country flowing with all the necessities and comforts of life."[10] Perhaps President Eisenhower best summed up the impact of civil religion when he said: "Our government makes no sense unless it is founded in a deeply felt faith—and I don't care what it is."[11]

Sixth, in at least some instances, religious or theological advice has been sought and given to presidents, including Reinhold Niebuhr to Franklin Roosevelt, Billy Graham to several presidents, such as Kennedy, Johnson, and Nixon and Jerry Falwell to Ronald Reagan. Sometimes their advice has been received both substantively and symbolically as when Presidents Kennedy, Johnson, and Nixon publicly announced and had pictures taken of their public policy discussions with Billy Graham.

Seventh, presidents cannot ignore, except at their own potential political peril, political movements with a theological base, such as the abolitionist movement prior to the Civil War that existed principally because of theological forces and the Nuclear Freeze and Moral Majority movements of today. The abolitionist movement with its uncompromising theologically based opposition to slavery kept "the feet of presidents to the fire" in the prosecution of their cause. The Nuclear Freeze movement whose troops are sprinkled liberally with persons of liberal theological convictions has forced President Reagan to acknowledge their presence by counter-attacking on this issue. Moral Majority, an umbrella for many conservative theological personalities, similarly served as a lightning rod for President Reagan's social and theological agenda on such issues as ERA, school prayer and abortion.

Church joining, if not faithful attendance, is an eighth reason for understanding the impact of theology and religion on presidents. Perhaps the best example of this occurred in 1952 when the Democratic candidate Adlai Stevenson, a Unitarian, became a Presbyterian, and a nonchurchmember, General Eisenhower, also became a Presbyterian. As shown in Table 6.1 presidents tend to be members of or to attend the safe or mainline denominational churches, such as Methodist, Presbyterian, Episcopalian, and Baptist. President Nixon

TABLE 6.1   Church Preferences of Presidents: Attendance and/or Membership

1.	George Washington	Episcopalian
2.	John Adams	Unitarian
3.	Thomas Jefferson	Unitarian*
4.	James Madison	Episcopalian
5.	James Monroe	Episcopalian
6.	John Quincy Adams	Unitarian
7.	Andrew Jackson	Presbyterian
8.	Martin Van Buren	Dutch Reformed
9.	William H. Harrison	Episcopalian
10.	John Tyler	Episcopalian
11.	James K. Polk	Methodist
12.	Zachary Taylor	Episcopalian
13.	Millard Fillmore	Unitarian
14.	Franklin Pierce	Episcopalian
15.	James Buchanan	Presbyterian
16.	Abraham Lincoln	Presbyterian*
17.	Andrew Johnson	Methodist*
18.	Ulysses S. Grant	Methodist
19.	Rutherford B. Hayes	Methodist*
20.	James A. Garfield	Disciples of Christ
21.	Chester A. Arthur	Episcopalian
22.	Grover Cleveland	Presbyterian
23.	Benjamin Harrison	Presbyterian
24.	Grover Cleveland	Presbyterian
25.	William McKinley	Methodist
26.	Theodore Roosevelt	Dutch Reformed
27.	William H. Taft	Unitarian
28.	Woodrow Wilson	Presbyterian
29.	Warren G. Harding	Baptist
30.	Calvin Coolidge	Congregationalist
31.	Herbert C. Hoover	Friend (Quaker)
32.	Franklin D. Roosevelt	Episcopalian
33.	Harry S Truman	Baptist
34.	Dwight D. Eisenhower	Presbyterian
35.	John F. Kennedy	Roman Catholic
36.	Lyndon B. Johnson	Disciples of Christ
37.	Richard M. Nixon	Friend (Quaker)
38.	Gerald R. Ford	Episcopalian
39.	Jimmy Carter	Baptist
40.	Ronald Reagan	Presbyterian

*Church Preference; never joined any church.

Source: Compiled by author.

took the unusual course of holding Sunday morning worship services in the White House with leading clergy from several denominations presiding.

The moderating influence of the safe or mainline churches on presidential behavior suggests a ninth reason. Or it could be said that politics itself tends to moderate the theological and religious convictions of presidents. Except for perhaps William McKinley and possibly Jimmy Carter, conservative and fundamental convictions appeared to have waned either before or during the presidencies of those presidents from such backgrounds like James A. Garfield and Warren Harding. With respect to Jimmy Carter one must wonder about how conservative or fundamental his theological and religious convictions were. Superficially they were deeply rooted if one remembers his Sunday School attendance with Bible in hand; however, his favorite theologians were liberal, and he did not appear to insist upon White House staff behavior consistent with his apparent personal convictions, Hamilton Jordan being the prime example of the prodigal. Although wooing conservative theological groups in his 1980 campaign, President Reagan generally tended to modify his statements and behavior during his presidency apparently in response to a broader American constituency.

The essential point is that like their political ideology, the theology of most Americans tends to be in the middle, i.e., neither hot nor cold. Thus, the middle of the electorate, we may reasonably argue, pressures presidents to conform to them.

Finally the national party platforms, particularly in recent years, present a contrast between conservative and liberal theological convictions perhaps best shown in the 1980 platforms wherein they differed sharply on such issues as school prayer, abortion, ERA (equal rights amendment for women) and others. That presidents feel the theological pressure from these platforms may be shown with respect to Jimmy Carter, who though personally opposed to abortion for theological reasons, would not take a stand against the mainstream of his party on this issue. Also, in 1980 George Bush had to agree to support the Republican Platform that contained several theologically based planks which he opposed.

Not only do these ten reasons offer sufficient justification for examining the relationships between presidential behavior and theological convictions, but they also begin to unveil differences between and among presidents. It is here that efforts have been made to classify presidents based upon religious and theological considerations. Our purpose now is to review these efforts and then to offer another classification scheme that shows relationships between theological and ideological aspects of presidential behavior.

REVIEW OF PRESIDENTIAL CLASSIFICATIONS

Of the three major efforts to classify presidents, two have used some form of religious or theological analysis. They are works by Robert S. Alley[12] and Michael Novak.[13] The third is the much more well known, but also highly controversial, work by James David Barber.[14]

Alley Classification. This scheme divides the presidents into three categories as described below:

Type A: "Goal-oriented" presidents generally of a deist persuasion early in American history who used the inoffensive language of civil religion that generally appeals to Catholics, Jews, and Protestants, such as, John Adams, Thomas Jefferson, John Q. Adams, Abraham Lincoln, and Andrew Johnson.

Type B: "Legalist" presidents scattered throughout American history who maintained relatively close ties to their religious or theological roots of a more conservative Christian persuasion, such as, Andrew Jackson, U. S. Grant, Grover Cleveland, William McKinley, Theodore Roosevelt, Woodrow Wilson, Warren Harding, Calvin Coolidge, Herbert Hoover, Harry Truman, Dwight Eisenhower, Lyndon Johnson, and Richard Nixon.

Type C; "Situation ethics" presidents primarily from established churches and/ or families who were pragmatic in their approach to theology, religion, and the presidency, such as, George Washington, Franklin Pierce, Chester Arthur, Franklin Roosevelt, and John F. Kennedy.

By Alley's own admission, his classification scheme raises many unanswered questions. Although we probably should not say it raises more problems than it resolves, certainly we can say it is in his words possessed of "obvious ambiguities" and room for disagreement is substantial.

Michael Novak provides the other religious or theologically oriented categorization of presidents based upon the nation's predominantly protestant experience, but without trying to classify them precisely as Alley does. Still his classification scheme is useful to the extent that it adds understanding to the impact of religion and theology on the presidency. His classification is five-fold:

(1) *Classic Mainline Protestantism* includes those generally associated with the "high-church" tradition, such as elements of the Episcopal, United, and northern Presbyterian churches, where wealth, family background, and political and social awareness cultivated in Ivy League education generally put forward a liberal ideological approach to public policy that is receptive to political compromise. Names like Nelson Rockefeller, John Lindsay, and Henry Cabot Lodge are on Novak's list in this category.

(2) *Lower Class Populist Tradition* concentrated in the South and the so-called Bible Belt of small towns and rural areas is a "low-church" tradition that is suspicious of formal authority and "outsiders" and that tends to follow strong leaders in religion and politics. This tradition tends to be absolutist in its understanding and advocacy of what is good and right and, therefore, is not as prone to political compromise. Novak includes such figures as George Wallace, Lyndon Johnson, Fred Harris, Lawton Chiles, Lester Maddox, and Estes Kefauver in this group.

(3) *Middle-Class Heartland Churches* typified by Methodism that is neither "high" nor "low" church is generally more midwestern and more receptive to structure, professionalism, bureaucracies and expertise than the lower class populist tradition generally found in the South. Mentioned in this category by Novak are such figures as Dwight Eisenhower, Hubert Humphrey, and Billy Graham.

(4) *Protestant Reform* from the Midwest also produces, in Novak's mind, a fourth type illustrated by William Jennings Bryan and George McGovern, who surface politically because of a burning moral issue like abolition, Wall Street, prohibition, civil rights, or the Vietnam War. This type, of course, tends to be cyclical in nature, dependent upon issues that will allow a leader to surface.

(5) *Black Protestantism* causes Novak to describe some white politicians at a black political gathering as "stiff and uncomfortable as an icicle in July." He finds that figures like Hubert Humphrey could bridge the gap, but George McGovern could not. The difference was in their ability to radiate "body heat" and "lively sensitivity" that blacks appreciate because of their emotional and experiential backgrounds.

The two principal groups overlooked in this protestant-oriented classification, Jews and Roman Catholics, have historically identified substantially more with the more liberally oriented Democratic Party in the era of the contemporary presidency, Franklin Roosevelt to the present. During this period the Democratic Party has been less bound by protestant tradition. Pragmatically, there were substantial reasons for these generally urban residents to identify with the party that usually controlled city governments and also advocated more social welfare programs and aid to the cities. Beginning in the late 1960s through the early 1980s, however, some of this support began to wane as Jews began to be attracted to the Republican Party's seemingly more consistent support of Israel and as Roman Catholics were attracted to the Republican Party's stance against abortion, ERA and other policies with a liberal theological bent. Since the Republican Party has attracted more conservatively oriented theological interests who revere the Old Testament tradition and hold to a more literal biblical interpretation, there is a greater tendency among Republicans to support the nation of Israel, right or wrong, since the Old Testament says she is "the apple of God's eye." Liberal Democrats in the last decade, generally with less conviction about biblical truth and precept, have not always been as consistent in their support of Israel. The presidential politics of conservatively and liberally oriented theological interest groups also show support for this analysis. Jerry Falwell's Moral Majority takes an exceedingly pro-Israeli stance, but the National Council of Churches has been more prone to look with favor on Arab interests in the Middle East. Additional support for this conclusion and analysis comes from an examination of elected political figures that show an increasing number of Jews and Roman Catholics elected as Republicans to the U.S. Congress, including such figures as Arlen Specter (R. Pa.) and Rudy Boschwitz (R. Minn.)

from the Jewish side, and Jeremiah A. Denton (R. Ala.) and Frank Murkowski (R. Ak.) from the Roman Catholic side.

James David Barber's much maligned, but very influential, typology divided the presidents into quadrants based upon a continuum of active to passive in their approach to the presidency and another from positive to negative in their personality and character. He, of course, did not treat the religious or theological component in classifying the presidents.

PRESIDENTIAL IDEOLOGY AND THEOLOGY

None of these principal efforts at classification of presidents relates the ideological and theological components of presidential leadership. Through application of the paradigm in Figure 6.2 and studying the principal biographical and autobiographical sources on all American presidents from Washington through Reagan, Figures 6.1-4 classify the presidents on an ideological continuum from conservative to liberal and on a theological continuum from conservative to liberal. Thus, a president of conservative ideological and theological convictions would generally conform to most of the theological and ideological precepts presented in Figure 1.2 of Chapter 1 while a president of liberal ideological and theological convictions would conform to the liberal precepts.

Some presidents present problems in classifying, such as Thomas Jefferson and Jimmy Carter. Jefferson, although obviously a liberal theologically, tended to support a conservative ideological stance in his writings; however, his presidential actions would generally lead to classifying him as a liberal ideologically. Jimmy Carter presents another problem. Symbolically at least he was a conservative theologically, but substantively his theological convictions appear to be more liberal, especially if one examines the writings of his favorite theologians who, as pointed out, were liberal.

Still another problem is in classifying the early presidents, especially those of the Unitarian persuasion which is today uniformly considered theologically liberal, since, during the early period of American history, Unitarian thought tended to be much more conservative than it is today. Thus, by today's standards, Unitarian presidents like the two Adams would generally fit the conservative side of the theological comparison more than the liberal.

While any classification system presents loopholes and difficulties in making precise classifications, they can be very helpful if one recognizes their limitations and does not try to press them to do more than what they were intended to do, namely to provide guidance in understanding presidential behavior. Among the conclusions that may be drawn from Figures 6.1-4 are these:

First, the ideological and theological components tend to reinforce one another. Liberal presidents ideologically also tend to be liberal presidents

FIGURE 6.1   The Ideological and Theological Tendencies of Presidents:
Washington—Buchanan

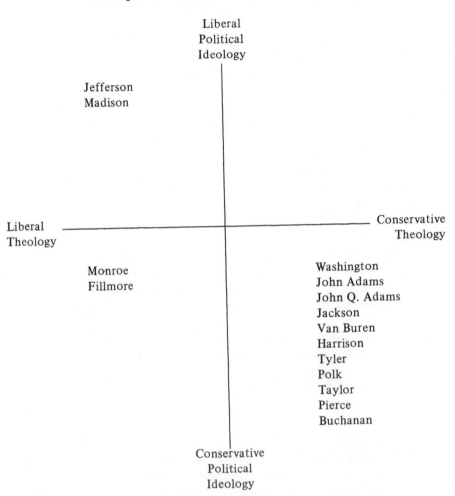

theologically while conservative presidents ideologically tend to be theologically conservative.

Second, one cannot always determine which came first, the "chicken or the egg," that is, whether a president is liberal primarily because of ideology or theology. Superficially, the safe conclusion would be that theology tends to reinforce ideology more than the other way around, but then we do not have sufficient evidence to conclude that firmly. One principal support for this conclusion is that presidents generally speak more about their ideology than their theology.

Third, some presidents appear never to give serious thought to their theological convictions, such as Harry S Truman and Dwight David Eisenhower.

In such instances theology would definitely tend to reinforce more than to direct their ideological positions.

Fourth, what cannot be shown are the degrees of conservatism and liberalism. To wit, Walter Mondale is clearly more liberal ideologically and theologically than Jimmy Carter, and Ronald Reagan is more conservative than Richard Nixon.

Fifth, those in the conservative-conservative quadrant are more likely to be Republicans and those in the liberal-liberal quadrant are more likely to be Democrats. This adds further evidence to the conclusion that theological liberals are more comfortable in the Democratic Party and theological conservatives are more at ease in the Republican Party.

Sixth, since Lyndon Johnson all presidents have either symbolically or substantively (or both) professed to be conservative theologically. This is at least a thread of evidence that strengthens the claim of ideological conservatives that there is a conservative resurgence in the nation. Another way to look at it is that from Nixon through Reagan, presidents have tended to go beyond the

FIGURE 6.2   The Ideological and Theological Tendencies of Presidents: Lincoln—McKinley

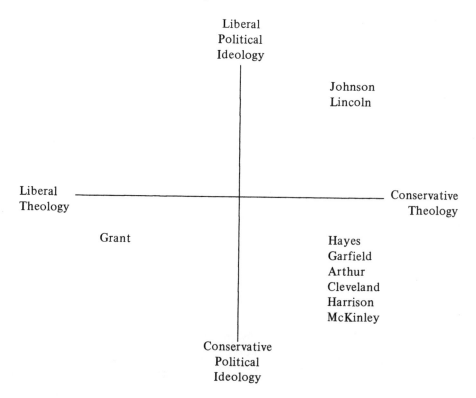

trappings of inoffensive civil religion to show the nation more clearly and dramatically their personal theological and religious convictions.

Seventh, the difficulty in placing Jimmy Carter also helps to reveal why he had difficulty governing. He made much use of theologically conservative symbols in capturing the Democratic nomination for president in 1976 and also in winning the office. Ironically the Democratic Party with a theologically liberal base in its platform and majority in Congress somewhat put President Carter in a vise between two irreconcilable points of view. He, a person of at least symbolically conservative theological convictions, had difficulty leading a party of definite liberal theological and ideological convictions.

Eighth, while presidents in the conservative-conservative quadrant dominated the first three eras of presidents, those in the liberal-liberal quadrant dominate the fourth era. This pattern conforms to the historical theological pattern as conservative theology dominated most of American history until the latest era. Now after a period of liberal theological domination, there has been a conservative theological resurgence that at least to some extent is reflected among the presidents as our most recent presidents have made greater efforts to appear more conservative theologically, evidently in response to a latent arousal of grassroots theological conservatism.

FIGURE 6.3   The Ideological and Theological Tendencies of Presidents: T. Roosevelt—Hoover

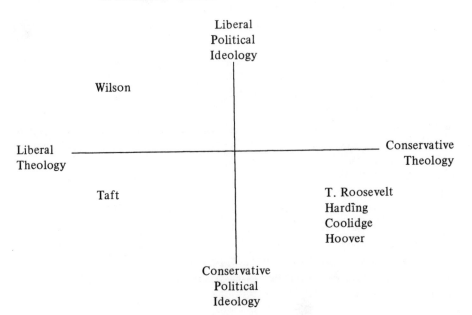

FIGURE 6.4   The Ideological and Theological Tendencies of Presidents:
F.D.R.—Reagan

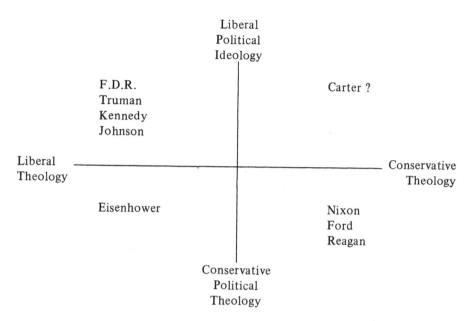

GENERALS OR FOOTSOLDIERS

The evidence tends to suggest that presidents are not generals on the theological battlefield. In a democratic sense as elected officials, they generally respond more to public pressures on theological issues than they lead the public. Then too as individuals they tend not to have strong theological convictions. The political experience, if not the presidency itself, evidently has the effect of moderating strongly held theological convictions among presidents. In an effort not to be offensive, presidents usually identify with mainline churches and use inoffensive language often called the language of the "civil religion" that attracts, but does not alienate, a cross-section of the religious among the electorate.

Presidents are not immune, however, to theological pressures for a variety of reasons. For example, theologically based political movements, such as liberally oriented ones on the Vietnam War and the nuclear freeze issues and conservative ones on issues like ERA and abortion, force presidents to respond. Party platforms with theologically based planks may also substantially influence presidential leadership.

In theological warfare over public policy then, presidents are important figures on the battlefield, but in rank they are probably somewhere between generals and footsoldiers.

NOTES

1. Michael Novak, *Choosing Our King* (New York: Macmillan, 1974), p. xv.

2. 1969 Inaugural Address.

3. As cited in Thomas E. Cronin, "The Textbook Presidency and Political Science," in *The Congressional Record*, October 5, 1970, p. S17106.

4. Clinton Rossiter, *The American Presidency*, revised edition (New York: New American Library, 1960), p. 239.

5. As cited in Novak, p. 154.

6. Presidential Address, March 4, 1933.

7. Presidential Address, March 15, 1965.

8. Conrad Cherry, *God's New Israel* (Englewood Cliffs, N.J.: Prentice-Hall, 1971), p. viii.

9. As cited in Perry C. Cotham, *Politics, Americanism and Christianity* (Grand Rapids, Mich.: Baker Book House, 1976), p. 51.

10. Ibid., p. 52.

11. In Robert N. Bellah, *Beyond Belief* (New York: Harper & Row, 1970), p. 170.

12. Robert S. Alley, *So Help Me God* (Richmond, Va.: John Knox Press, 1972), pp. 24-28.

13. Novak, *Choosing Our King*, pp. 131-34.

14. James David Barber, *Presidential Character*, 2nd Ed. (Englewood Cliffs, N.J.: Prentice-Hall, 1972), pp. 12, 13, 95-97, 146, 172, 174, 206, 210, 211.

7 A THEORY OF AMERICAN POLITICAL THEOLOGY

This severing of much connection of political theory from religion and theology . . . has unfortunately served to separate them precisely at a moment when religion . . . is gaining an unprecedented political influence . . . this self-isolation of political theory, the result of its own modernist methodology, is itself in part responsible for the radicalization of theology because this latter discipline almost never receives the sobering wind of analysis that ought to come from political theory at its best about what we might expect of men in the world.[1]

JAMES V. SCHALL

Rhetorical radiation from verbal bombs dropped in heated combat between groups like People for the American Way on the left and the Moral Majority on the right poses perplexing problems for American democracy. Both sides speak fervently with absolute assurance that their view of American democracy is the correct one. Both cannot be right.

Two of the best known intellectuals in America reveal the strikingly dramatic contrast between these polarized positions as they address the theological overtones of secular humanism. Aleksandr I. Solzhenitsyn in his 1978 Harvard University commencement address charged that humanism "started Western civilization on the dangerous trend of worshipping man and his material needs. . . . As humanism in its development was becoming more and more materialistic, it also increasingly allowed its concepts to be used first by socialism and then by communism."[2] Yale University President A. Bartlett Giamatti

171

condemned groups like the Moral Majority by saying they "would sweep before them anyone who holds a different opinion."[3]

Whether intellectuals of the caliber of Solzhenitsyn and Giamatti or groups like Moral Majority and People for the American Way, basic theological issues with political consequences are being raised. The liberal theological position among Jews, Protestants, and Roman Catholics has made its presence felt on such issues as the nuclear freeze while the conservative theological position has influenced public policy on issues like anti-abortion and school prayer. Without liberal and conservative theological support for these and other issues, the respective sides of the disputes would have been sapped of considerable support.

Although this book pretends neither to alleviate the animosities nor to eliminate the antagonisms between the "religious right" and the "religious left," it does propose to provide more detached observers with a clearer understanding of the origins, goals, strengths, and weaknesses of the contending sides.

The primary conclusions of this book are expressed in seven propositions about the nature of American political theology:

1. that fundamental differences and similarities between conservative and liberal theology affect how, why, and when they influence the political process;
2. that economic, political, social and theological issues are interdependent;
3. that theological unity is closely related to economic, political, and social unity;
4. that theological influence on politics and society follows a cyclical pattern of action and reaction;
5. that educational institutions significantly help to determine the dominance of a theological viewpoint in politics and society;
6. that the theological moderation of the American people together with their political moderation tend to lessen the strength of deviating theological points of view; and
7. that presidents and other political leaders tend to reflect rather than to direct theological influences on politics and public policy.

These seven propositions not only serve as conclusions for the analysis of this book, but they are also a statement of hypotheses about how theology affects American politics. In short, they are a theory about American political theology.

Proposition 1. *Fundamental differences and similarities between conservative and liberal theology affect how, why, and when they influence the political process.*

While the book's analysis and illustrations verify the differences between conservative and liberal theology set forth in Figure 1.2 of Chapter 1, it would be helpful here to explore at least two previously unmentioned differences. First conservative theology has a basically different conception of law as illustrated in Figure 7.1 below, "Conservative Theology's Pyramid of Laws and Their Sources." According to the conservative theological mind, the Bible should be the foundation of all law and, therefore, any law contrary to it should be considered unconstitutional or illegal. Liberal theology with a generally lower view or lesser regard for the Bible does not try to conform its political and social positions clearly to biblical postulates, but rather leans heavily upon nature and human reason for guidance in these matters. This is at least one of the reasons why liberal theology has been far more susceptible to change than conservative theology.

Sometimes one may wonder why theological conservatives are less concerned about nuclear weaponry and development than liberals. Part of the answer is due to their theological differences with respect to God and not just that conservatives are more nationally and militarily minded while liberals are more internationally minded. Conservatives generally look upon God as sovereign; therefore, nuclear war and catastrophe will only happen if God allows. Liberals with their greater emphasis upon the will and work of mankind do not have a similar trust in the sovereignty of God; hence, they are more prone to engage in efforts to halt or to limit the spread of nuclear weaponry.

Historically conservative theology has thrived more in an agrarian setting while liberal theology has thrived more in an impersonal urban setting. Indeed,

FIGURE 7.1   Conservative Theology's Pyramid of Laws and Their Sources

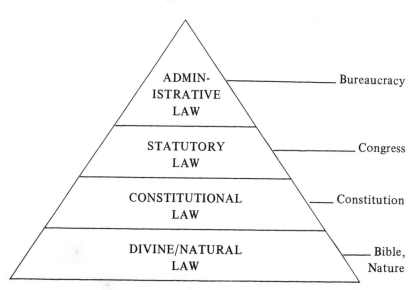

the growth of liberal theology parallels the growth of the urban environment in America. Although not the only reason for liberal ascendance, certainly urbanization is one.

Contrasts also exist between conservative and liberal theology as to when they are more likely to be successful in influencing politics and public policy. The conservative requires a more stable and healthy economy that allows conservative moral issues to be considered very important to the public. That is, in a depressed economy, economic issues tend to push the moral issues of conservative theology out of the picture. In 1980, conservative moral issues were important influences in the presidential election despite a troubled economy because the challenger, Mr. Reagan, was attacking the incumbent, Mr. Carter, economically and theologically. In 1982 with a continuingly troubled economy, theological issues of a conservative nature were not as successful. Liberal theology, on the other hand, has done better, such as during the Great Depression and the New Deal, with an unhealthy economy. Depressed economic conditions are more likely to help serve as a catalyst to achieve liberal theological goals with respect to public policy. Generally desiring a larger role for government and the strengthening of the national government in relationship to state and local government, unstable economic conditions have sparked greater liberal successes.

Historically conservative and liberal theology have differed with respect to their strategies for influencing government and politics. Conservatives have generally followed an "outside" and an "indirect" strategy while liberals have observed an "inside" and a "direct" strategy. The conservative position molded by Charles Finney (see Chapter 3) holds that successful governmental and social reform cannot take place without first spiritual regeneration of the heart; therefore, conservatives have historically emphasized an indirect approach to governmental and social reform, proclamation of the gospel to save souls of men who, when regenerated, would bring about governmental and social change. Liberals, on the other hand, molded by William Lloyd Garrison's strident opposition to slavery, have sought to bring about quicker governmental and social reform by direct governmental action. In conclusion we can see that conservatives have tended to work outside the governmental and political system in an indirect manner while liberals have done the opposite. Until recent years with the advent of the Moral Majority and other conservative religious interest groups, this has been the generally accepted conservative model. Because they have customarily emphasized the "inside" and "direct" approaches to governmental and social reform, liberal denominations and churches have probably enhanced their numbers in politics. Conservative denominations and churches, by contrast, have been more likely to emphasize the call to preach and the proclamation of the gospel and, thus, fewer of their number have been encouraged to enter the political realm. The last ten years in particular have begun to change the conservative emphasis, however, and if history is an accurate predictor, we will probably see more persons of conservative theological persuasion entering the political battlefield.

One of the outcomes of the politicization of the liberal denominations and churches, especially from the turn of the century until now, has been the loss of membership. That is, the more these denominations and churches address social and political issues, the less successful they have been in recruiting new members. Conservative church bodies, however, have been the dominant growth force in the church realm as people have responded more to the preaching of the Bible and presentation of the gospel message of salvation. Some conservative churchmen now fear that the latent political involvement of conservative churches will dampen their growth as their members are turned from "soul winning" to political action.

Is the church more powerful when it is political or nonpolitical? In the shortrun, it would appear that the church can exercise substantial political power when it is politicized. Certainly it did so prior to the Civil War, prior to the New Deal and now on such issues as the nuclear freeze and abortion. The question remains, however, if that power can be sustained when the church emphasizes the political to the neglect of the spiritual. Here data on the declining membership of the liberally dominated Methodist church and the extraordinary growth of conservative churches suggest that in the longrun politicization of the church will weaken it.

Also to be pointed out is that as the church turns to the government as the catalyst for action, the government becomes stronger and the church weaker in the performance of historically accepted roles. The most dramatic example of this is social welfare programs that prior to the New Deal were almost wholly within the province of the local church.

When religious groups follow a "direct" and an "inside" strategy for influencing government and politics, they necessarily seek to form political alliances with nonreligious groups. In the shortrun there is an apparent increase in theological strength by virtue of such alliances. Evidence of the religious element of the abolitionist movement aligning with political forces, the alignment of the social gospel and neo-orthodox movements with New Deal programs and the contemporary theological and political alignments of the left and right reinforce this conclusion. Once again the question remains, however, whether such alliances ultimately weaken the religious body as it begins to fight spiritual battles on the political level.

Among these and many other differences that could be cited are several interesting similarities, but one in particular. Both tend to address the highly moral and emotional issues rather than the more mundane. Of course, during the last decade their methods have become very similar as conservative theology has begun to adopt more of a "direct" and an "inside" strategy like liberal theology.

Although protestant and Roman Catholic theology have fundamental differences, their respective conservative and liberal public policy interests intersect in supporting such groups as People for the American Way, Moral Majority, and Eagle Forum. Hence, a conservative Roman Catholic like Phyllis Schlafly boasts a substantial protestant membership in her Eagle Forum as does protestant Jerry Falwell boast a substantial Roman Catholic membership in his Moral Majority. Liberal Roman Catholic Theodore Hesburgh of Notre Dame and liberal protestant James M. Dunn, Executive Director of the Baptist Joint Committee on Public Affairs, work together within People for the American Way.

Proposition 2. *Economic, political, social, and theological issues are interdependent.*

Examination of the deterioration of conservative theological dominance from the founding era to the present reveals that economic, political, and social causes are at least partly responsible. For example, the advent of modern science with its emphasis upon evolution challenged the conservative theological position of creation by a direct act of God. Second, the zenith of conservative theology occurred in a more personal and agrarian society that was challenged by the emergence of modernization, urbanization, and industrialization, creating a more impersonal society that weakened the hold of conservative theology. Third, the influx of Roman Catholic and Jewish immigrants in large numbers that generally aligned with the political causes of liberal protestant theology significantly weakened the conservative Christian dominance in American political life.

These and many other reasons that could be cited show that theological tension is a part of larger tensions in society and that there is a degree of mutual interdependence among them.

Proposition 3. *Theological unity is closely related to economic, political, and social unity.*

In the eighteenth and nineteenth centuries, theological division was relatively minor, except for the Civil War era when conservative theology divided over the Bible's teaching on slavery. In the twentieth century, however, there has been an increasingly greater gap between conservative and liberal theological forces. As theological unity has broken down, economic, political, and social unity have also broken down.

During the Founding era, only modest differences existed between conservative and liberal theology at least as compared to the differences today. Thus, the two sides could generally make common cause with respect to the policy issues they faced. During the pre-Civil War era, however, theological unity broke down between conservative northern and conservative southern theology, helping to spark the breakdown in the party system and the proliferation of third parties. During the pre-New Deal era, a huge gap began to develop between the two theological forces over the economic and social roles of government that liberal theology thought should be used to usher in the kingdom of God on earth while conservatives believed that this kingdom would not come about until God personally intervened to bring it about. During the post New Deal era or the present time, acute theological tension sparks pitched battles between conservative and liberal theological forces on an array of social issues, such as school prayer, abortion, and nuclear development.

Using the present time to illustrate the theological tension within and between the major parties the Democratic Party reflects in its platform an almost wholly liberal theological posture while the Republican Platform is generally the opposite. It is increasingly uncomfortable for theological conservatives to remain in the Democratic Party and for theological liberals to remain in the Republican Party.

Civil religion that has so successfully helped to glue society together on religious grounds appears to be breaking down as the language and symbols of civil religion lack the sustaining power to bridge the increasingly wider gulf that is fixed between the two theological poles. Where modest and inoffensive references to God, prayer, and other heretofore more neutral religious terms were widely accepted, efforts with at least some liberal theological support have increased to remove the trappings of civil religion, such as seeking to eliminate military chaplains, removing Christmas displays, and not allowing the Ten Commandments to be displayed on public school classroom walls.

In summary, theological tension is not only part of, but also a contributing cause of national unity or disunity; moreover, the record suggests that there cannot be national unity without theological unity.

Proposition 4. *Theological influence on politics and society conforms to a cyclical pattern of action and reaction.*

Liberal theology, departing from historically accepted conservative theology, established the pattern of cyclical action and reaction. For example, during the Founding era, liberal Unitarian theology grew out of conservative protestant theology. Initially Unitarian theology was only modestly different from its conservative counterpart, but the gap has been widened during the succeeding 200 years.

Conservative theology, remaining essentially constant, has been forced to react to continuing changes in liberal theology as the latter departed more from historically accepted conservative theology. We can see this during the present era not only with respect to protestant theology, but also Roman Catholic and Jewish theology. The liberalization of Roman Catholic and Jewish theology has sparked counterattacks from adherents of conservative theology in those two religious bodies as conservative Roman Catholics have reacted to liberal doctrine and political practices and conservative and orthodox Jews have grown in response to the secularization of Jewish theology via reformed Judaism.

Politically we can suggest that this cyclical pattern of action and reaction precedes political and social change and helps to set the boundaries of debate on political and social issues. For example, theological liberalism in the form of the social gospel and neo-orthodoxy dominated the political battlefield during the New Deal era and together with humanist theology there was little or no significant reaction, at least visibly, to their political achievements until the 1970s when conservative theology awakened from its political lethargy to see that its positions on vital social issues, such as school prayer, homosexuality, and abortion were being challenged. Thus, a latent conservative reaction occurred in response to liberal theological success on certain moral issues.

There appears to be no final resolution of theological disputes in the political realm as the two forces vie for dominance. The basic philosophy of society as to what is right and wrong, thus, continues to change as the two forces compete for the upper hand.

Proposition 5. *Theological moderation of the American people together with their political moderation tend to lessen the strength of deviating theological points of view.*

President Abraham Lincoln's point of view on the Civil War was first to sustain the Union and only much later as the abolitionist sentiment grew did he take the emancipation position espoused by theological interest groups. What we are suggesting is that the bulk of the American electorate is in the middle not only politically, but also theologically, and that usually only as that middle changes its viewpoint will an astute and successful politician do so.

Certainly the rhetoric of the civil religion is an indication of this fact. Neutral and inoffensive, it speaks abstractly of God and prayer, but does not specify to whose God and what kind of prayer should be made. The rhetoric of civil religion has been historically acceptable to a broad range of Americans in the middle. With the so-called revival of religious conservatism of the 1970s and early 1980s, other terms began to be used by Presidents Carter and Reagan like "born again" that had heretofore not been a part of the acceptable civil religion rhetoric. An expanding conservative theological base encouraged utilization of these terms.

Presidents, then, as well as other political leaders, tend to be bridges between and among competing theological points of view. The lowest common denominator of their rhetoric sufficient to appeal to the center of the electorate in the middle is the course of action generally followed.

Propostion 6. *Presidents and other political leaders tend to reflect rather than to direct theological influences on politics and public policy.*

Presidents with strong religious upbringings tend to lose those convictions or preferences, at least overtly, by the time they enter the presidency, if not before. This has been especially true of a number of presidents with very conservative theological roots, such as Presidents Garfield and Harding, who upon becoming president, or before, began to act much more like mainstream Americans theologically. President Nixon also epitomized a middle-of-the-road theological position when he hosted Sunday services at the White House addressed by an array of establishment religious figures from Jewish, Protestant, and Roman Catholic backgrounds.

On the contemporary scene, Presidents Reagan and Carter while molding an alliance with conservative theological leaders, astutely avoided close identification with them once elected president. Their more overt campaign activities designed to woo conservatively oriented theological voters became more covert as their respective presidencies progressed. A dramatic example of this occurred when President Reagan, who had carefully cultivated the fundamental/conservative constituency of Bob Jones University with alumni in every state during the campaign, quickly ran for cover when its biblical position on separation of the races began to cause him political embarrassment. President Reagan spoke to the 6,000-plus BJU student body during the 1980 campaign, but would not allow his Secretary of Education to deliver a special lecture there later in his administration. While unopposed to integration, Bob Jones University will not allow interracial dating among Blacks, Orientals, and Caucasians.

Proposition 7. *Educational institutions are important components in establishing the primacy of a theological viewpoint in political and public policy realms.*

The veracity of this proposition has been demonstrated in many ways. For example, prior to the Civil War, educational institutions like Oberlin College and others became fountainheads of abolitionist agitation. Prior to the New Deal, denominational machinery and leading colleges and universities, such as Ivy League schools like Yale, Harvard, and Princeton, became battlegrounds in the adoption of social gospel and neo-orthodox theology. As those institutions fell into liberal theological hands, they became training grounds for points of view about government and its role that had been opposed by preceding generations of conservative domination. Prior to the civil rights movement, the future leaders of the movement like Martin Luther King were frequently receiving their theological education in colleges and seminaries controlled by liberal theological points of view.

Often overlooked is the fact that millions of Americans listen to sermons in church each Sunday morning and that the impact of those sermons can significantly affect the daily points of view of members. Certainly the civil rights movement would have lost much of its fervor if it had been absent of the motivational force of theologically liberal sermons. This is not to say that conservatives are opposed to integration, but rather to show that while conservatives preach more about spiritual and eternal matters, liberals preach more about physical and daily matters.

Humanist theology with its deemphasis upon God, rejection of absolute standards of right and wrong, and disavowal of nationalism among other things is a formidable force in the public school educational establishment. Reaction to humanist strength there is a principal reason for the growth of Christian grade schools, high schools, and colleges, especially from the 1960s to the present.

CONCLUSION

Our goal has been not only to examine emotion-charged issues dispassionately and objectively, but also to provide a framework for analyzing political and theological relationships. In short, the purpose of this book has been to explore the links between politics and theology and to suggest new ways of thinking about them. The theory set forth here can now be tested elsewhere. Put still another way, our purpose has been to simplify complex issues by developing diagrams, paradigms and figures that make it easier to understand the importance and significance of American political theology.

NOTES

1. James V. Schall, "Political Theory: The Place of Christianity," *Modern Age* 25 (Winter 1981): 31.
2. Aleksandr I. Solzhenitsyn, *A World Split Apart* (New York: Harper & Row, 1978), p. 53.
3. The New York *Times*, September 1, 1981, p. 1.

BIBLIOGRAPHY

Ahlstrom, Sidney E., Ed., *Theology in America: The Major Protestant Voices from Puritanism to Neo-Orthodoxy*. Bobbs-Merrill, 1967.

Alley, Robert S. *So Help Me God: Religion and the Presidency: Wilson to Nixon*. John Knox Press, 1972.

Anderson, Charles H. *White Protestant Americans: From National Origins to Religious Group*. Prentice-Hall, Inc., 1970.

Arnold, Thurman. *The Symbols of Government*. Harcourt, Brace and World, Inc., 1935.

Baker, Tod A., et al., eds. *Religion and Politics in the South*. Praeger, 1983.

Bellah, Robert N. *Beyond Belief: Essays on Religion in a Post-Traditional World*. Harper & Row, 1970.

Bellah, Robert. *The Broken Covenant*. Seabury, 1975.

Bellah, Robert N. *On Morality and Society*. University of Chicago Press, 1973.

Bellah, Robert N. and Hammond, Phillip E. *Varieties of Civil Religion*. Harper & Row, 1982.

Benson, Peter L. *Religion on Capitol Hill*. Harper & Row, 1982.

Berger, Peter L., and Neuhaus, Richard J. *Movement and Revolution: On American Radicalism*. Anchor, 1970.

Berger, Peter L. and Neuhaus, Richard J. *To Empower People: The Role of Mediating Structures in Public Policy*. American Enterprise Institute, 1977.

Brown, Harold O. *The Reconstruction of the Republic: A Modern Theory of the State 'Under God' and Its Political, Social and Economic Structures*. Arlington House, 1977.

Buchanan, Patrick J. *The New Majority*. Girard Bank, 1973.

Bunzel, John. *Anti-Politics in America*. Knopf, 1967.

Carroll, Peter N., ed. *Religion and the Coming of the American Revolution.* Ginn-Blaisdell, 1970.

Cherry, Conrad, ed. *God's New Israel: Religious Interpretations of American Destiny.* Prentice-Hall, Inc., 1971.

Cole, Charles C., Jr. *The Social Ideas of the Northern Evangelists, 1826-1860.* Columbia University Press, 1954.

Cole, Franklin P. *They Preached Liberty.* Liberty Press, 1979.

Commager, Henry S. *The American Mind.* Yale, 1950.

Commager, Henry S. *Jefferson, Nationalism and Enlightenment.* Braziller, 1975.

Cone, James. *Liberation.* James Lippincott, 1970.

Cothan, Perry C. *Politics, Americanism, and Christianity.* Baker Book, 1976.

Cousins, Norman. *The Religious Beliefs and Ideas of the American Founding Fathers.* Harper & Row, 1958.

Cuddihy, John Murray. *No Offence: Civil Religion and Protestant Taste.* Seabury, 1978.

Davis, Charles. *Theology and Political Society.* Cambridge, 1980.

Dillenberger, John and Welch, Claude. *Protestant Christianity.* Charles Scribner's Sons, 1954.

Dohen, Dorothy. *Nationalism and American Catholicism.* Oxford University Press, 1968.

Doob, Leonard. *Patriotism and Nationalism.* Yale University Press, 1964.

Dulce, Berton and Richter, Edward J. *Religion and the Presidency.* Macmillan, 1962.

Duncan, Hugh D. *Symbols in Society.* Oxford University Press, 1968.

Edelman, Murray. *The Symbolic Uses of Politics.* University of Illinois Press, 1967.

Eliopoulos, Nicholas C. *Oneness of Politics and Religion.* Vantage Books, 1978.

Falwell, Jerry. *Listen, America!* Doubleday and Company, 1980.

Felsentha, Carol. *The Sweetheart of the Silent Majority: The Biography of Phyllis Schlafly*. Doubleday, 1981.

Fowler, Robert Booth. *A New Engagement: Evangelical Political Thought, 1966-1976*. Eerdmans, 1982.

Fowler, Robert Booth, ed., "Religion and Politics," *Humanities in Society*. 6 (Winter, 1983).

Gaustad, Edwin S. *A Religious History of America*. Harper & Row, 1966.

Goldwin, Robert A. and Schambra, William A., eds. *How Democratic Is the Constitution?* American Enterprise Institute, 1980.

Greinacher, N. and Mueller, Alois, eds. *Political Commitment and Christian Community*. Seabury, 1973.

Hallowell, John. *The Decline of Liberalism as an Ideology*. Fertig, 1971.

Hallowell, John. *The Moral Foundations of Democracy*. University of Chicago Press, 1954.

Hanna, Mary. *Catholics and American Politics*. Harvard University Press, 1979.

Harkmen, Gergia E. *The Modern Rival of Christian Faith: An Analysis of Secularism*. Greenwood, 1978 (reprint of 1952 edition).

Hartz, Louis. *The Liberal Tradition in America*. Harcourt Brace, 1955.

Henderson, Charles P., Jr. *The Nixon Theology*. Harper & Row, 1972.

Henley, Wallace. *Rebirth in Washington: The Christian Impact in the Nation's Capital*. Good News, 1977.

Herbert, Will. *Protestant-Catholic-Jew: An Essay in American Religious Sociology*. Doubleday, 1955.

Hofstadter, Richard. *The American Political Tradition*. Knopf, 1948.

Hudson, Winthrop S., Ed. *Nationalism and Religion in America: Concepts of American Identity and Mission*. Harper & Row, 1970.

Jersild, Paul, ed. *Moral Issues and Christian Response*. Holt, Rinehart, and Winston, 1976.

Johnson, John W. *Political Christians: A Guide for Christians in Public Service*. Augsburg, 1979.

Kelley, Dean M. *Why Conservative Churches Are Growing*. Harper & Row, 1972.

Kurland, Philip B. *Religion and the Law*. University of Chicago Press, 1978.

LaHaye, Tim. *The Battle for the Mind*. Fleming H. Revell Company, 1981.

Lawrence, Jerome and Lee, Robert E. *Inherit the Wind*. Bantam, 1969.

Lee, Robert and Marty, Martin E. *Religion and Social Conflict*. Oxford University Press, 1969.

Levy, Mark R. and Kramer, Michael S. *The Ethnic Factor: How America's Minorities Decide Elections*. Simon and Schuster, 1972.

Linder, Robert D. and Pierard, Richard. *Politics: A Case for Christian Action*. Inter Varsity, 1973.

Malbin, Michael J. *Religion and Politics: The Intention of the Authors of the First Amendment*. American Enterprise Institute, 1978.

Mansfield, Harvey. *The Spirit of Liberalism*. Harvard University Press, 1978.

Marty, Martin. *A Nation of Behavers*. University of Chicago Press. 1980.

Marty, Martin. *Pro and Con of Religious America*. Word Books, 1975.

Marty, Martin. *Righteous Empire: The Protestant Experience in America*. The Dial Press, 1970.

Mason, Alpheus T. *The Supreme Court from Taft to Warren*. Norton, 1964.

Matusow, Alan J. *The Unraveling of America: A History of Liberalism in the 1960s*. Harper & Row, 1984.

McLoughlin, William G. *Revivals, Awakenings and Reform*. University of Chicago Press, 1978.

McWilliams, Wilson Carey. *The Idea of Fraternity in America*. University of California Press, 1973.

Mechling, Jay, ed. *Church, State, and Public Policy*. American Enterprise Institute, 1979.

Meyer, Donald B. *The Protestant Search for Political Realism: 1919-1941*. Greenwood, 1973 (reprint of 1960 edition).

Miller, Perry, ed. *The Legal Mind in America: From Independence to the Civil War*. Cornell University Press, 1962.

Miller, Perry. *Nature's Nation*. Harvard-Belknap, 1961.

Moltman, Jurgen, et al. *Religion and Political Society*. E. Melen, 1976.

Morgan, Richard E. *The Politics of Religious Conflict: Church and State in America*. University Press of America, 1980.

Mouw, Richard. *Political Evangelism*. Eerdmans, 1973.

National Conference of Catholic Bishops. *The Challenge of Peace: God's Promise and Our Response*. Origins, National Catholic Documentary Service, May 19, 1983.

Neuhaus, Richard J. *Christian Faith and Public Policy: Thinking and Acting in the Courage of Uncertainty*. Augsburg, 1977.

Niebuhr, H. Richard. *The Church Against the World*. Willett, Clark and Co., 1935.

Niebuhr, Reinhold. *Christian Realism and Political Problems*. Kelley, 1953.

Niebuhr, Reinhold. *Moral Man and Immoral Society*. Charles Scribner's Sons, 1932, 1960.

Niebuhr, Reinhold. *The Children of Light and the Children of Darkness*. Charles Scribner's Sons, 1960.

Niebuhr, Reinhold. *The Irony of American History*. Charles Scribner's Sons, 1952.

Niebuhr, Reinhold. *The Self and the Dramas of History*. Charles Scribner's Sons, 1955.

Niebuhr, Reinhold. *Faith in Politics*. Stone, Donald H., ed. Braziller, 1968.

Niebuhr, Reinhold. *Christianity and Power Politics*. Anchor Books, 1969.

Novak, Michael. *Choosing Our King*. Macmillan, 1974.

Novak, Michael, ed. *Democracy and Mediating Structures*. American Enterprise Institute, 1980.

Novak, Michael, ed. *Moral Clarity in the Nuclear Age*. Nelson, 1983.

Novak, Michael, ed. *The Spirit of Democratic Capitalism*. Simon and Schuster, 1982.

Parrington, Vernon L. *Main Currents in American Thought*. Harcourt, Brace and Co., 1930.

Rauschenbusch, Walter. *A Theology for the Social Gospel*. Macmillan, 1917.

Richardson, John D., ed. *A Compilation of Messages and Papers of the President*. U.S. Government Printing Office, 1896.

Richey, Russell E. and Jones, Donald G., eds. *American Civil Religion*. Harper & Row, 1974.

Richter, Edward J. and Dulce, Berton. *Religion and the Presidency*. Harper & Row, 1974.

Rochester, Stuart I. *American Liberal Disillusionment in the Wake of World War I*. Penn State University Press, 1972 (reprint of 1959 edition).

Rosenman, Samuel I., ed. *The Public Papers and Addresses of Franklin D. Roosevelt*. Random House, 1938.

Rushdoony, Rousas J. *The Nature of the American System*. Thoburn Press, 1978.

Rushdoony, Rousas J. *This Independent Republic*. Thoburn Press, 1978.

Sandeen, Ernest R. *The Roots of Fundamentalism: British and American Millenarianism 1800-1930*. The University of Chicago Press.

Scammon, Richard M. and Wattenberg, Ben J. *The Real Majority*. Berkeley Publishing Corporation, 1970.

Siegfried, André. *America Comes of Age*. Da Capo, 1974.

Singer, Gregg. *A Theological Interpretation of American History*. Presbyterian and Reformed Publishing Co., 1964.

Smith, Elwyn A., Ed. *The Religion of the Republic*. Fortress Press, 1971.

Smith, Harry E. *Secularization and the University*. John Knox, 1968.

Solzhenitsyn, Aleksandr I. *A World Split Apart*. Harper & Row, 1978.

Stark, Rodney and Glock, Charles Y. *American Piety: The Nature of Religious Commitment*. Berkeley, The University of California Press, 1968.

Stokes, Anson Phelps, ed. *Church and State and the U.S.* Harper & Row, 1950.

Streiker, Lowell D. and Strober, Gerald S. *Religion and the New Majority: Billy Graham, Middle America, and the Politics of the '70s*. Association Press, 1972.

Strout, Cushing. *The New Heavens and New Earth: Political Religion in America.* Harper & Row, 1974.

Stumpf, Samuel E. *Democratic Manifesto: The Impact of Dynamic Christianity upon Public Life and Government.* Vanderbilt University Press, 1978.

Sweet, William Warren. *Religion in the Development of American Culture, 1765-1840.* Charles Scribner's, 1952.

Swisher, Carl Brent. *The Growth of Constitutional Government.* University of Chicago Press, 1963.

Templeton, Kenneth S., ed. *The Politicization of Society.* Liberty Press, 1979.

Thornton, John Wingate, ed. *The Pulpit of the American Revolution.* Franklin and Co., 1970.

de Tocqueville, Alexis. *Democracy in America.* Vintage Books, 1954.

Tuveson, Ernest L. *Redeemer Nation: The Idea of America's Millennial Role.* University of Chicago Press, 1978.

Viguerie, Richard A. *The New Right: We're Ready to Lead.* The Viguerie Company. Distributed by Caroline Hoose.

Wallis, Charles, ed. *Our American Heritage.* Harper & Row, 1970.

Warner, W. Lloyd. *American Life: Dream and Reality.* The University of Chicago Press, 1953, 1962.

Whitehead, John W. *The Separation Illusion.* Mott Media, 1977.

Wilhelmsen, Frederick D. *Christianity and Political Philosophy.* University of Georgia Press, 1978.

Zinn, Howard, ed. *New Deal Thought.* Bobbs-Merrill, 1966.

INDEX

ABOUT THE AUTHOR

CHARLES W. DUNN, Clemson University professor and Head of the Department of Political Science, previously taught at Florida State University and the University of Illinois.

Among his books are *The Future of the American Presidency* (1975) and *American Democracy Debated* (Second Edition, 1982). Some of the scholarly journals publishing articles by him are the *American Journal of Political Science*, *American Politics Quarterly*, *Presidential Studies Quarterly*, and *Humanities in Society*.

He has also served as a senior staff aide for members of the U.S. Senate and U.S. House of Representatives, for a governor, and also for the 1970 Illinois Constitutional Convention.

Illinois State University awarded him the Alumni Achievement Award in 1982.